DEFENSE OF THE JAPANESE HOMELAND
JAPANESE ARMY MANUALS 1943~1945
TRANSLATED BY ERIC SHAHAN

Copyright © 2023 Eric Michael Shahan
All Rights Reserved.
ISBN: 978-1-950959-72-3

ERIC SHAHAN

Defense of the Japanese Homeland
Table of Contents

How to Fight With a Bamboo Spear October 1943 Page 1~	Building Fortifications April 1945 Page 89~
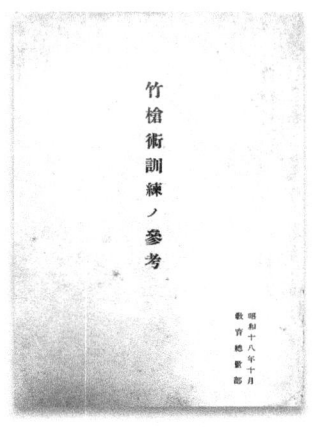	
National Resistance Manual April 1945 Page 153~	Weekly Photo Report Magazine (excerpt) July 1945 Page 267~

ERIC SHAHAN

DEFENSE OF THE JAPANESE HOMELAND

竹槍術訓練ノ参考

How to Fight With a Bamboo Spear: A Reference Manual For Training

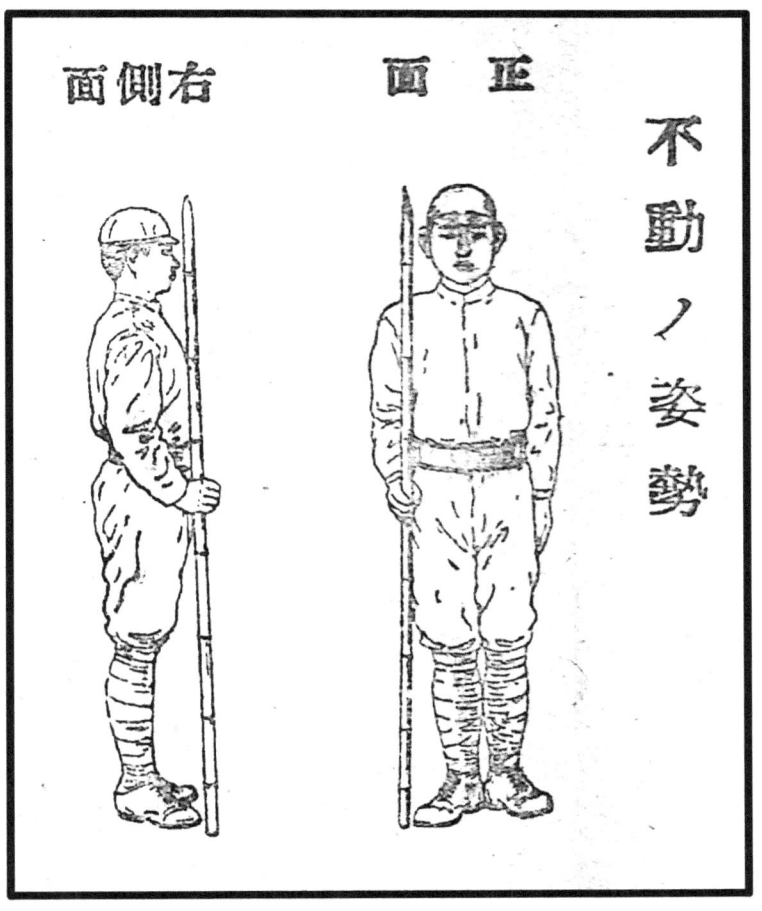

Published in 1943 by the Education Division of the Japanese Army

ERIC SHAHAN

Translator's Note: This booklet consists of two rectangular pages, one on top of the other, folded into a booklet. The top sheet is for students and the bottom sheet is for instructors. The instructor's sheet covers the same topics as the student's sheet but details the training objectives for instructors. While this isn't stated, it seems likely the instructor would rip off the bottom sheet and hand the top sheet to the learner.

For Learners:

For Instructors:

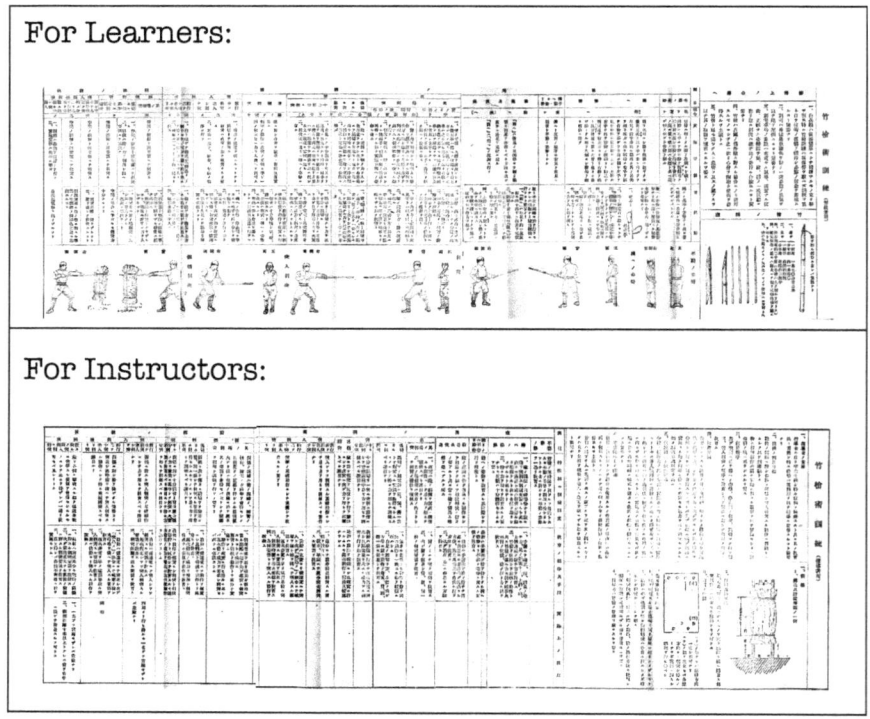

Most of the illustrations are in the guide for students.

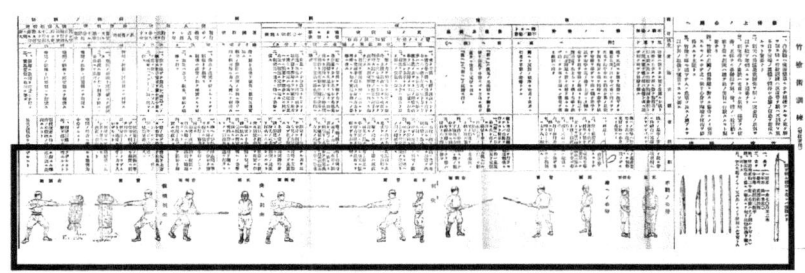

However, the instructor's guide contains a diagram and instructions for constructing practice targets, in addition to a schematic showing how to arrange multiple practice targets.

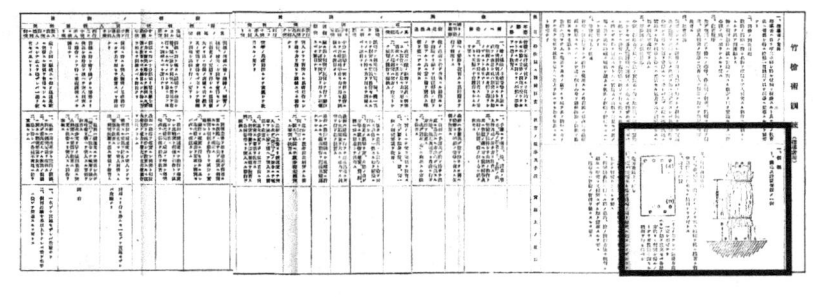

The information is arranged in horizontal columns in both the guide for learner as well as for instructors. For example, the highlighted boxes show the information regarding proper stance in the guide for learners (top) and the one for instructors (bottom.)

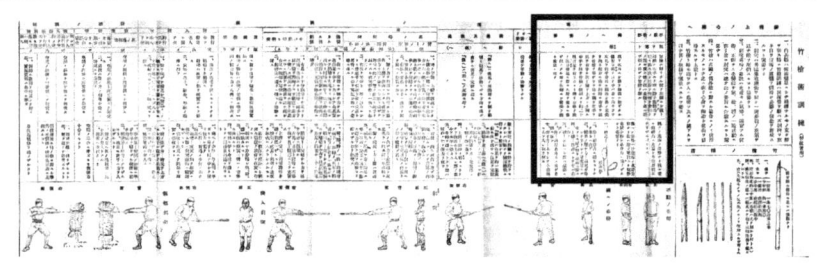

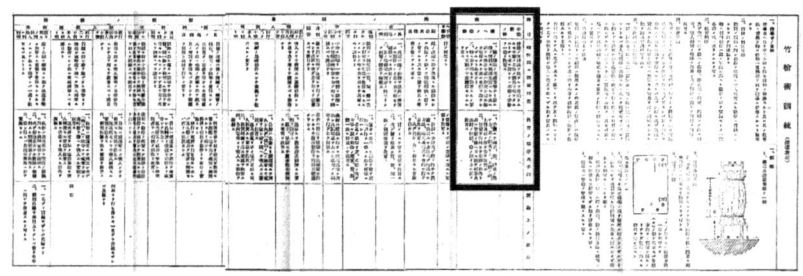

The primary word used for describing attacks with the spear is *Shitotsu*. This is a word that uses the following Kanji:

Sasu 刺 "to stab or pierce"

Tsuku 突 "to strike or stab"

The way the Kanji are read changes when combined so this word is pronounced *Shitotsu*, and means *to stab or attack with an edged weapon*. For for the purposes of this book, *piercing thrust*.

The word *Tsuku* is also used as a command and appears as *Tsuke!* Stab!

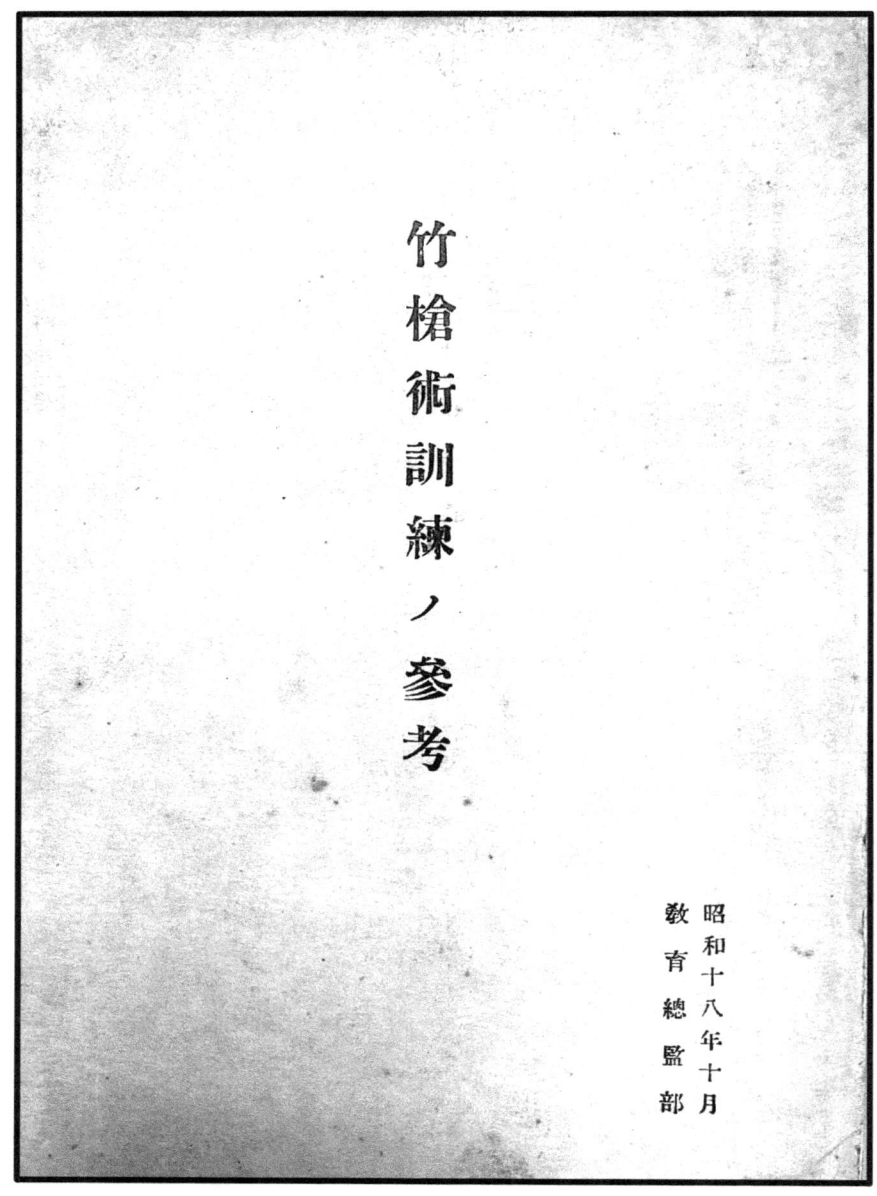

竹槍術訓練ノ參考

昭和十八年十月
教育總監部

Takeyari Jutsu Kunren no Sanko

竹槍術訓練ノ参考

How to Fight With a Bamboo Spear: A Reference Manual For Training

18th Year of the Showa Emperor (1943)

Published by the Education Division of the Japanese Army

竹槍術訓練 （習技者用）

修得上ノ心構ヘ

一、白兵戰ハ使術者當中ニシテ槍術鍛錬ナルモノ克ク勝ヲ制ス特ニ竹槍訓練ハ度々戰勢ヲ厭ハズ訓練ヲ重ネ自ラ使術ノ眞髓ヲ體得シ必勝ノ信念ヲ養成スルコト緊要ナリ

二、刺突ハ勇猛果敢機先ヲ制シ一突必殺ノ意氣ヲ以テ敵ヲ壓倒スルコト緊要ナリ

三、刺突奏功ノ要訣ハ充實セル氣勢、確實ナル使術、正確ナル姿勢卽チ氣、槍、體ノ一致活動ニ在リ故ニ刺突ハ總テ此ノ要旨ニ合致スルコト緊要ナリ

四、竹槍ハ君國ノ爲外敵ニ對スル場合ニノミ使用スルモノニシテ之ニ依リ心身ヲ陶冶シ使術ヲ修得スルヲ主眼トス

五、竹槍ト雖モ過ツテ人ニ危害ヲ及ス〻虞アルヲ以テ其ノ取扱ヲ愼重ニスルヲ要ス

How to Fight With a Bamboo Spear (Learner's Guide)

Important Things to Remember When Training

1. When engaging in hand-to-hand or close quarters combat, the best way to achieve victory is to use a simple weapon that you have trained thoroughly. In particular, you should not be negligent in continually drilling bamboo spear techniques. It is essential that you train until they develop an understanding of how to use this weapon. Developing the confidence that the techniques are effective will lead to certain victory in an engagement.
2. It is essential that when launching a piercing thrust with your spear, you do so with dauntless courage. Your attack should break through your opponent's offense. A strike should be launched with the intent that it will deliver certain death to the enemy. The enemy should be flattened no matter how he resists.
3. The key to a successful thrust is having a determined spirit, a solid understanding of technique and proper posture. Thus the following three should all be operating in unison:
    Ki – Your spirit
    Yari – The spear
    Tai – Your body
It is vital that you understand a proper piercing thrust is a combination of spirit, spear and body.
4. The bamboo spear should only be used to defend the Emperor and the nation against its foreign enemies. Therefore, citizens should focus on cultivating their body and spirit while developing a practical knowledge of this weapon.
5. Since the *Takeyari*, bamboo spear, is a weapon that can cause people harm, it is essential that it be handled carefully and in accordance with procedure.

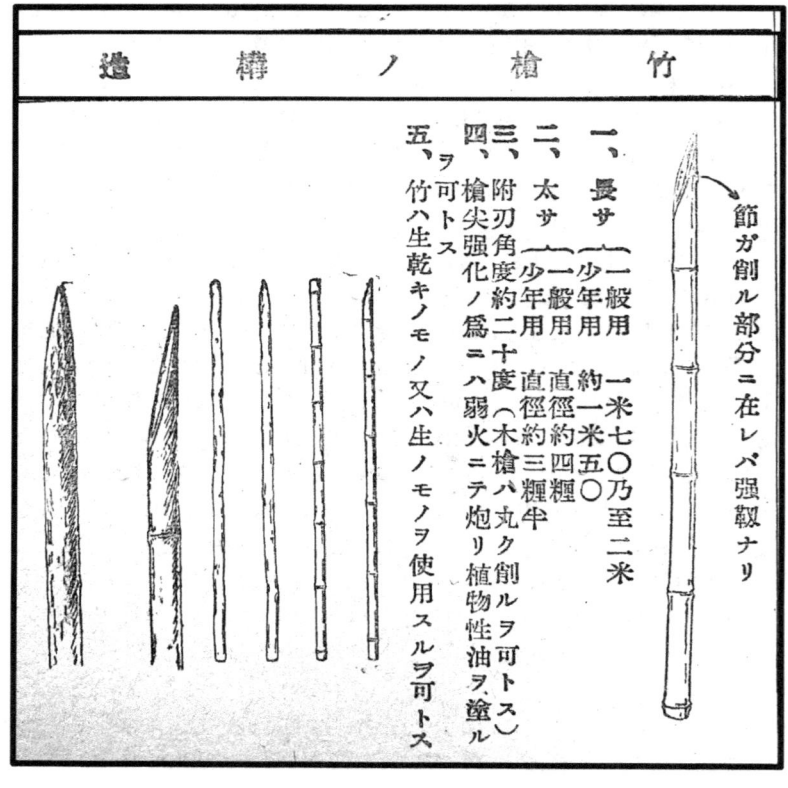

竹槍ノ構造

節ガ削ル部分ニ在レバ強靱ナリ

一、長サ（一般用　約一米七〇乃至二米
　　　　少年用　約一米五〇
二、太サ　一般用　直徑約四糎半
　　　　少年用　直徑約三糎半
三、附刃角度　約二十度（木槍ハ丸ク削ルモ可トス）
四、槍尖強化ノ爲ニハ弱火ニテ炮リ植物性油ヲ塗ルヲ可トス
五、竹ハ生乾キノモノ又ハ生ノモノヲ使用スルヲ可トス

Takeyari no Kozo
Construction of a Bamboo Spear

When cutting the bamboo to make a spear-point, be sure your cut goes through one of the joints. This will give it additional strength

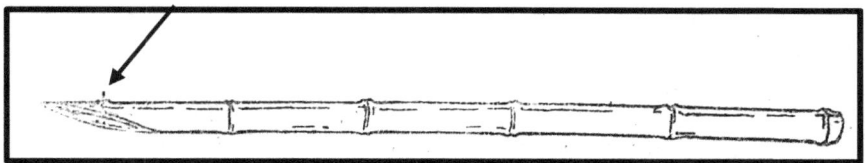

1. Length
For adults: 1.7 meters ~ 2 meters
For youth[1]: 1.5 meters

2. Diameter
For adults: 4 centimeters in diameter
For youth: 3.5 centimeters in diameter

3. Angle of Cut for Spearpoint
The cut should be approximately 20 degrees. (For wooden spears, the end should be shaved into a conical point.)

4. Final Preparation
To increase the strength of the spearpoint, lightly braise it over a flame then rub it with vegetable oil.

5. Note
Both cut and dried bamboo as well as freshly cut bamboo can be used.

---

[1] In 1943, all males over 20 were subject to enlistment. In 1944, they included men over the age of 15. By the end of the war in 1945, the range had been expanded 15~60 years old for men and 17~40 for women.

Part 1
Kukan no Kunren
Training Against an Imaginary Target

Fudo no Shisei
Immovable Stance (At Attention)

Right Side   Front

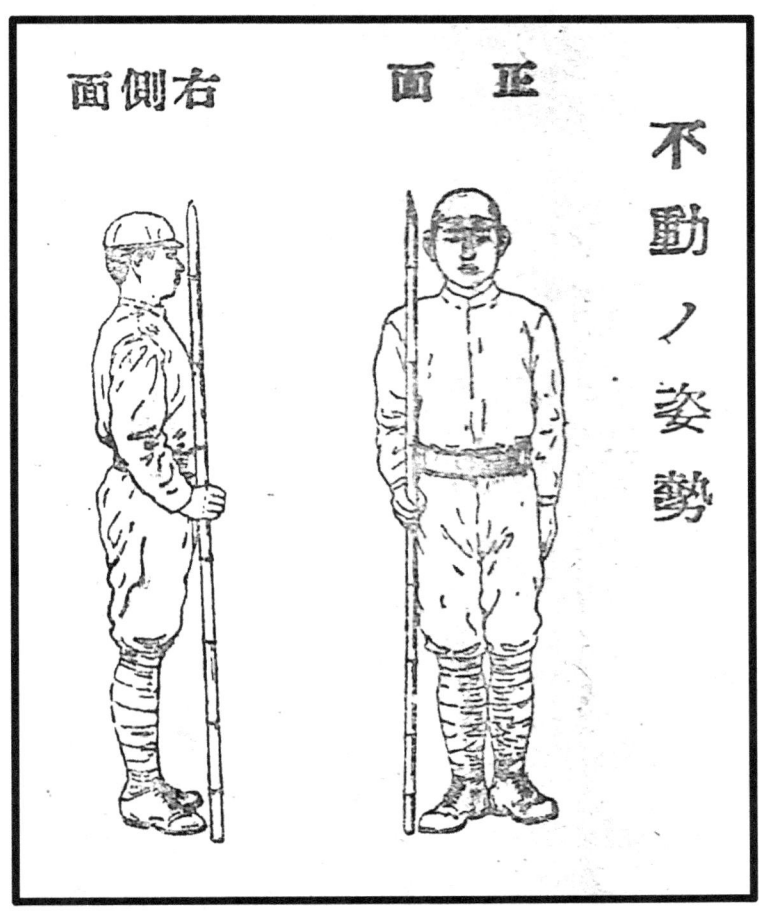

課目號令	實施要領	著眼點
不動ノ姿勢	氣ヲ著ケ	竹槍ハ削リタル面ヲ左側ニシ銃(テイビ)ト同樣ニ右手ニテ握ルヲ卽チ腕關節ヲ稍々前ニ出シ竹槍ヲ拇指ト食指ノ間ニ置キ他ノ指ハ食指ト共ニ閉ヂ輕ク曲ゲテ竹槍ヲ握ル	總テノ基本ノ姿勢ナリ故ニ常ニ精神內ニ充溢シ外嚴肅端正ナラザルベカラズ

Fudo no Shisei
Immovable Stance (At Attention)

Command:
Ki wo Tsuke
Attention!

Operational Guide:
Hold the spear in your right hand, with the cut end facing left. This is similar to how you hold a rifle. Your wrist should be slightly forward with the spear held between your thumb and forefinger. Your other fingers are curled beside your index finger, holding the spear lightly.

Important Points:
This is the basic stance used in all drills. Therefore, it is important to have the proper state of mind. Your manner should not be anything other than serious and orderly.

Kamae no Shisei
Ready Stance

Ride Side View   Back View

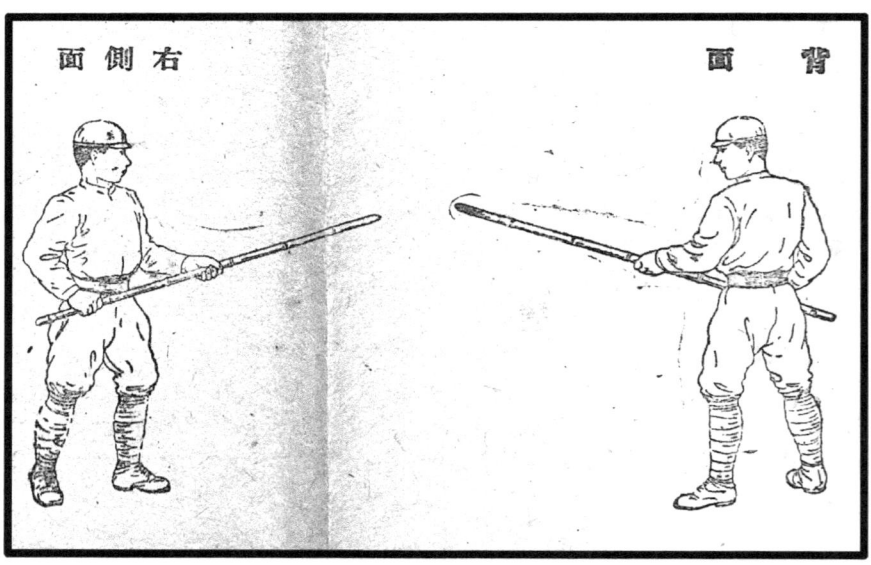

構ヘノ姿勢

構　ヘ

頭ヲ正面ニシ眼ヲ敵眼ニ注ギタル儘右足尖ヲ以テ半歩右ニ向キツツ左足ヲ約半歩前ニ踏出シ其ノ足尖ヲ概ネ敵方ニ向ケ同時ニ右手ヲ以テ竹槍ヲ擧ゲツツ前ニ倒シ左手ヲ以テ右手ニ近ク槍ヲ上方ヨリ握ル右手ヲ以テ竹槍ノ後端ヨリ約二十糎附近ヲ右上方ヨリ握リ右拳ヲ右腋骨附近ニ置キ左肘ヲ僅カニ曲ゲ削リタル面ヲ左側ニシ槍尖ヲ概ネ敵眼ニ向ク

構ヘノ姿勢ハ竹槍術ノ基礎姿勢ナリ故ニ敵ヲ壓伏スル氣勢充實シ特ニ心身共ニ凝ラザルコト必要ナリ

一、兩足ー約半歩

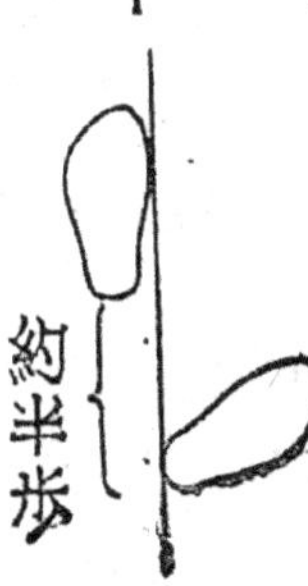

二、膝ー兩膝共ニ凝ルコトナク僅カニ曲グ

三、體重ノ懸ケ方ー兩足平等ニシテ主トシテ足尖ニ支フルモ踵ハ輕ク地面ニ接ス

四、上體ー眞直ニシテ半バ右ニ向ク

五、頭ー正面ニシ眼ハ敵眼ニ向ク

六、肘ー兩肘共僅カニ曲ゲ自然ニ保ツ

七、握リ方ー主トシテ小指側ニ力ヲ入レ弱ク握ル

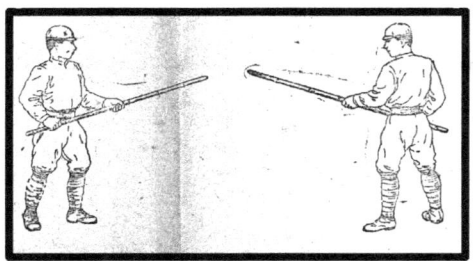

How to Take Kamae

Command:
Kamae!
Ready!/Take your Stance!

Operational Guide:
Face forward and direct your gaze into the enemy's eyes as you press down with the toes of your right foot. Take a half step forward with your left foot and rotate your right foot clockwise. The toes of your left foot should be directed at the enemy.

As you step, your right hand lifts the spear off the ground. Allow it to fall forward before gripping it with your left hand, close to your right hand. Then slide your right hand back towards the end of the spear and grab at a point about 20 centimeters from the end. Your right fist should be on your right hipbone. Your left elbow is slightly bent. The angled cut on the end of the spear should be facing to your left with the tip of the spear pointed at the enemy's eyes.

Important Points:
The body positioning described above is the fundamental way of standing for Takeyari Jutsu, Bamboo Spear Fighting. You should be infused with the feeling of subduing your enemy, and your body and mind prepared to react without hesitation.

1. Diagram of Foot Position

Approximately one half-step distance from heel to heel.	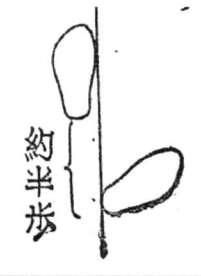

2. Knees
Your knees should not be rigid, but rather bent slightly.

3. Body Weight Distribution
Your weight should be distributed evenly over both feet. However, the focus of the weight should be on your toes, with the heels only lightly touching the ground.

4. Upper Body
Your upper body should be straight with your chest facing to the right.

5. Head
You should be facing your enemy squarely and staring into his eyes.

6. Elbow
Keep both your elbows slightly bent, maintaining a natural position.

7. Grip
Generally speaking, your little finger should grip the strongest. Overall, grip lightly.

欅ヨリ姿勢ヘノ不動
直レ
欅ヘト反對ノ順序ニ右足ヲ左足ニ引著ケ不動ノ姿勢トナル

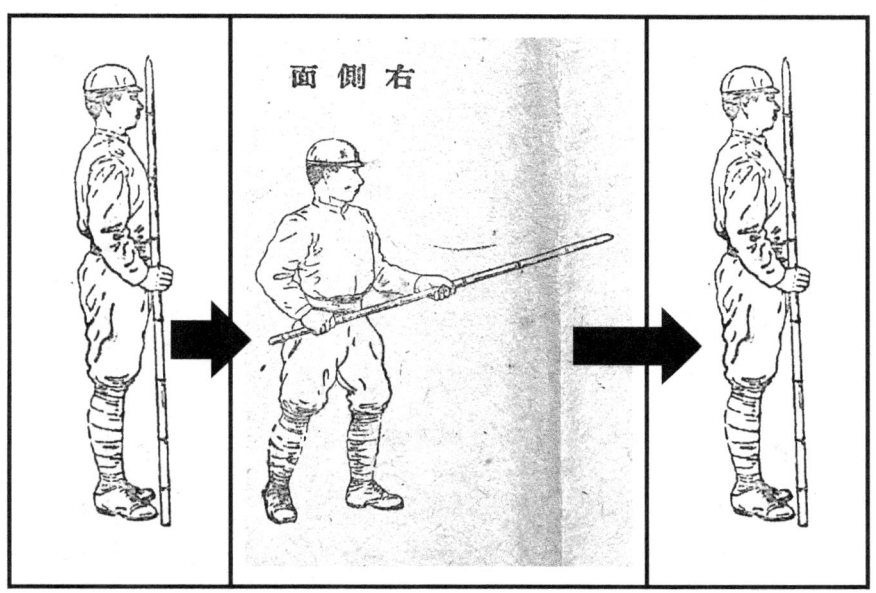

Shifting From Ready Stance to Immovable Stance

Command:
Naore!
Return!

Operational Guide:

Return to your original stance by reversing the previous instructions. Your right foot pulls back beside your left and you return to Immovable Stance.

Important Points:
None

前進及後退	
前へ	（後へ）
「前ヘ」ハ後足ノ足尖部ニテ輕ク踏切リ前足ヲ移動スベキ方向ニ出シ直チニ後足ヲ定位ニ送ル	「後ヘ」ハ「前ヘ」ノ反對ニ行フ

敵ト至近ノ距離ニ於テ行フモノナレバ油斷ナク敏速輕快ニ行フコト緊要ナリ

一、「前ヘ」ハ前足ヲ約一足長ニ出シ直チニ後足ヲ定位ニ送ル

二、踏切リ方ハ前ヘ（後ヘ）ハ後足（前足）ノ足尖部ニテ輕ク踏切ルリ

三、ク足ノ踏著ケ方—足尖部ヨリ輕ク地ニ著ク

四、上體—姿勢ヲ崩スコトナク下腹部ニ力ヲ入レ體ノ重心ヲ水平ニ動カス

五、身體ヲ凝ルコトナクばねノ如ク彈力ヲ保ッ膝ハ

How to Advance and Retreat

Command:
Mae-eh! Forward!
Ushiro-eh! Back!

Operational Guide:
At the command of *Mae-eh!* or *Forward!*, press the toes of your rear foot lightly into the ground and use your front foot to move in the appropriate direction. Next, pull your rear foot up so it is the proper distance behind your front foot.

Important Points:
Since you will be drawing close to your enemy with this movement, it is essential that you do not make a careless error. Your movements should be quick and nimble.

1. Responding to Commands
At the command of *Mae-eh!* or *Forward!*, step a maximum of one foot span forward, then immediately bring your back foot up to its proper position.

2. How to Step
When the command *Forward!* or *Back!* is given, lightly press down with your toes. When moving forward, put pressure on your back toes, when moving back, put pressure on your front toes.

3. How to Plant Your Foot After Stepping
The toes of your foot should make contact with the ground lightly

4. Upper Body
Be sure your posture remains straight and focus all your power in your lower abdomen. When moving be sure your center point moves parallel to the ground.

5. Overall
Don't allow your body to become rigid. Be sure to keep some spring in your knees so you can respond flexibly.

Choku Tsuki
Straight Thrusts
Front View : *Shitotsu* Piercing Thrust

DEFENSE OF THE JAPANESE HOMELAND

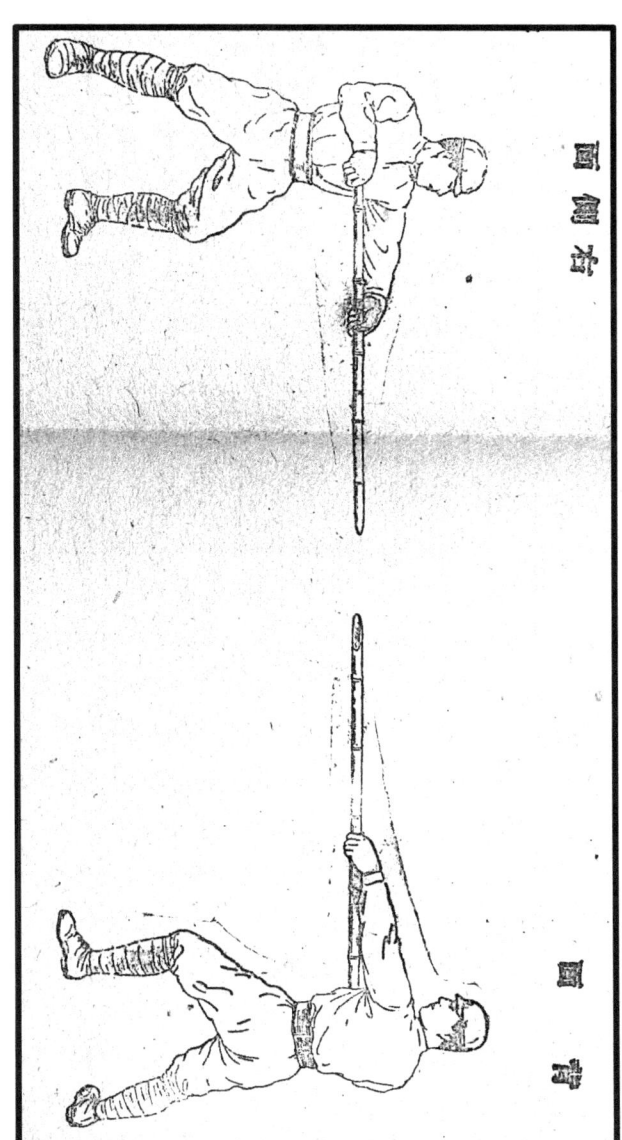

Shitotsu Piercing Thrust
View From the Right Side View From the Back

臂ノミノ動作

突ケ

一、突クノ要領ハ上體ヲ眞直ニシタルマゝニ右拳ハ構ヘノ位置ヨリ前上方ニ進メ概ネ左乳ノ前方ニ進ム此ノ際槍ハ兩方ニ進ム

二、拳突ヲ以テ水平ニ握締ス此ノ際敏速ニ引抜クノ要領兩手ハ捷路ヲ經テ構ヘノ位置ニ復ス

一、右肘ハ概ネ直角ニ曲ゲ殊更ニ張ルコトナク前膊ノ内側ニ槍ヲ抱込ム

二、左肘ヲ十分伸バス刺突ノ瞬時ノ姿勢ト兩拳ノ握締メ刺突ノ經路ハ何レモ最後ノ位置ト

三、強ク握リ經路ヲ通ル

四、ノ間ノ捷路

Sonoba Shitotsu
Training Thrusts In Place

Part 1
Stabbing by Using the Elbows Only

Command:
Tsuke! Stab!
If conducting training step-by-step, then use the command, *Nu-ke!* Pull out!

Operational Guide:
1. Tsuku: The Essential Points of the Stabbing Thrust. While keeping your upper body straight, move your right fist forward and up from where it is positioned on your hip. The motion should continue until your fist is in front of and below your left breast. At the same time your left fist should move forward. Just as your right fist reaches the spot below your left breast, grip tightly with both hands. You should thrust your spear forward rapidly, ensuring the spear is travelling parallel to the ground.
2. Hiki-Nuku: The Essential Points of Withdrawing Your Thrust. Both hands should deftly trace the same path back until they arrive at their original positions.

Important Points:
1. Your Right Elbow
Your right arm should be bent at a right angle, but not flexed hard. When thrusting push the spear into the inside of your front arm.
2. Your Left Elbow
Make sure you extend your left arm forward sufficiently.
3. Gripping With Both Fists
The moment you strike, grip the spear tightly with both hands.
4. The Path Your Two Fists Should Travel
Your fists should travel the shortest distance between where your hands are positioned in the ready stance to where the spear is extended forward.

臂脚一致ノ動作
分解教育ノ場

一、腰ノ力ヲ利用シテ刺突スル動作ヲ上體ヲ眞直ニシタル儘腰ヲ僅カニ左膝ヲ曲ゲテ兩手ヲ以テ行フス此ノ刺突動作ヲ腰ノ推進ト一致スル如ク前方ニ出シ刺突ス

二、タルヲ引拔ク要領上體ヲ眞直ニシ腰ノ後退ト同時ニ兩手ノ引拔ト儘拔ク勢ニ復スルナルガ如ク實施シ構ヘノ姿勢

一、膝ノ曲ゲ方ー左膝頭ト左足尖トハ概ネ同一垂直線トス

二、腰ノ送出シ方ー腰ハ眞直ニ送ル腰ノ送出シ方ー前足ハ膝ニ

三、兩足ノ蹠著ケ方シ後足ハ平ニ地面ニ接著ヲ地面ヨリ離サザル如ク彈力ヲ保チ踵刺突ス

Moving the Elbows and Legs in Unison

Command:
Tsuke! Stab!
If conducting training step-by-step, then use the command,
Nu-ke! Pull out!

Operational Guide:
1. How to Generate Power In Your Hips for a Stabbing Thrust
While keeping your upper body straight, thrust your hips forward. Your left knee should bend as you stab forward. Your hips and hands should move in unison when doing this strike.

2. The Essential Points of Withdrawing Your Thrust
Keeping your body straight, pull the spear out, while simultaneously shifting your hips back. Finally, return to your original ready position with the spear.

Important Points:
1. How to Bend Your Knee
Your left knee should bend forward until your kneecap is directly over your toes. You should be able to draw a straight vertical line from your kneecap to the end of the toes on your left foot.

2. How to Move Your Hips Forward
Thrust your hips directly forward.

3. How to Step Evenly With Both Feet
Your front foot is planted evenly on the ground. The knee of your back foot should be ready to respond in a moment's notice. The heels of your feet should not break contact with the ground as you stab forward.

僅カニ切リ	二ニ刺ス	蹈突
合	「八」	拔

一、前ヘノ要領ニテ輕ク力ヲ入レ進出量ヲ少クシテ右足尖ニテ蹈切リ左足ヨリ僅カニ前ニ出ルト同時ニ兩手ヲ以テ停止間ノ動作ト同要領ニテ槍ヲ突出ス

二、引拔ク要領ハ停止間ノ動作ニ準ズ

一、臂、脚、體ノ一致ー刺突時ノ兩手ノ握締メ、左足ノ蹈著ケ、腰ノ推進ヲ一致セシムニノ蹈切リヲ主トシテ右足尖

二、ニテ短切ナルカヲ以テ蹈切ル

三、左足ノ蹈著ケー平ニ蹈著ク

How To Stab Stepping Slightly Forward

Command:
Same as above

Operational Guide:
1. This is done the same way as the previous technique. Gently add additional power into the toes of your right foot to propel yourself forward. As you do this your left foot should move slightly forward. At the same time stab the spear forward with both hands. This action should be as described before, both hands and the spear move from where they are stopped at your waist to where they stop extended out in front.

2. Withdrawing the spear should be done as previously described. The hands should follow the path from where the spear is stopped extended in front of you, to where it stops at your waist.

Important Points:
1. Unification of Elbows, Legs and Body
When stabbing with the spear, the following should occur simultaneously:
Your hands should grip.
Your left foot should contact the ground.
Your hips should end their forward motion.

2. How to Step
You should focus your weight in the toes of your right foot. Push off that foot to take a short step forward.

3. How You Should Plant Your Left Foot
Your left foot should move parallel to the ground before making contact.

突
十分踏切ル突刺
（ス令ヲ

一、右足ニテ十分踏切リ左足ヨリ以テ迅速ニ進出スルト同時ニ兩手ヲ突檜ヲ握締メツツ敏速ニ前方ニ突出スル兩足ハケメツ地面ニ近ク左足ハ平踏スル爾足ハ敏速ニ定位ニ體重ヲ之ニ托シ

二、復スシ突後ハ速カニ構ヘノ姿勢ニ

一、踏切リ短切ナル力ヲ以テ十分ノ踏地ト同時ニ左膝ヲ曲ゲ且下腹部ニ力ヲ充實

二、左足ノ薯地ト同時ニ力ヲ

三、體ヲ上體ノ安定―刺突瞬時身ヲ動搖セザルコト

四、槍尖ノ威力―刺突ノ速度ヲ逐次ニ大ナラシムルコト

How To Stab While Taking Full Step Forward

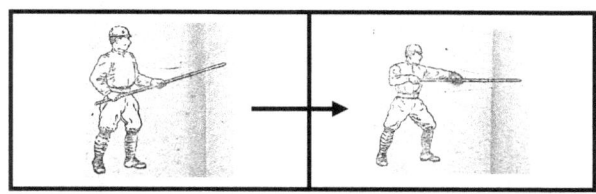

Command:
Tsuke! Stab!
If conducting training step-by-step, then use the command, *Nu-ke!* Pull out!

Operational Guide:
1. Put a sufficient amount of pressure on your right toes and step forward rapidly with your left foot. At the same time rapidly thrust the spear forward with both hands and grip firmly. Do not raise your feet high when stepping, both feet should stay near the ground. Your left foot should move parallel to the ground before making contact, then shift all your weight onto your left foot. This will allow you to rapidly pull your right foot up to its proper position, behind your left foot.
2. After stabbing your target, rapidly return to your starting stance.

Important Points:
1. Stepping Forward
Add more power to your back foot than in the previous method of taking just a short step forward.
2. The Left Foot
The moment your left foot makes contact with the ground, bend your left knee forward and focus your power in your lower abdomen.
3. Upper Body Stability
Ensure that moment you stab, your upper body does not become unbalanced.
4. The Force of the Spear
The faster you stab with the spear the greater the damage it will inflict

連續刺突

續イテイケ突

敵ニ對シ直突ヲ敏活ニ數回反復實施ス
刺突ノ動作ハ直突ノ要領ニ準ジ一回ノ刺突毎ニ力ヲ入換ヘテ刺突ス

一、最初ハ動作ヲ緩徐ニシ刺突及引拔ク動作ヲ確實ニ行フコト
二、刺突ハ十分伸暢シ氣、槍、體一致スルコト
三、引拔ハ確實ニ構ヘノ姿勢ニ復スルコト
四、習熟ニ伴ヒ身體ヲ凝ルコトナク圓滑且迅速ニ行フコト

Attacking With Successive Strikes

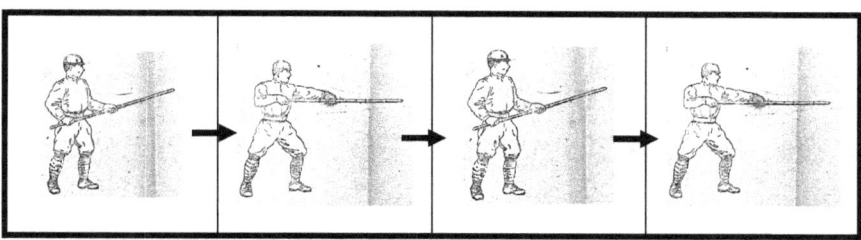

Command:
None

Operational Guide:

When confronting an enemy, you are attacking with spear-thrusts in rapid succession. Though you are attacking multiple times, these straight thrusts should be done as previously described. Each thrust should be done with the same amount of power.

Important Points:
1. Initially do the steps slowly, being sure to accurately thrust and withdraw the spear.
2. When thrusting forward be sure to extend your arms sufficiently. Your Spirit, Spear and Body should be moving in unison.
3. After withdrawing the spear, return to the correct starting position.
4. By doing extensive review of these lessons your body will lose its hesitancy and you will be able to attack with your spear rapidly and smoothly.

Totsunyu Shitotsu
Advancing Forward, Piercing Thrust

View From the Right   View From the Front

突　入	
數行	
步ヲ	
前突	
進入	
シ刺	
テ突	
突込メ	

一、前進ノ速度ヲ緩ムルコトナク踏切リテ刺突ス　刺突ハ直突ノ如ク確實ナルヲ要ス

二、實施ハ速歩、駈歩、早駈ノ順序ニ行フ

一、構ヘノ姿勢ー停止間ニ準ズルモ兩手ヲ以テ少シク槍ヲ後方ニ引ク

二、步行ハ普通ノ步行ノ如クス

三、刺突ハ直突ノ如ク確實ニ刺突シ特ニ刺突直前ニ躊躇セザルコト

四、引拔ハ左足ニテ踏切リ確實ニ引拔クコト

Totsunyu Shitotsu
Advancing Forward, Piercing Thrust

Advancing Several Steps, Then Piercing Thrust

Command:
Tsuki Kome!
Stab In!

Operational Guide:

1. Without allowing your speed to decrease, step forward and do a piercing thrust.
2. When training, increase the speed of your advance as follows:
Sokuho: Fast Walk
Kake Ashi: Quick Trot
Hayaga: Run

Important Points:
1. Proper Stance
Shift both hands back from where the spear is stopped at your hip, pulling the spear back
2. Walking Forward
Advance at a normal walk

3. Stabbing Thrust
This is a straight thrust and you should be sure to stab accurately. It is particularly important not to hesitate the moment before you strike.
4. Yank Out
Press your left foot down firmly so you can yank your spear out completely.

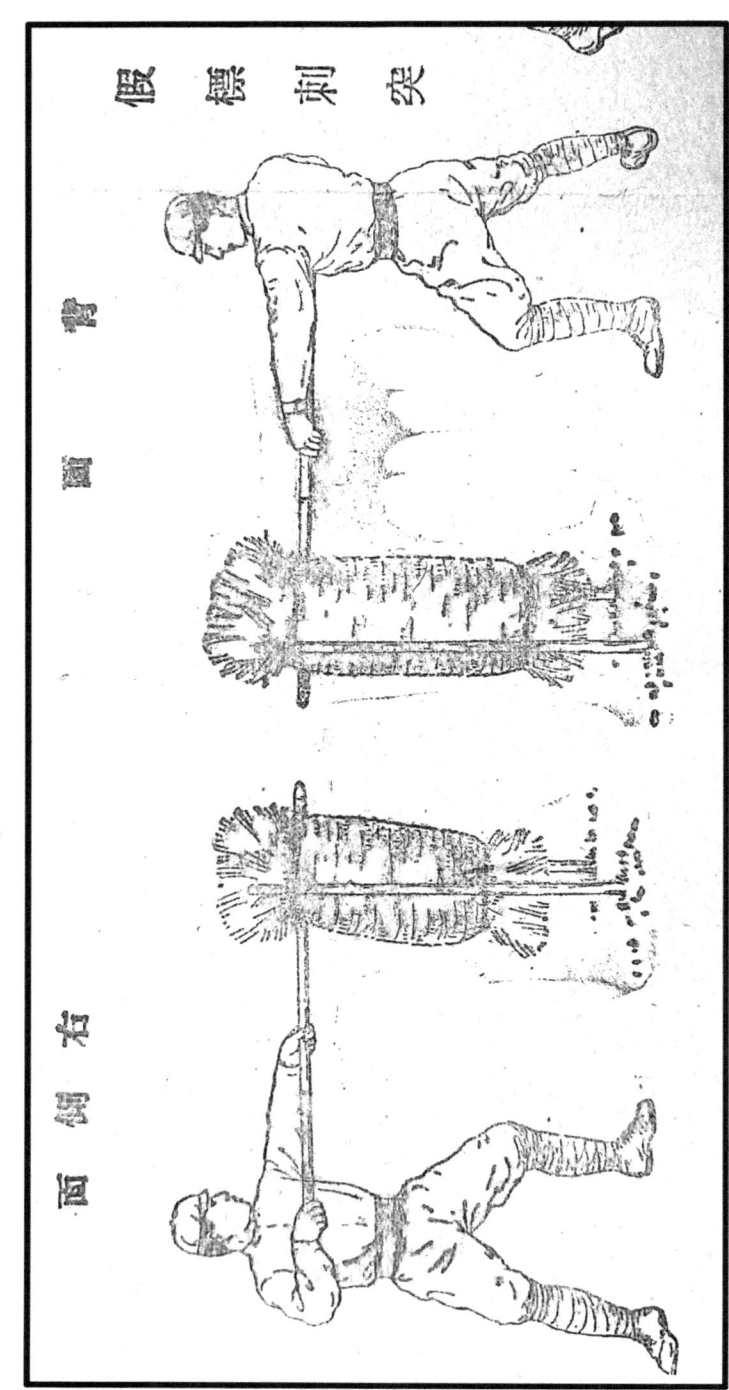

Kahyo Shitotsu Piercing Thrust on a Practice Target

Kahyo no Kunren
Piercing Thrust on a Practice Target

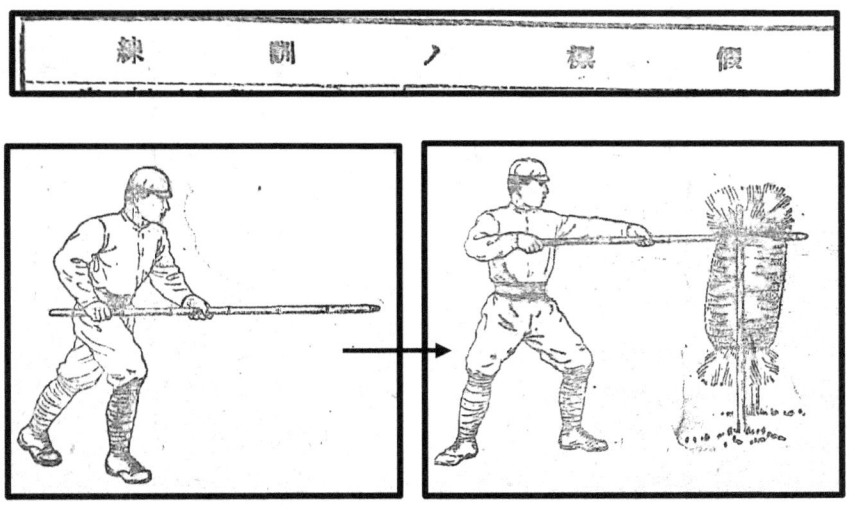

假標刺突

其ノ場刺突	位置ニ佶ル刺突 踏ニカル刺突 十分ナル踏切刺突 切突
突ケ	
空間ノ訓練ト同要領ニテ刺突ス	一、空間ノ訓練ト同要領ニテ刺突ス 二、引抜ハ腰ノ力ヲ利用シ後ヘノ要領ニテ引抜ク	空間ノ訓練ト同要領ニテ刺突ス
一、刺突量ハ空間ノ訓練ニ準ジ姿勢ヲ崩サザル程度ニ於テ刺突スコト、過度ニレザルコト 二、刺突法ハ押突トナラザルコト、左手ニカヲ入レザルコト	一、シ其ノ量大トナルコト 二、眞直ニ引抜クコト 刺突量ハ其ノ場刺突ニ比	空間ノ場合ニ準ズルモ刺突力十分ナルコト

Kahyo Shitotsu
Piercing Thrusts on a Practice Target

Part 1
How to Do a Piercing Thrust in Place

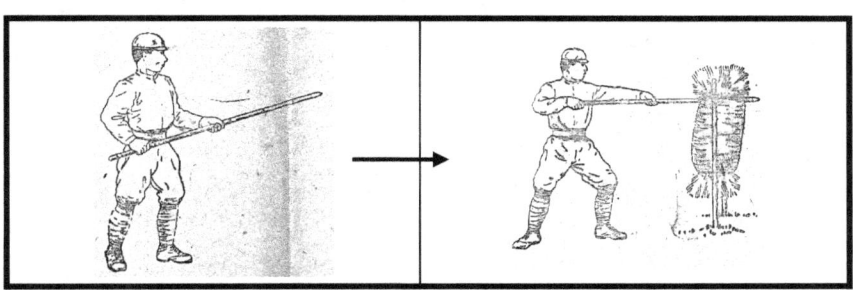

Command:
Tsuke! Stab!

Operational Guide:
The technique is done according to the same parameters as *Training in Place Against an Imaginary Target.*

Important Points:
1. Penetrating Power
Execute your piercing thrust with the same feeling as when training against an imaginary target. Be sure not to lose your balance when doing this attack.
2. A Proper Piercing Thrust
Do not allow this attack to be a pushing thrust. Prevent this by putting sufficient power in your left hand.

Stepping Slightly Forward Before Piercing Thrust

Command:
Tsuke! Stab!

Operational Guide:
1. The technique is done according to the same parameters as the previously chapter *Training in Place Against an Imaginary Target*.
2. Yank your spear out of the target as was previously described. Be sure to use the power of your hips when yanking the spear out.

Important Points:
1. When comparted to *Training in Place Against an Imaginary Target* the penetrating power must be greater.
2. Be sure to yank the spear out in a straight line.

Taking a Big Step Forward Then Piercing Thrust

Command:
Tsuke! Stab!

Operational Guide:
The attack is done according to the same parameters as *Training in Place Against an Imaginary Target*.

Important Points:
The attack should be considered the same as *Training in Place Against an Imaginary Target*, however be sure to put sufficient power in your piercing thrust.

突入假標刺突		
數步前進シテ突入シ突刺ヲ行フ突入突刺	約二十米ヲ行リ突入シ突刺ヲ行フ突入突刺込	敵ニ對スル突入突刺メ
空間ノ訓練ト同要領ニテ刺突ス	空間ノ訓練ト同要領ニテ刺突ス	一、假標ハ數箇ヲ設置シテ行フ 實施要領ハ前項ニ準ズ
二、刺突距離ヲ誤ラザルコト 腰ヲ落シテ刺突スルコト	引拔後更ニ他ノ敵ニ對スル準備ノ爲假標ノ後端迄迅速ニ進出スルコト	最後迄氣勢ヲ弛メザルコト

Advancing On The Practice Target, Then Launching a Piercing Thrust

Part 2
Advancing Several Steps Then Piercing Thrust

Command:
Tsuke Kome!
Advance and Attack!

Operational Guide:
The attack is done according to the same parameters as *Training in Place Against an Imaginary Target*.

Important Points:
1. Be sure to judge the distance to the point you launch your piercing thrust accurately.
2. Drop your hips as you launch your piercing thrust forward.

Advancing 20 Meters, Then Piercing Thrust

Command:
Tsuke Kome! Advance and Attack!

Operational Guide:
The attack is done according to the same parameters as *Training in Place Against an Imaginary Target.*

Important Points:
After you yank your spear out, immediately ready yourself to engage the next enemy by continuing rapidly past the practice target.

Advancing Forward Then Launching Piercing Thrusts Against Multiple Enemies

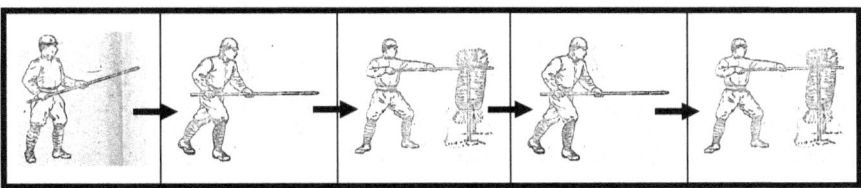

Command:
Tsuke Kome!
Advance and Attack!

Operational Guide:
1. Set up several practice targets for this training.
2. The training is done the same way as previously described.

Important Points:
Be sure to maintain the same intensity throughout the exercise.

ERIC SHAHAN

DEFENSE OF THE JAPANESE HOMELAND

Takeyari Jutsu Kunren Shidosha Yoh
Bamboo Spear Fighting
Training Manual
· Instructor's Guide ·

Kahyo no Kunren
假表ノ訓練
Training With a Practice Target

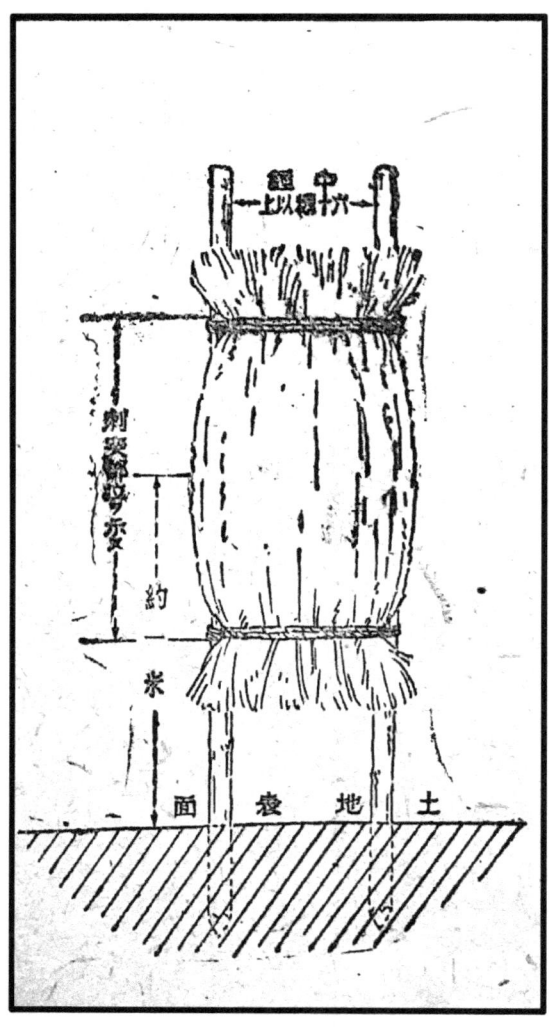

1. Illustration of the Construction of a Practice Target and How to Set it Up

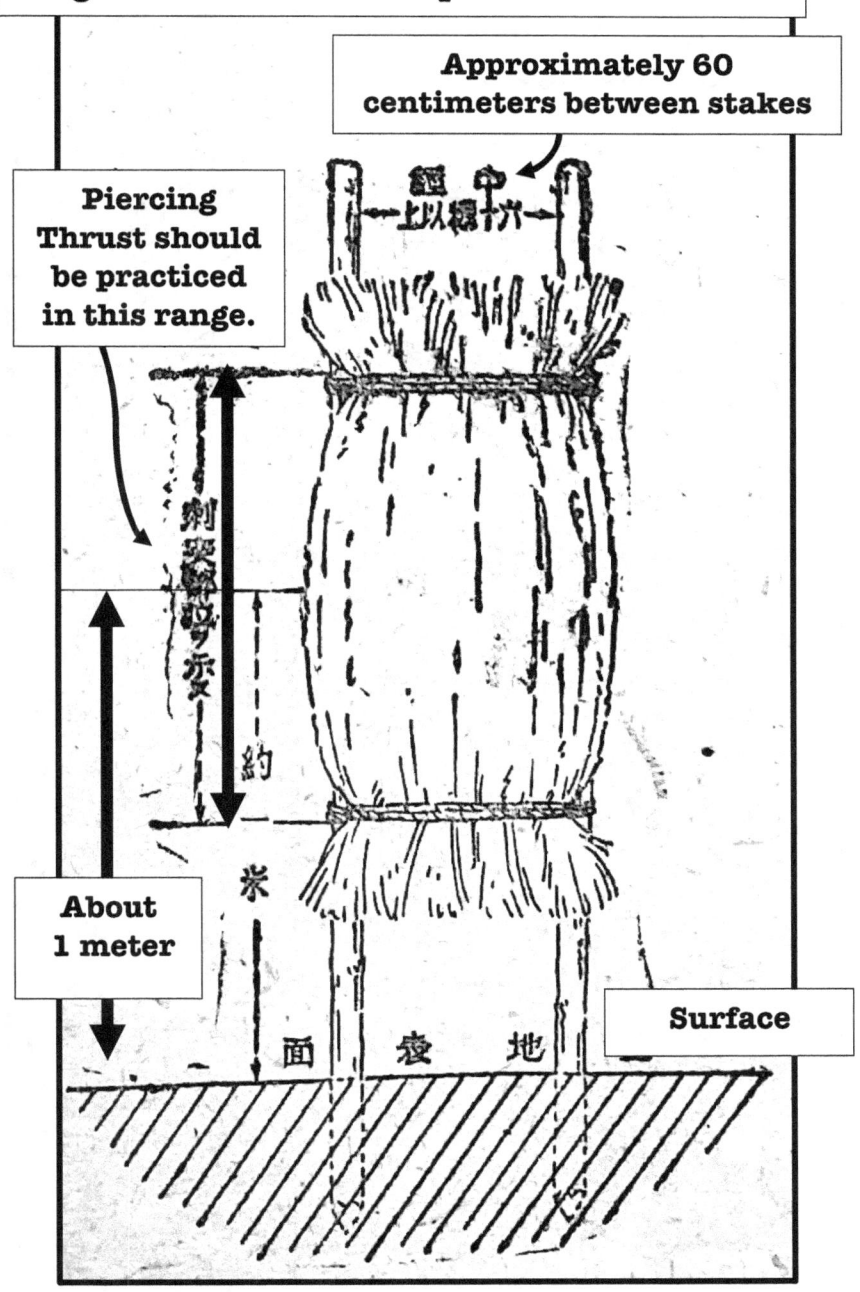

一、假標

1、構造及設置要領ノ一例

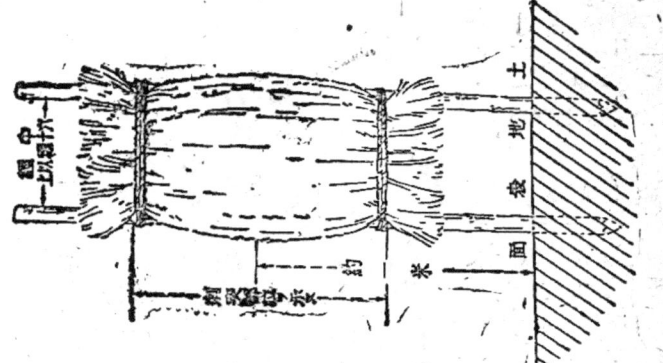

2、材料及結束法

麥藁、笹、草等柔カナル藁類ヲ可トス
突部位ニハ結束セル木ノ束ヲ可トス
設置ニハ兩端ヲ杭ニ繋著スル

3、設置ノ位置

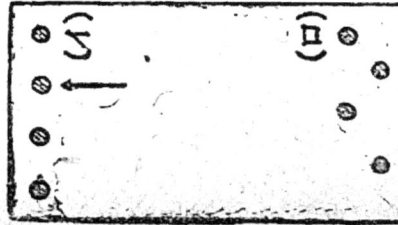

(イ)ノ如ク一定ノ方向ニ植立セル各個ノ刺突ニ對シ得ベカラザル如ク數箇ヲ行フヲ可トス
(ロ)ノ如ク方向ヲ異ニシ得ル訓練ヲ行フモ可ナリ

二、危害豫防上ノ注意

1、槍ヲ使用スル場合ハ槍尖ノ附近ニ在ル者ニ指先ヲ觸レザルコト
2、訓練ハ必ズ統制ヲ以テ一齊ニ行ヒ各自ニ行ハシメズ
3、刺突後舊位ニ復スル際又ハ刺突セザル如ク退路ヲ留意スル要ス
4、指導者ハ竹槍ノ管理ヲ嚴ニスルヲ要ス

名ヅケ刺突ノ時ハ假標ニ刺突スル
刺突携行方法モ統制シ
相互ニ衝突シ刺突セザル如ク注意ス

Part 1
Kahyo Practice Target

1. (previous page)
2. **Construction Materials & Tying Method**
Make a bundle of Wara (rice straw,) Mugi-wara (barely straw,) Sasa-kusa (bamboo grass straw) or other such soft material. Tie each end of the bundle securely with cord. Note that the area that you will be doing piercing thrusts on should not be tied.

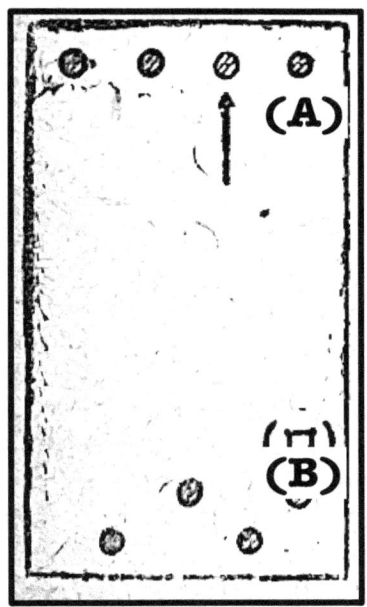

3. Positioning the Practice Targets
(A) Positioning the targets in this manner means you can only use them for training in one direction, so this should not be done.

(B) Positioning the targets as shown here not only means students can practice piercing thrusts in multiple directions, but also they can train attacking multiple targets.

Part 2
How to Avoid Dangerous Injuries

1. When spears are being used during training, no one should stand near where the spearpoints can reach.
2. It is absolutely essential that instructors maintain control of training. In particular, when students are training piercing thrusts against a practice target. Students should not practice randomly, rather the instructor should call students forward one at a time and that student should practice piercing thrusts.
3. Following practice against the target, the instructor should designate the path the student takes back to their original position. In addition, the way the students carry the spear when travelling this path should be standardized, to prevent students from colliding and injuring each other. Finally, instructors should maintain awareness so no situation arises that results in one student doing a piercing thrust on another.
4. The instructor should maintain strict control over the use and storage of the Takeyari, bamboo spears.

一、指導者ノ實務
　指導者ハ自ラ率先垂範スルト共ニ其ノ敎育法ニ習熟シ時ニ終始一貫熱意ヲ以テ指導ニ從事スルコト緊要ナリ

二、訓練ノ到達目標
　敎官ハ假標ニ對シ必勝ヲ確信シ突入刺突スル動作ヲ習熟セシムルヲ以テ到達點トス
　併シ刺突動作ハ眞ニ實敵ニ對スル觀念ヲ以テ實施セシメ一突必殺ノ域ニ至ラシムルヲ要ス

三、敎育順序
　先ヅ塁同ニ於テ稱ヘノ姿勢、停止間ノ刺突、突入刺突ノ順序ニ敎育シ次テ假標ニ對シテ前記ノ順序ニ適切ヲ行フ則

四、敎育要領
　敎育セントスル課目ノ目的及精神ヲ知ラシメ模範ヲ示シ實施
　分解シテ行ヒ要領ヲ會得セシムルニ至レハ先ヅ正確ニ次テ迅速ニ刺突セシムル
　法ノ概要ヲ説明シ所要ノ注意ヲ與へ次テ要スヘキ氣力ヲ充實セシムル
　漸次要求程度ヲ高ムル如ク實施スルヲ要ス
　部隊訓練ト個性指導

五、少數ヲ以テ多數者ニ對シ短時間ニ訓練ヲ實施セントセハ多人數同時ニ造リ訓練スルコトヲ得ズ止ムヲ得ズ外形ノ齊一ヲ
　然レドモ敎育ハ個々造應シテ行フモ實施者ノ缺點ヲ發見セシムルモノ
　ニ因リ場ニ於テ適時的確ニ編正シ速ニ使術ノ眞髓ヲ體得セシムルニ努ムルヲ要ス

六、竹槍使用上ノ注意
　竹槍ハ銃ノ代用トシテ之ヲ使用スル
　訓練ニ依リ心身ヲ假練陶冶シ使術ヲ修得セシメ其ノ如クニ留意スル以テ直接外敵擊
　得スル誡メニ使用スルモノニテ人ニ危害ヲ與ヘザル如ク統制ヲ全ウスルヲ主眼トシ殊ニ攻防ヲ假設スル如キ場合ニ於テハ他人ニ危害ヲ及ホサザル如ク留意スルコト緊要ナリ

Instructor's Manual

1. The Instructor's Responsibility
It is essential that instructors set an example worth following. Thus, an instructor should have trained these techniques extensively and also be intimately familiar with the teaching method. It is particularly important that the instructor maintains intense focus while teaching, and that his instruction is consistent from beginning to end.

2. Achievement Goal for Training
The training goal can be considered to have been achieved if a learner is able to advance on a series of targets and accurately launch piercing thrusts capable of completely incapacitating the enemy.

3. Instruction Order
The first phase, *Training in Place Against an Imaginary Target,* teaches the proper stance and how the arms move the spear forward from the ready position. Next, stepping and doing a piercing thrust as well as advancing then attacking with a piercing thrust are taught.

Having completed the above, the same drills should be repeated in the same order against a practice target.

4. Outline of the Teaching Method
The instructor should clearly explain the curriculum as well as the proper state of mind learners should maintain while training. Further, the instructor should clearly explain the essential points and model how the techniques are to be executed. Instructors also need to highlight points that require particular attention or caution. By breaking down the techniques and gradually progressing through the material, learners will gradually develop an understanding of the essential points. Initially, the focus of instruction should be on accuracy, then to a rapid execution of the technique. The final

result of this gradual implementation of requirements are students that can execute an accurate piercing thrust at with the proper intensity.

5. Training in Groups and Instructing Individual Students

The fact is a small number of instructors are now required to teach a large number of students simultaneously in a short amount of time. However, part of educating the students in this course requires the instructor to adapt his lessons to the students. Instructors should not become trapped in futilely attempting to unify the outward appearance of all the students. Rather, if you find a learner is deficient in some aspect, give the proper correction then and there before continuing to develop all the students. There is an urgent need for students to become proficient users of this weapon, so they need to develop a fundamental understanding of its operation through repeated practice.

6. Cautions Regarding the Use of the Bamboo Spear

The bamboo spear is being trained in place of a rifle. The purpose of training is to destroy foreign invaders to our imperial lands. Thus the purpose of training is to forget the body and spirit so that students can become proficient at this weapon.

Since the bamboo spear can do injury to a person, the training method should be strictly regulated by the instructor. It is essential that instructors remain vigilant so that students do not cause injury to each other.

課目	特性竝ニ訓練程度	教育ノ順序及手段
空	不動姿勢ノ動勢 / 構ヘノ姿勢	
	竹槍ノ保持法ヲ教フルヲ目的トス コルモ不動ノ姿勢ノ訓練ヲ受ケタル トナキ者ニ對シテハ不動ノ姿勢 ヲ一通リ教育ス	
	一、槍ノ操法ノ基礎姿勢ナリ故ニ 敵ヲ突刺スル氣魄充實スルト共ニ 堅確ナルト必要ナリ 直チニ前進シ或ハ刺突シ得ルガ如 クナルコト必要ナリ 二、特ニ力ヲ用ヒテ教育スルノ要 ヲ要ス要點ハ十分體得セシムル	一、手腰ニテ兩足、膝、體重ノ懸 ケ方、足ノ踏著ケ方、上體ノ向 上體及頭ノ保持チ方ヲ教育ス 二、竹槍ヲ保持シテ前號ノ動作ト 共ニ竹槍ノ構ヘ方ニ就テ 兩肘ノ位置、槍ノ握リ方ニ就テ 教育ス

Training Against an Imaginary Target

Fudo no Shisei
Immovable Stance

Focus of Training
The purpose it to teach students how to hold the Takeyari. Students that have not received training in the Immovable Stance should be given an overview of this stance.

Kamae Eh no Shisei
Going Into the Ready Stance

Focus of Training
1. This is the basic starting stance when manipulating the spear, therefore it is important the students execute the piercing thrust with sufficient vigor. The students should also become able to immediately advance and execute a skilled piercing thrust. It is essential that this be done in conjunction with developing a body that will not freeze at the crucial moment.
2. It is not necessary for the instructor to teach with extreme strictness, rather the goal should be for the students to develop sufficient ability.

Order of Teaching & Methodology
1. Instructors should teach about proper positioning of the hands and hips, as well as the knees. In addition how to balance, how to plant the feet, how the upper body should be angled and how the head should be held throughout the exercise.
2. Continuing from the previous step, where students were taught how to hold the bamboo spear, instructors teach how to transition into this stance with the bamboo spear. In particular, instructors should show the proper positioning of the fists, the elbows and how the spear should be gripped.

構ヘノ姿勢ヲ教育スル為附隨シテ行フ程度トス	構リノヘ不姿ヨ動勢
敵ノ直前ニ於テ進退スル動作ニシテ油断ナク極メテ敏捷輕快ニ行フノ要アルト共ニ常ニ槍ヲ突出ス準備ヲ整ヘアルヲ要ス	前進及後退
一、最初ハ手腰次デ槍ヲ持チテ眞直ニ前進スル方法次デ後退スル方法、前進及後退ヲ自由ニ行フ方法ヲ教育ス 二、次デ斜左（右）ニ前進スル方法ヲ教育ス	最初ハ手腰次デ槍ヲ持チタル構ヘノ姿勢ヨリ不動ノ姿勢ニ復スル要領ヲ教育ス

Transitioning From Ready to Immovable Stance

Focus of Training
This should be taught as part of the training in the Ready Stance.

Order of Teaching & Methodology
First teach about how the hands and hips should be positioned, then how the spear should be held when going into Ready Stance. Finally, instruct them in how to return to Immovable Stance.

Advancing as well as Retreating

Focus of Training
Students should learn how to either advance towards or retreat away from an enemy. It is essential that this movement should be done without faltering and in a rapid and fluid manner. At the same time, students should be ready to attack with their spear.

Order of Teaching & Methodology
1. First teach how the hands and hips should be positioned and then how to hold the spear. After that, show how to advance in a straight line and then how to withdraw. Students should be taught to be able to either advance or retreat smoothly and without hesitation.
2. Following that, students should be taught how to advance on a left or right diagonal.

直突	突	
其ノ場突刺	僅ニカル切刺突蹈突	十分ニル蹈刺切突
一、直突ハ敵ノ胴體ヲ眞直ニ刺突スル動作ニシテ最モ力ヲ用ヒテ訓練スベキ課目ナリ 二、其ノ場刺突ハ突方ノ内主トシテ兩臂ノ操作ヲ演練ス	蹈切ッテ刺突スル特ニ臂、脚、體一致シテ刺突スル要領ヲ修得セシムルモノニシテ特ニ力ヲ用ヒテ訓練スベキ課目ナリ	十分ニ蹈切リ一突ニ突刺ス動作ニシテ竹槍訓練中最モ力ヲ用ヒテ訓練スベキ課目ナリ
一、臂ノミニテ突ク要領ヲ教育ス 二、次デ腰ヲ推進シ臂、腰、脚一致ノ刺突要領ヲ教育ス	一、僅カニ進出スル動作ト一致スル如ク槍ヲ突出ス動作ト一致スル如ク緩徐ニ行ハシム 二、右足ノ蹈切リ方、左膝ノ曲ゲ方、體ノ一等ニ就キ動作ノ確實、臂、脚、體一致ニ留意シテ教育ス	最初ハ緩徐ニ行フモ逐次迅速ニ出シ且蹈切量ヲ大ニシ威力アル刺突ヲ行フ如ク教育ス

Choku Tsuki
Straight Thrust

A Stationary Piercing Thrust

Focus of Training
1. The straight thrust should be to the enemy's torso. The instructor should focus on the students executing this thrust with the maximum amount of power.
2. When teaching how to do spear thrusts in place the focus should be on the movement of the spear, with particular attention paid to how the elbows move.

Order of Teaching & Methodology
1. The main point instructors should teach about this thrust is how this is done with the elbows.
2. Next, instructors should show how to thrust the hips forward. Then show how to move the elbows, hips and legs in unison to execute a piercing thrust.

Stepping Slightly Forward, then Piercing Thrust

Focus of Training
When executing a piercing thrust while stepping forward, it is important to ensure the elbows, legs and body all move in unison. This combination needs to be trained extensively. The instructor's focus should be demonstrating how to apply power.

Order of Teaching & Methodology
1. Instructors should focus on ensuring the learners unify the slight step forward and spear-thrust. The training should be conducted at a slow speed.
2. Instructors should emphasize how the weight should be shifted to the right foot and how the left knee should bend. Check that these movements are accurate. Watch to make sure the students' elbows, legs and body are moving in unison.

突	連刺 續突
十分ニ蹈切リ一突ニ突刺ス動作ニシテ竹槍訓練中最モ力ヲ用ヒテ訓練スベキ課目ナリ　蹈分切刺突	敵ニ對シ刺突ヲ反復シテ行フ動作ニシテ直突ニ次デ力ヲ用ヒテ訓練スベキ課目ナリ
最初ハ緩徐ニ行フモ逐次迅速ニ突出シ且蹈切量ヲ大ニシ威力アル刺突ヲ行フ如ク教育ス	最初ハ動作ヲ緩徐ニシ且確實ニ行ハシムルモ逐次動作ヲ圓滑且敏速ナラシム

Taking a Full Step Forward, Then Piercing Thrust

Focus of Training
The action of taking a full step forward and then stabbing in a piercing thrust is the aspect of bamboo spear training that should employ the most strength. Instructors should focus on this aspect of training.

Order of Teaching & Methodology
Initially, instructors should do the training at a slow pace before gradually increasing the speed. Further, instruct the students to maximize the distance the front foot travels to increase the force of the piercing thrust.

Launching Multiple Piercing Thrusts

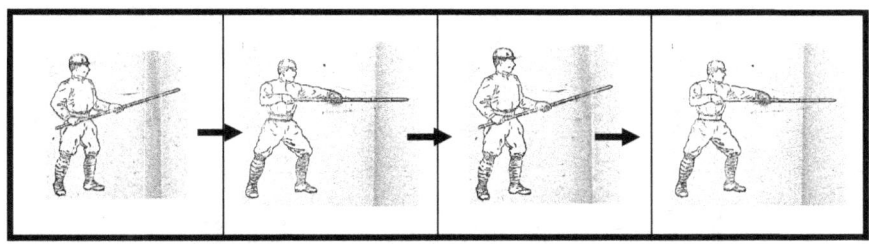

Focus of Training
This is launching repeated piercing thrusts at the enemy. Instructors should focus training on how to put power into each piercing thrust.

Order of Teaching & Methodology
Initially the training should be done slowly, but moreover accurately. The speed should gradually be increased so the action is smooth and, in particular, fast.

練	
突　刺　入　突	
リ　ヨ　　十　二　約 突　刺　　突　フ　行	テ　進前　步 シ　刺入　突 突刺　入突　數 ナリ　　　　フ
突撃ノ基礎動作ニシテ重視シテ教育スルノ要アリ	突入シツツ刺突スル基礎動作ニシテ最モ力ヲ用ヒテ訓練スベキ動作
四、演練ス各種姿勢ヨリ突入スル動作ヲ 三、刺突時腰ヲ落ス要領ヲ教育ス 二、入リ逐次突歩度ヲ早メ猛烈果敢ニ突刺スル要領ヲ教育ス 一、聲ヲ發シ槍ヲ構ヘテ突入スル要領ヲ教育ス最初ハ立姿ヨリ緩速度ニテ突入シ次デ「突込メ」ノ號令ニテ喊	二、駈步、早駈ニテ數步疾走刺突スル要領ヲ教育ス 一、速步ニテ數步前進刺突スル要領ヲ教育ス

Totsunyu Shitotsu
Advancing Then Piercing Thrust

Advancing Several Steps, Then Piercing Thrust

Focus of Training
Instructors should put maximum effort into training students to be able to execute a piercing thrust, the fundamental movement, while advancing.

Order of Teaching & Methodology
1. Instructors should teach all aspects of how to advance several steps before executing a piercing thrust.
2. Instructors should teach all aspects of how to advance using *Kake Ashi* : Quick Trot, as well as *Hayaga* : Run.

Advancing About 20 Meters, Then Piercing Thrust

Focus of Training
Instructors should focus on ensuring learners can execute a piercing thrust, the fundamental movement.

Order of Teaching & Methodology
1. First have the learners start from a standing position and then move forward slowly before stabbing with their spear. Next, instructors should teach students how to respond to the command of "*Tsuki Kome!*" by going into the ready stance, ad advancing and attacking.
2. Instructors should gradually increase the speed of the attack until students can advance and launch a piercing attack with furious intent.
3. Instructors should ensure students are aware that they should drop their hips the moment they launch a piercing thrust.
4. Students should demonstrate advancing and attacking from any starting position.

假　標		
假標突刺		突刺踏切　分ル十
其ノ場ノ刺突	僅カニ踏切ッテ刺突	分ルノ力ヲ十分ニ發揮
假標ノ訓練ハ槍ノ握締メ、兩臂ノ操作、槍尖ノ方向等ヲ會得セシメ且刺貫クノ實感ヲ得シムル為價値大ナリ故ニ空間ノ訓練ニ於テ概ネ其ノ要領ヲ會得セバ主トシテ假標ヲ利用シ訓練ヲ行フノ要アリ	假標ニ對シ僅カニ踏切ツテ前進シ臂、脚一致シテ刺突スル要領ヲ會得セシムルモノニシテ最モ力ヲ用ヒテ訓練スベキ課目ナリ	假標ノ力ヲ對シ十分踏切リ臂及腰全體ニ集中シテ刺突スル特ニ要領ヲ教育スベキ課目ナリ
一、刺突姿勢ヲ取リ槍尖ガ假標ニ當ル距離ニ起チ先ヅ確實ニ刺突スルコトヲ演練ス刺突動作ヲ施セシム逐次ニ槍ノ威力ヲ確實ニ行ヒ得ルニ至レバ直チニ引拔カシム　二、逐次刺突ト引拔ク動作ヲ區分シ實ニ引拔ク動作ヲ要求シ刺突セ	一、最初ハ緩速度ニテ動作ヲ確實ニシ且刺突ト引拔ク動作ヲ區分シテ教育ス槍尖ノ威力ヲ増加シ刺突教育ス　二、分シテ教育ス槍尖ノ威力ヲ増加シ刺突ス最後直チニ引拔	最初ハ動作ヲ確實ニシ動作ヲ區分シテ教育スル刺突ト引拔動作逐次槍尖ノ威力ヲ増大シ且引拔ヲ次迅速ナラシム

Kahyo
Practice Target
Kahyo Shitotsu
Piercing Thrusts on a Practice Target

Part 1
Stationary Piercing Thrust

Focus of Training
When training using the practice target instructors should ensure students understand how to grip the spear tightly and bend both elbows properly when attacking and are orienting the cut end of the bamboo spear correctly. Moreover this training will add the tactile feeling of penetration which is very valuable. Thus if students have developed an understanding of the technique through Training Against an Imaginary Target then the remainder of training should focus on training against a practice target.

Order of Teaching & Methodology
1. Have the students stand ready to attack, close enough for the point of the spear to hit the practice target. First practice doing a piercing thrust.
Have the students practice doing a piercing thrust and yanking out the spear separately.
2. As the students' accuracy improves the instructor should encourage the students to attack with more force and to yank the spear out immediately after doing a piercing thrust.

假標突刺		其ノ場ノ刺突
十分踏切突刺	僅ニ踏切ル刺突	
假標ニ對シ十分踏切リ臂及腰ノ全體ノ力ヲ槍尖ニ集中シテ刺突スル要領ヲ教育スベキ課目ナリ	假標ニ對シ僅カニ踏切ッテ前進シ臂、脚一致シテ刺突スル要領ヲ會得セシムルモノニシテ最モ力ヲ用ヒテ訓練スベキ課目ナリ	假標ノ訓練ハ槍ノ握締メ、兩臂ノ操作、槍尖ノ方向等ヲ會得セシメ且刺貫クノ實感ヲ得シムル爲價値大ナリ故ニ空間ノ訓練ニ於テ概ネ其ノ要領ヲ會得セバ主トシテ假標ヲ利用シ訓練ヲ行フノ要アリ
一、最初ハ動作ヲ確實ニシ刺突ト引拔クノ動作トヲ區分シテ教育スルモノ次ク槍尖ノ威力ヲ増大シ且引拔動作ヲ迅速ナラシム	一、最初ハ緩速度ニテ動作ヲ確實ニシ且刺突ト引拔クノ動作トヲ區分シテ教育スルモノトシテ槍尖ノ威力ヲ増加シ刺突ス 二、分シテ教育スル槍尖ノ威力ヲ増加シ刺突ス後直チニ引拔ク動作	一、刺突姿勢ヲ取リ槍尖ガ假標ニ當ル距離ニ起チ先ヅ確實ニ刺突スルコトヲ演練スルコト刺突ト引拔ク動作トヲ區分シ實施セシム動作ヲ確實ニ行ヒ得ルニ至レバ逐次槍ノ威力ヲ要求シ刺突セ 二、バ直チニ引拔カシム

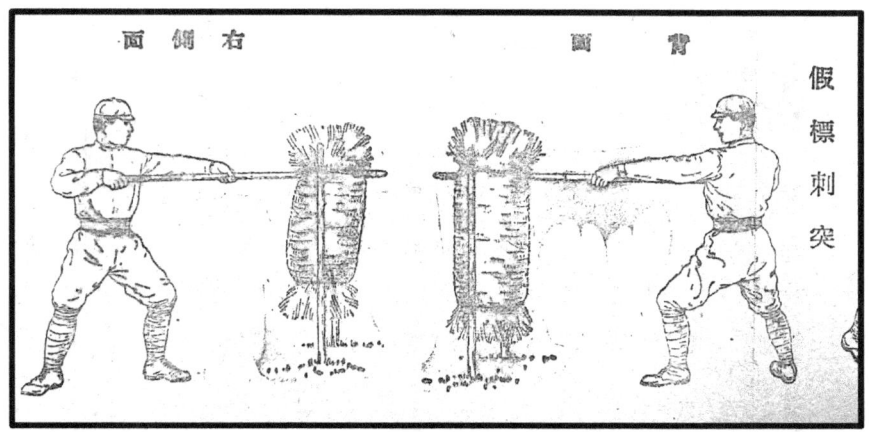

Stepping Slightly Forward, Then Piercing Thrust

Focus of Training
The instructor should teach the proper way to advance a small step forward before attacking with a piercing thrust that uses the elbows and legs moving in unison. Instructors should devote their energy to training students until they are able to demonstrate this attack.

Order of Teaching & Methodology
1. Initially students should practice at a slow speed in order to learn the proper movements. Instructors should teach how to do the piercing thrust and how to yank the spear out separately.
2. Instructors should have the students gradually increase the power they are putting into the spearpoint and after attacking with a piercing thrust, be taught how to yank the spear out.

假標		
假標刺突 其ノ場突	僅カニ刺突スル蹈切	十分ナル蹈切分刺突切突
假標ノ訓練ハ槍ノ握締メ、兩臂ノ操作、槍尖ノ方向等ヲ會得セシメ且刺貫クノ實感ヲ得シムル爲價値大ナリ故ニ空間ノ訓練ニ於テ概ネ其ノ要領ヲ會得セバ主トシテ假標ヲ利用シ訓練ヲ行フノ要アリ	假標ニ對シ僅カニ蹈切ッテ前進シ臂、脚一致シテ刺突スル要領ヲ會ヒテ訓練スベキ課目ナリ	假標ニ對シ十分蹈切リ臂及腰全體ノ力ヲ槍尖ニ集中シテ刺突スル特ニ力領ヲ敎育スベキ課目ナリ
一、刺突姿勢ヲ取リ槍尖ガ假標ニ當ル距離ニ起チ先ヅ確實ニ刺突スルコトヲ演練ス刺突ト引拔ク動作トヲ區分シ實施セシム 二、動作ヲ逐次ニ槍ノ威力ヲ要求シ刺突セシムバ直チニ引拔カシム	一、最初ハ緩速度ニテ動作ヲ確實ニ且刺突ト引拔ク動作ヲ區分シテ敎育ス槍尖ノ威力ヲ増加シ刺突ス 二、後直チニ引拔ク動作ヲ敎育ス	最初ハ動作ヲ確實ニシ刺突スルモ逐次槍尖ハ動作トヲ區分シテ敎育シ次ク槍尖ノ威力ヲ増大シ且引拔ヲ迅速ナラシム

Taking a Full Step Forward, Then Piercing Thrust

Focus of Training
Students should be taught to take a full step forward, advancing on the practice target and attack with a piercing thrust. The whole body, particularly the elbows and hips, should move forward in unison with all the power focused in the tip of the spear. Instructors should pay particular attention when training students in this skill.

Order of Teaching & Methodology
Initially instruction should focus on accurate movements. Teach attacking with a piercing thrust and yanking the spear out separately. Later instruct the students to apply more force to their thrusts and yank the spear out quickly.

闘練			ノ入突	
突刺	標假		突入	
對ニ突刺	標假ノ入突	數箇ノ突刺	ヨリ突刺	十米突入	約二フ行	シテ突刺	進入前突	數箇行フ
敵ヲ各個ニ撃破スル如ク迅速果敢ニ突撃スル要領ヲ會得セシムルノミニシテ止ムヲ得ザレバ一通リ教育セバ足レリトス	假標ニ對シ槍ヲ提ゲタル姿勢ヨリ突進シ適時槍ヲ搆ヘテ突入刺突ル動作ニシテ特ニ重視訓練スベキ課目ナリ		假標ニ對スル突入刺突ノ基礎動作ニシテ力ヲ用ヒデ教育スベキ課目ナリ	
三、實施セシム 二、對スル刺突要領ヲ教育スル為ニシ刺突要領ヲ得レバ各種不齊地ニ於テ 一、最初ハ前後差少キ數箇ノ假標ニ次デ前後差大ナル數箇ノ假標	三、演練ス 二、逐次步度ヲ早メ猛烈果敢ニ突入スル動作ヲ更ニ伏姿ヨリ突入スル要領ヲ教育ス 一、最初ハ緩速度ニテ突進シ次デ「突込メ」ノ號令ニテ喊聲ヲ發シ適時槍ヲ搆ヘテ突入スル要領		三、刺突後腰ヲ落ス要領ヲ教育ス 二、要領ヲ逐次疾走シツツ突入刺突スル教育ス 一、最初ハ緩速度ニテ突入シツツ刺突要領ヲ教育ス	
二、假標距離十米以上トナレバ槍ヲ右手ニ提ゲテ前進スルヲ可トス 一、一名ヅツ實施セザレバ危險ナリ	同右		四周ヨリ行ヒ得ルモ一名ヅツ實施セザレバ危險ナリ	

Totsunyu Kahyo Shitotsu
Advancing On The Practice Target Then Launching a Piercing Thrust

Part 2
Taking Several Steps Forward, Then Piercing Thrust

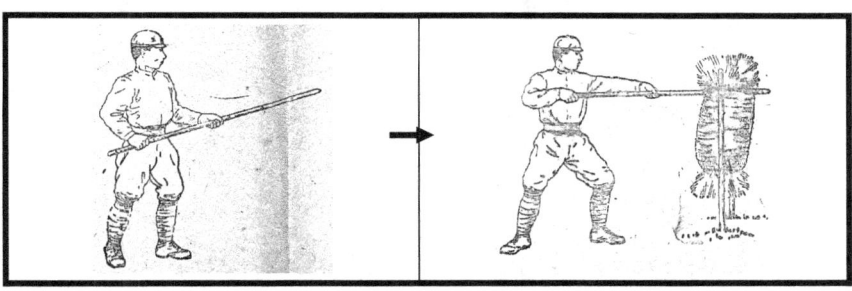

Focus of Training
The instructor should continue to develop the students using the practice target, building on the foundation learned in *Advancing Toward the Enemy, Then Piercing Thrust*.

Order of Teaching & Methodology
1. Initially the speed which the students advance towards the target and attack with a piercing thrust should be kept slow.
2. The instruction should then focus on increasing the speed until the students are running towards the target and stabbing with a piercing thrust.
3. Teach to drop the hips after the piercing thrust.

Cautions During Instruction
Students should stand outside the training area and be called forward one at a time. Failing to do this will result in injury.

突入	訓 練	練 突 刺
歩数行／進前突入突入シテ突刺	約十米ニ突入 假標ノ突刺 標 リ ヨ 突 刺	数 行 ス ル 假ノ突入 標箇入 對ニ突刺
假標ニ對スル突入刺突ノ基礎動作ニシテ力ヲ用ヒデ教育スベキ課目ナリ	假標ニ對シ槍ヲ提ゲタル姿勢ヨリ突進シ適時槍ヲ構ヘテ突入刺突ル動作ニシテ特ニ重視訓練スベキ課目ナリ	敵ヲ各個ニ擊破スル如ク迅速果敢ニ突擊スル要領ヲ會得セシムルモノニシテ止ムヲ得ザレバ一通リ教育セバ足レリトス
一、最初ハ緩速度ニテ突入シツツ刺突ノ要領ヲ教育ス 二、逐次疾走シツツ突入刺突スル要領ヲ教育ス 三、要領ヲ刺突後腰ヲ落ス要領ヲ教育ス	一、最初ハ緩速度ニテ突進シ次デ「突込メ」ノ號令ニテ喊聲ヲ發シ適時槍ヲ構ヘテ突入スル要領ヲ教育ス 二、逐次步度ヲ早メ猛烈果敢ニ突入刺突スル要領ヲ教育ス 三、更ニ伏姿ヨリ突入スル動作ヲ演練ス	一、最初ハ前後差少キ数箇ノ假標ニ對スル突刺ノ要領ヲ演練ス 二、次デ前後差大ナル数箇ノ假標ニ對スル刺突ノ要領ヲ教育ス 三、實為シ得レバ各種不齊地ニ於テ實施セシム
四周ヨリ行ヒ得ルモ一名ヅツ實施セザレバ危險ナリ	同 右	一、一名ヅツ實施セザレバ危險ナリ 二、假標距離十米以上トナレバ槍ヲ右手ニ提ゲテ前進スルヲ可トス

Advancing 20 Meters, Then Piercing Thrust

Focus of Training
Instructors should pay particular attention to teaching students how to advance on the practice target with their spear held low, then, at the appropriate distance, shift to the proper stance and attack with a penetrating thrust.

Order of Teaching & Methodology
1. Initially, the students should be taught to advance slowly. Later, students should respond to the command Tsuki Kome!, with a battle cry and advance, shifting into the proper stance at the right time.
2. Gradually increase the speed the students are walking, emphasizing the goal of advancing in a decisive manner and attacking with a penetrating thrust that has ferocious intensity.
3. Instructors should also teach how to rise and advance from a prone position.

Cautions During Instruction
Students should stand outside the training area and be called forward one at a time. Failing to do this will result in injury.

突刺ノ訓練

突入 步行シテ突進前進入突刺	假入標 約行フ二十米入リ突刺	刺標 數ルス箇ノ突刺	突刺 對二突刺 假ノ突入
假標ニ對スル突入刺突ノ基礎動作ニシテ力ヲ用ヒデ教育スベキ課目ナリ	假標ニ對シ槍ヲ提ゲタル姿勢ヨリ突進シ適時槍ヲ構ヘテ突入刺突スル動作ニシテ特ニ重視訓練スベキ課目ナリ	敵ヲ各個ニ擊破スル如ク迅速果敢ニ突擊スル要領ヲ會得セシムルモノニシテ止ムヲ得ザレバ一通リ敎育セバ足レリトス
一、最初ハ緩速度ニテ突入シツツ刺突スル要領ヲ敎育ス 二、逐次疾走シツツ突入刺突スル要領ヲ敎育ス 三、刺突後腰ヲ落ス要領ヲ敎育ス	一、最初ハ緩速度ニテ突進シ次デ「突込メ」ノ號令ニテ喊聲ヲ發シ適時槍ヲ構ヘテ突入スル要領ヲ敎育ス 二、刺突スル要領ヲ敎育ス 三、更ニ伏姿ヨリ突入スル動作ヲ演練ス	一、最初ハ前後差少キ數箇ノ假標ニ對スル刺突要領ノ演練ヲ得タル後差大ナル數箇ノ假標ニ對スル刺突要領ヲ敎育ス 三、爲シ得レバ各種不齊地ニ於テ實施セシム
四周ヨリ行ヒ得ルモ一名ヅツ實施セザレバ危險ナリ	同右	一、一名ヅツ實施セザレバ危險ナリ 二、假標距離十米以上トナレバ槍ヲ右手ニ提ゲテ前進スルヲ可トス

Attacking Multiple Targets With a Piercing Thrust

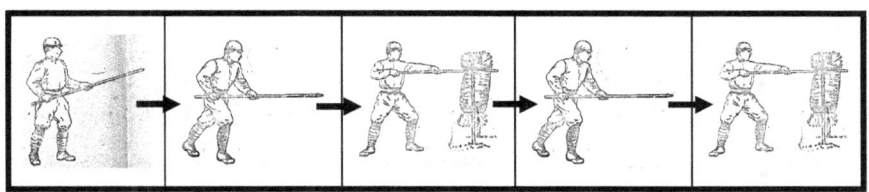

The goal of this lesson is for the student to advance on each enemy and destroy them. The piercing attacks should be quick and decisive. If there are time constraints, then having each student practice one time will be sufficient.

1. At first the number of targets should be kept small. Have the students advance on one target in front of them and one target behind them and attack each with a piercing thrust.
2. Next, the instructor should increase the number of practice targets the students attack with piercing thrusts, both in front and behind.
3. If all the criteria above are met, then training should be conducted on different types of uneven ground.
4. It is dangerous to train more than one student at a time.
5. When more than 10 meters from the target the spears can be held low in the right hand as the students advance.

How to Fight With a Bamboo Spear
End

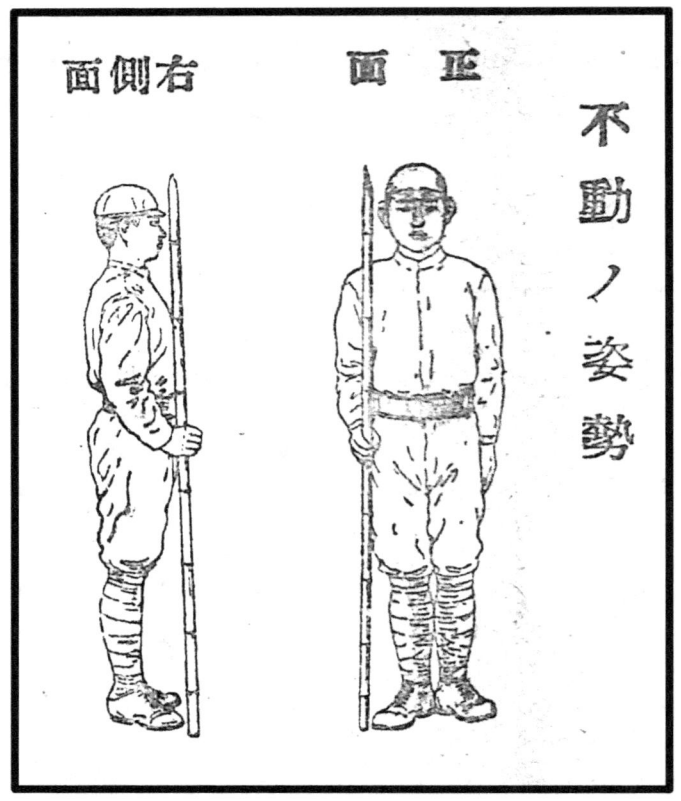

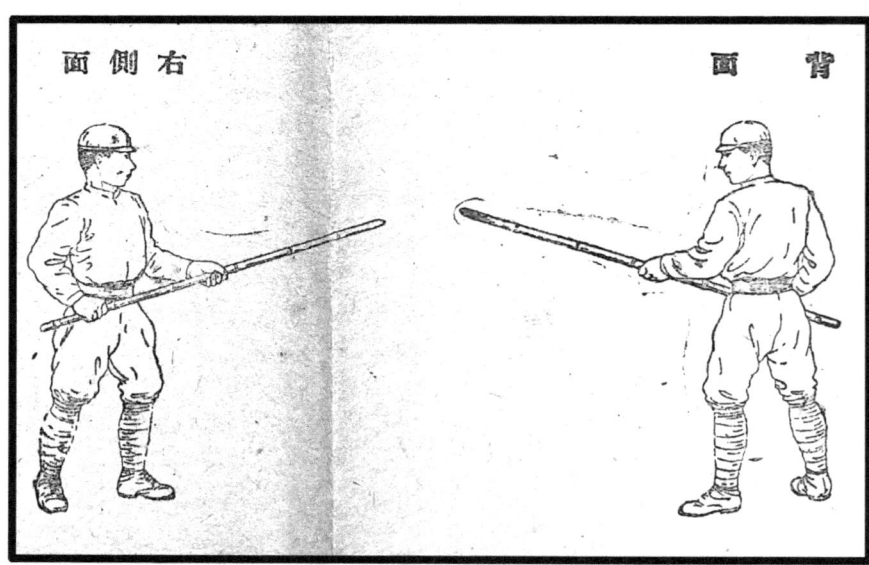

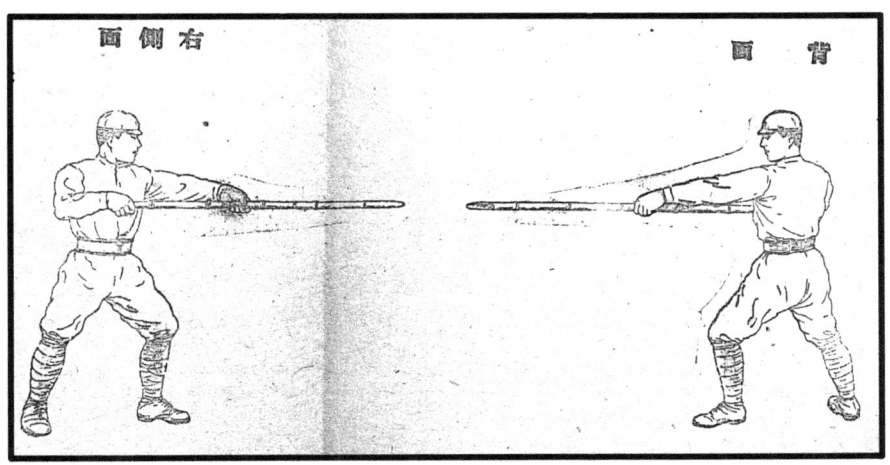

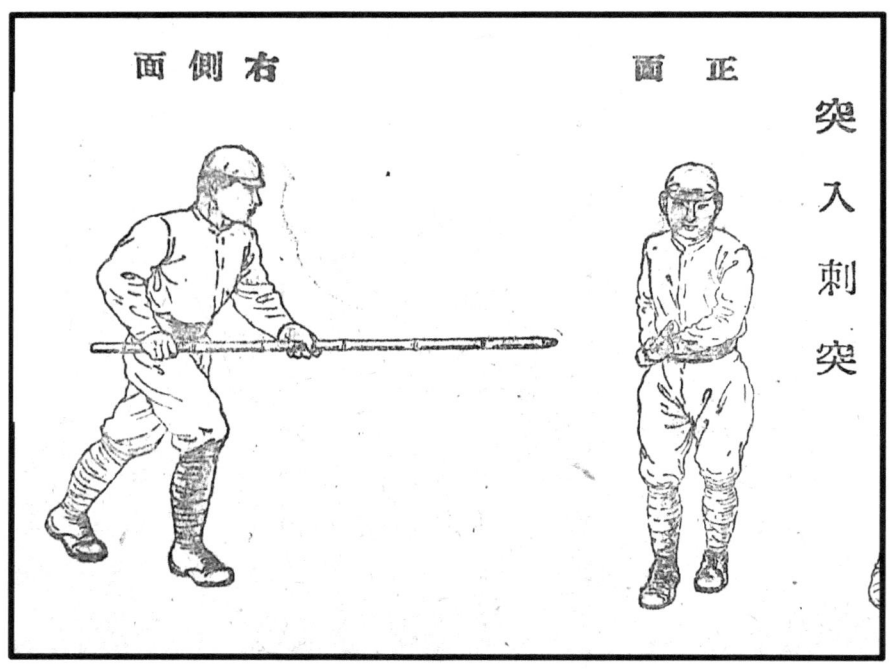

突入刺突　正面　右側面

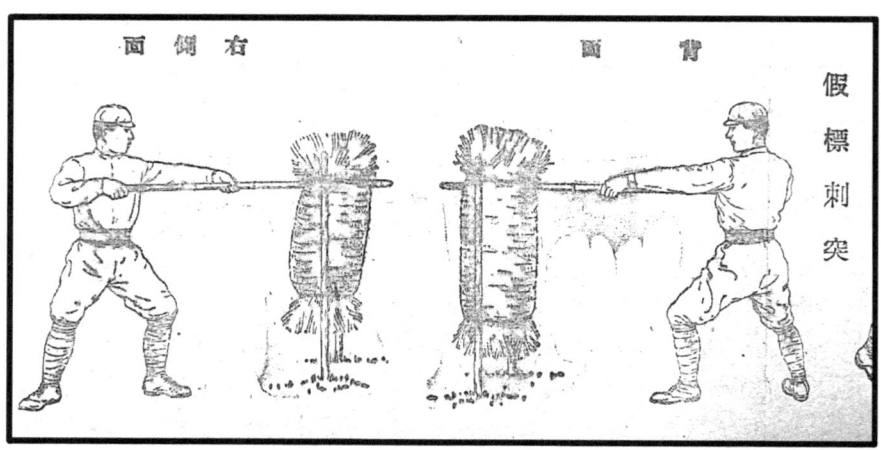

假標刺突　背面　右側面

Translator's Note: Pictures of Bamboo Spear Training from the Late 1940s. These pictures were not included in the manual and are for reference.

DEFENSE OF THE JAPANESE HOMELAND

DEFENSE OF THE JAPANESE HOMELAND

ERIC SHAHAN

DEFENSE OF THE JAPANESE HOMELAND

国民築城必携
Building Fortifications : The Citizen's Essential Guide

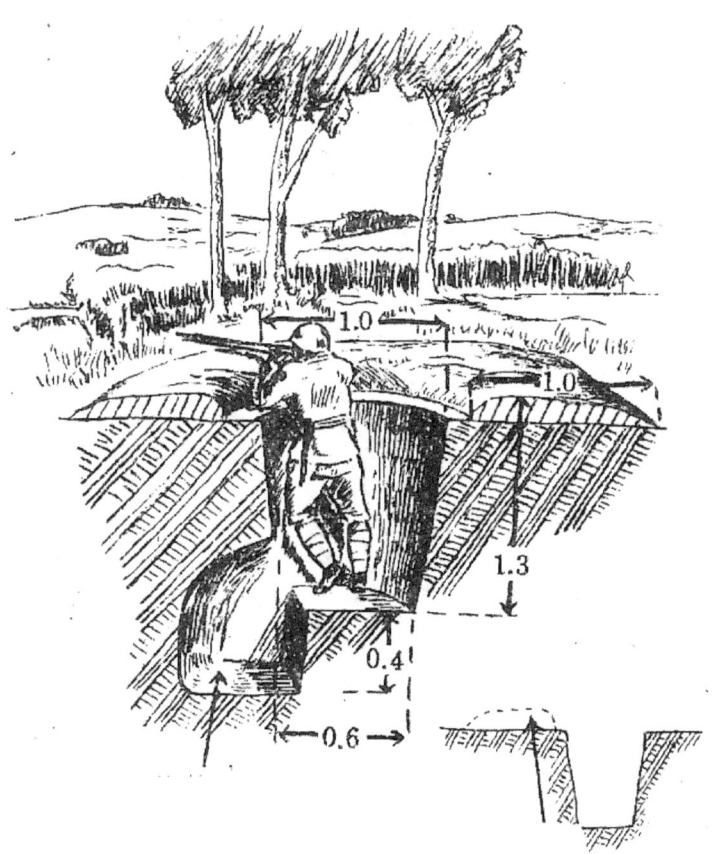

Japanese Army Manual

Published April 12 Showa 20 (1945)

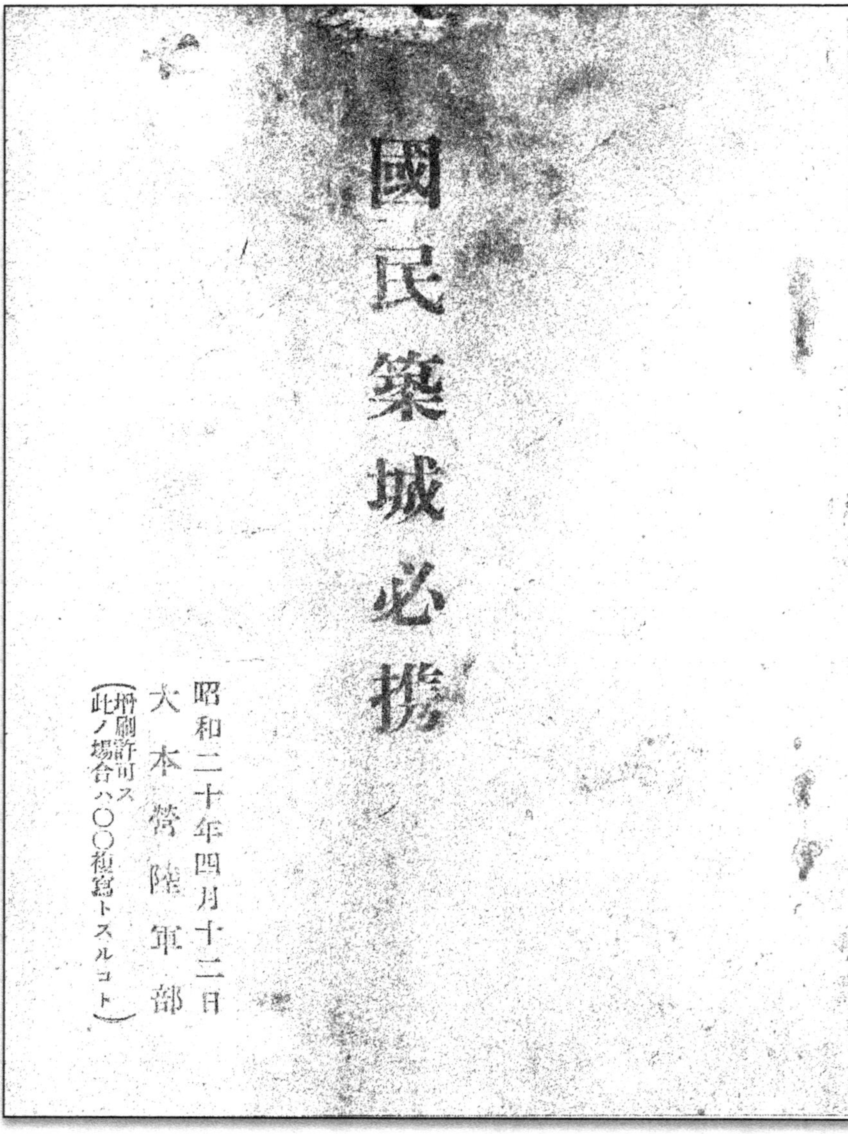

國民築城必携

昭和二十年四月十二日
大本營陸軍部
（增刷許可ス
此ノ場合ハ〇〇複寫トスルコト）

DEFENSE OF THE JAPANESE HOMELAND

Kokumin Chikujo Hikkei
Building Fortifications :
The Citizen's Essential Guide

Published April 12 Showa 20 (1945)
The Imperial General Headquarters Army Division[2]

(Reprinting is authorized. Record the number printed in each run.)

---

[2] The Imperial General Headquarters was part of the Supreme War Council and was established in 1893 to coordinate efforts between the Imperial Japanese Army and Imperial Japanese Navy during wartime.

要　旨

一、築城ハ軍ノ指導ノ下ニ造ルヲ立前トスル本册子ハソノ作リ方ノ參考デアル

二、軍指導以外ノ土地モ皇國守護ノ爲全國民ハ各人ノ郷土ヲ要塞化シ對敵戰鬪ヲ容易ナラシムル爲築城ヲ實施セネバナラヌ

三、築城ノ中最モ大切ナノハ對戰車障碍デアル

四、敵モシ來寇スル時ハ軍ノ指導ニ從ヒ各人ハ其ノ郷土要塞ニ據ツテ戰鬪シ徹底的ニ抗戰セネバナラヌ

DEFENSE OF THE JAPANESE HOMELAND

Outline

1. While in principle the construction of fortifications will be done under the direction of the military, this guide has been produced as a reference.
2. In order to protect the lands under control of the Emperor, people in areas not under direct military control should fortify their local area. This will make the area easy to defend from enemy assault or launch attacks from.
3. When fortifying an area, the most important thing to build are anti-tank obstacles.
4. In the event an enemy invades, all persons are expected to follow the instructions given by the military and dedicate themselves entirely to the task of defending the fortified local area.

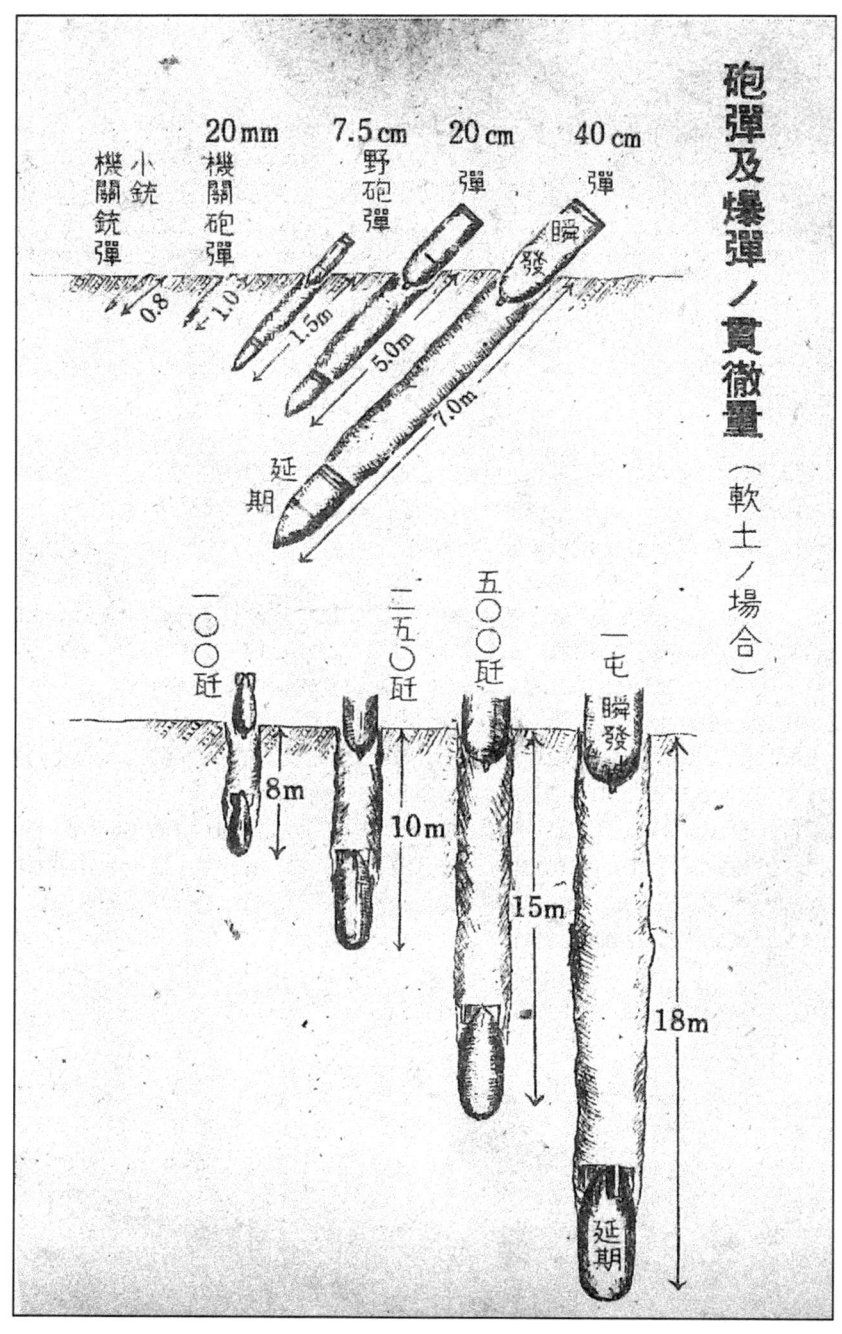

Penetrating power of Artillery Shells and Bombs (If on soft earth.)
1. 40 Centimeter Artillery Shell: 7 meters
2. 20 Centimeter Artillery Shell: 5 meters
3. 7.5 Centimeter Field Artillery Shell: 1.5 meters
4. 20 Millimeter Autocannon: 1 meter
5. Small arms or Machine Gun Rounds: 0.8 meters

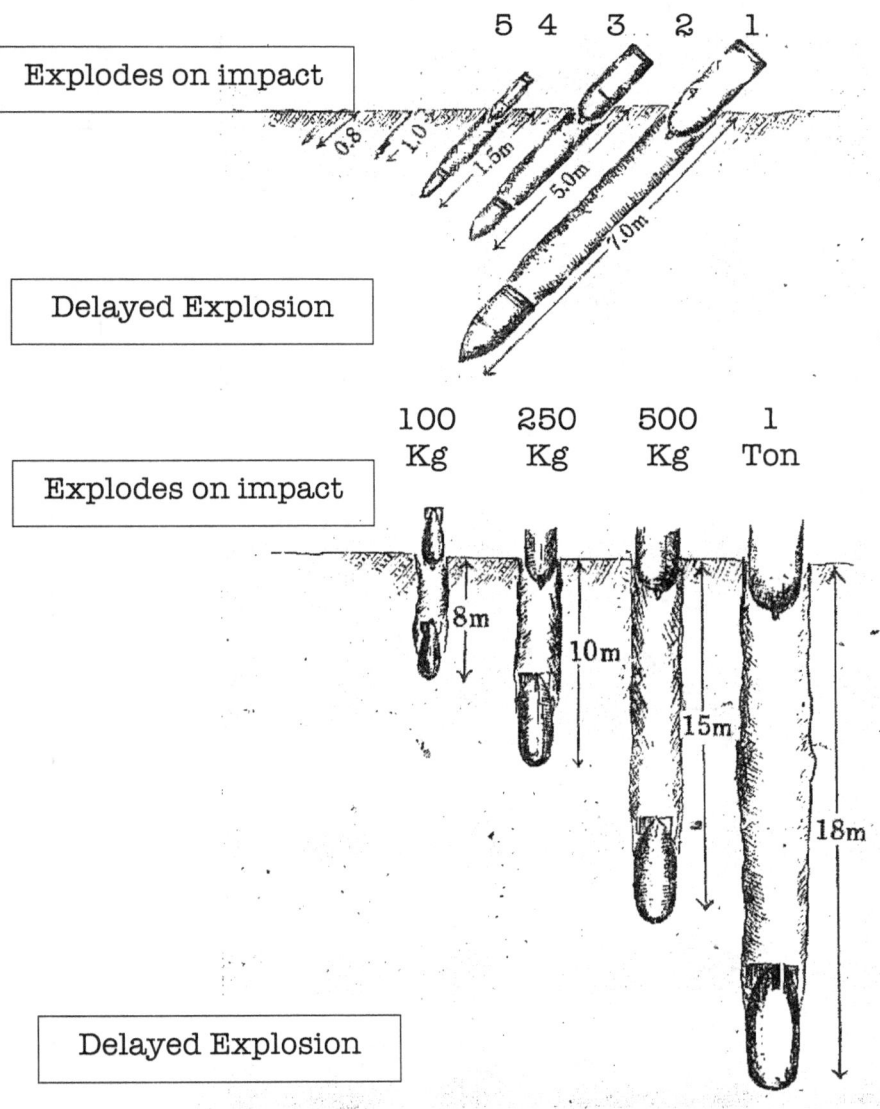

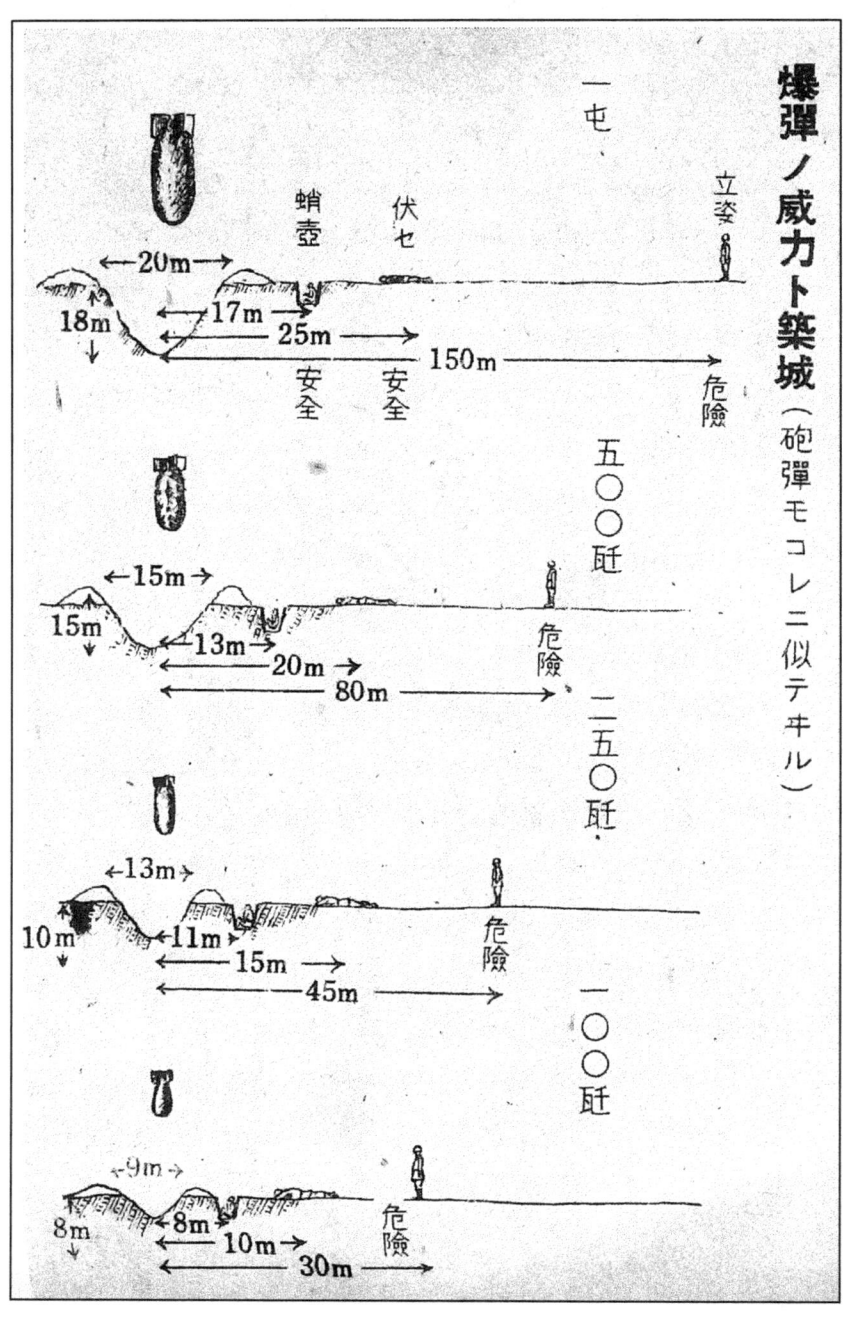

DEFENSE OF THE JAPANESE HOMELAND

Bombs Explosive Force and Fortifications
(This also applies to artillery shells)

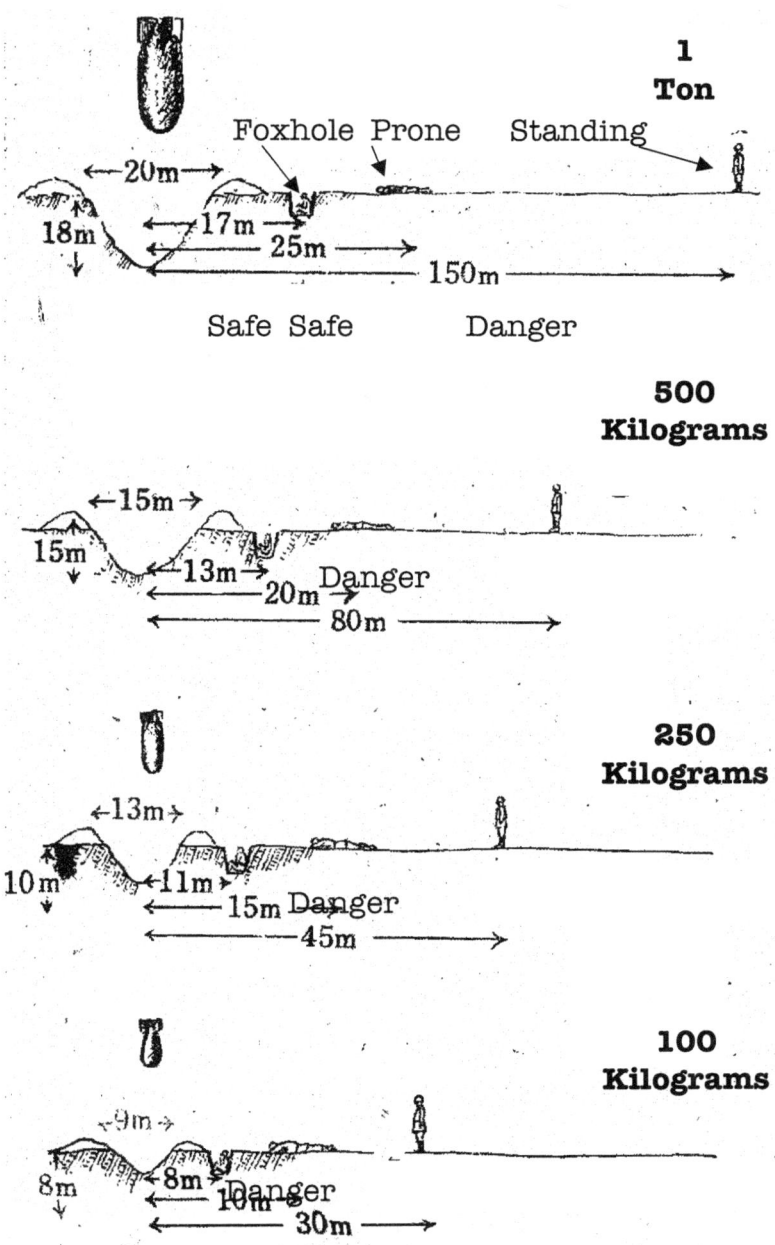

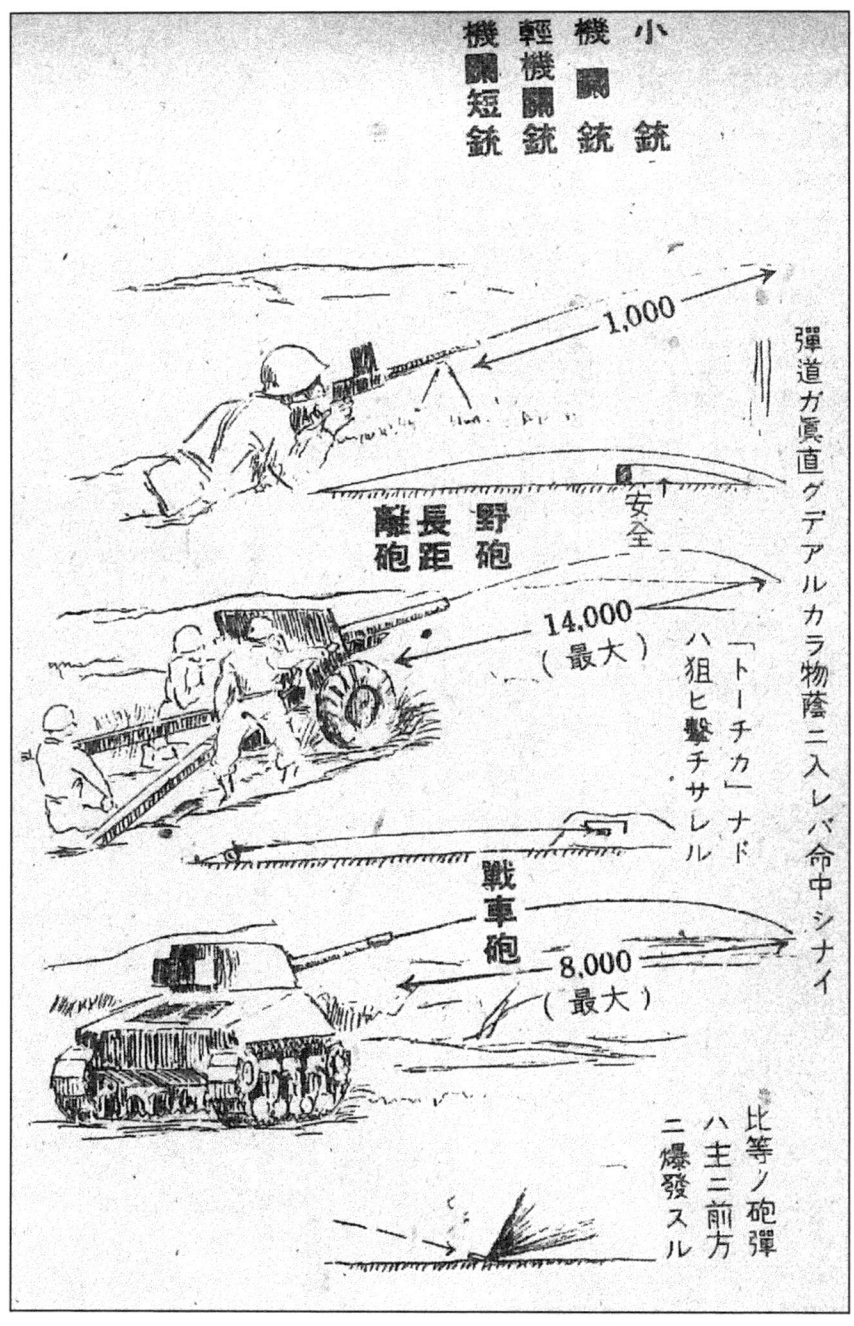

Small Arms · Machine Guns
Light Machine Gun · Sub Machine Gun

These guns have a range of 1000 meters. The bullets travel on a straight path so if you hide behind something, you won't be struck.

Safe

Field Artillery · Long Range Gun
(Maximum) Range 14,000 meters

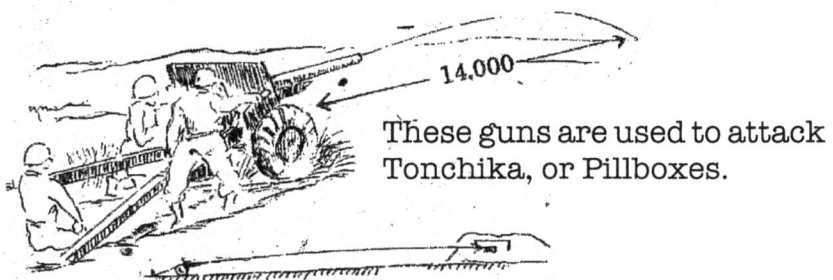

These guns are used to attack Tonchika, or Pillboxes.

*Tonchika is a Russian word used by the Japanese.

Tank Shells
(Maximum Range) 8,000 meters

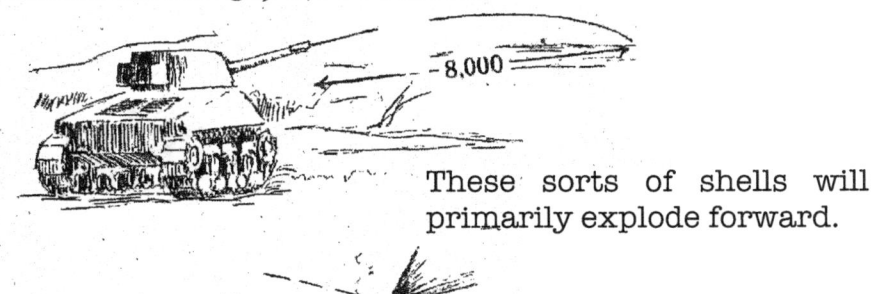

These sorts of shells will primarily explode forward.

Rocket Shells

3,000 ~ 7,000 meters

Since rockets travel on an arcing path, they can strike on the far side of mountains. You can observe a fiery tail behind rockets as they fly, which makes them easy to see.

Mortar Shells

(A maximum of) 5,000 ~ 8,000 meters

These types of rounds explode in all directions

Bombardment by Naval Artillery

40-centimeter shells have a range of 30,000 meters

12.7 ~ 20-centimeter shells have a range of 15,000 meters.

These guns can strike targets from an extreme distance and the shells fired have a great destructive power. However, if you have constructed fortifications, there is nothing to fear.

Level Flight Bombing

The bombs can be dropped all at once or in sequence. Generally dropped from above 2,000 meters and below 10,000 meters.

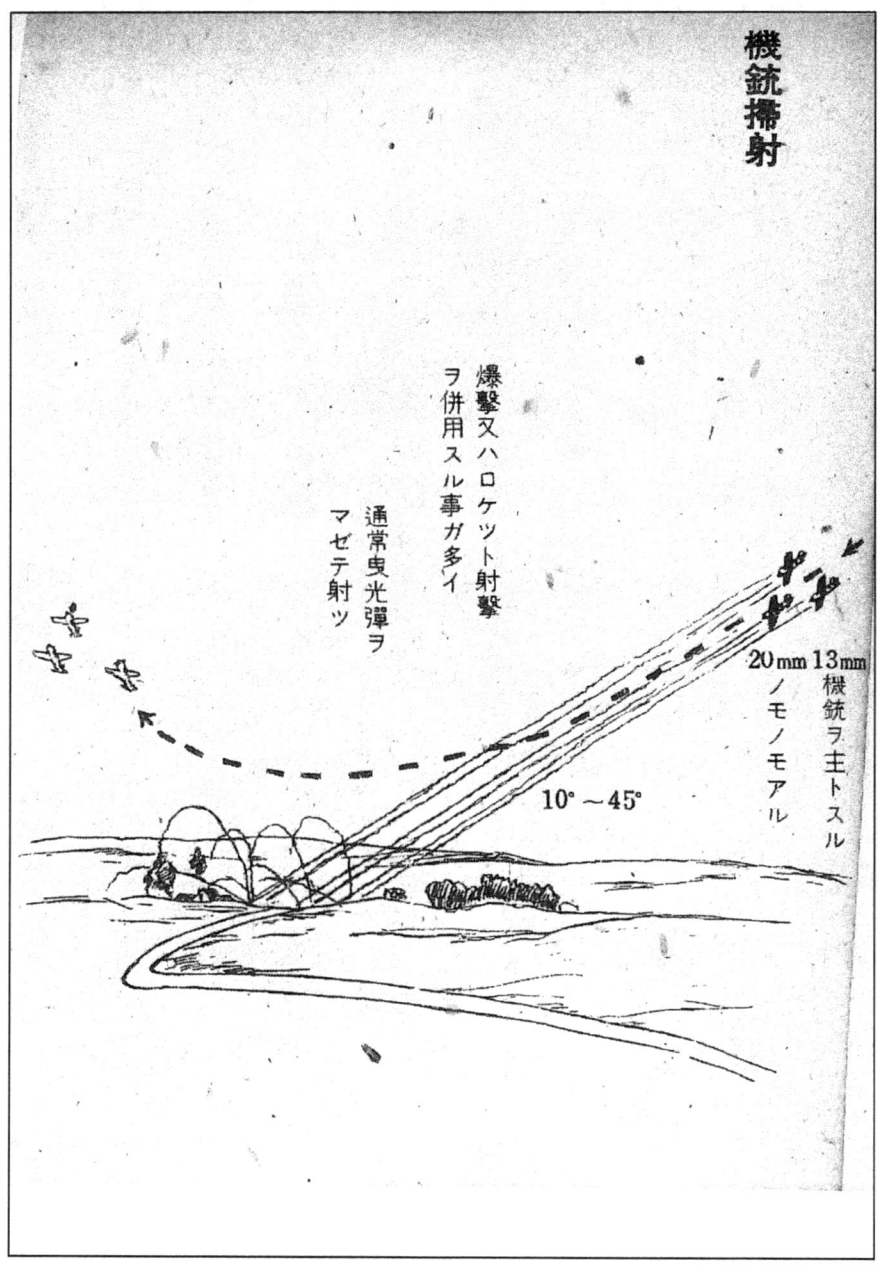

Machine Gun Strafe
- Angle of attack is 10 ~ 45°
- The primary rounds fired are 33-millimeter, however 20-millimeter are also used.
- A machine gun strafe is often done in conjunction with bombing or rocket attacks.
- Typically, tracer rounds are mixed in with the regular ammunition.

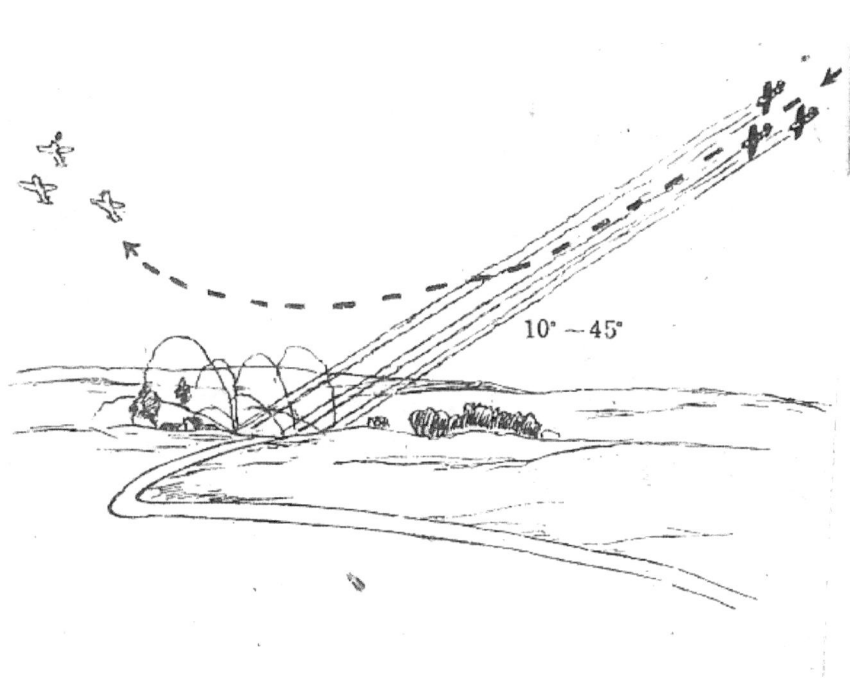

How to Position Your Unit
1. Near a Village
Shoot the troops accompanying the tanks.³ To destroy the tanks used Nikuhaku Kogeki,⁴ close attack.

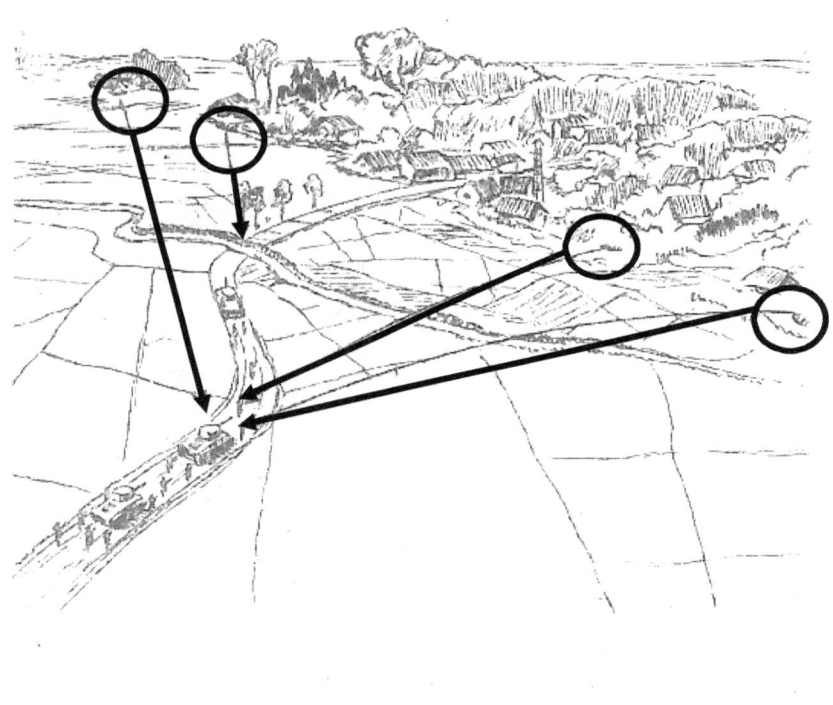

---

³ Circles show what seem to be the recommended firing points or sniper positions, though no additional information is given.

⁴ Nikuhaku Kogeki is comprised of two Kanji, Meat 肉 and Thin 薄. It means to be close enough so that your flesh is pressing against the enemy. In this case a tank.

How to Position Your Unit
#2 At a Narrow Road or Bridge

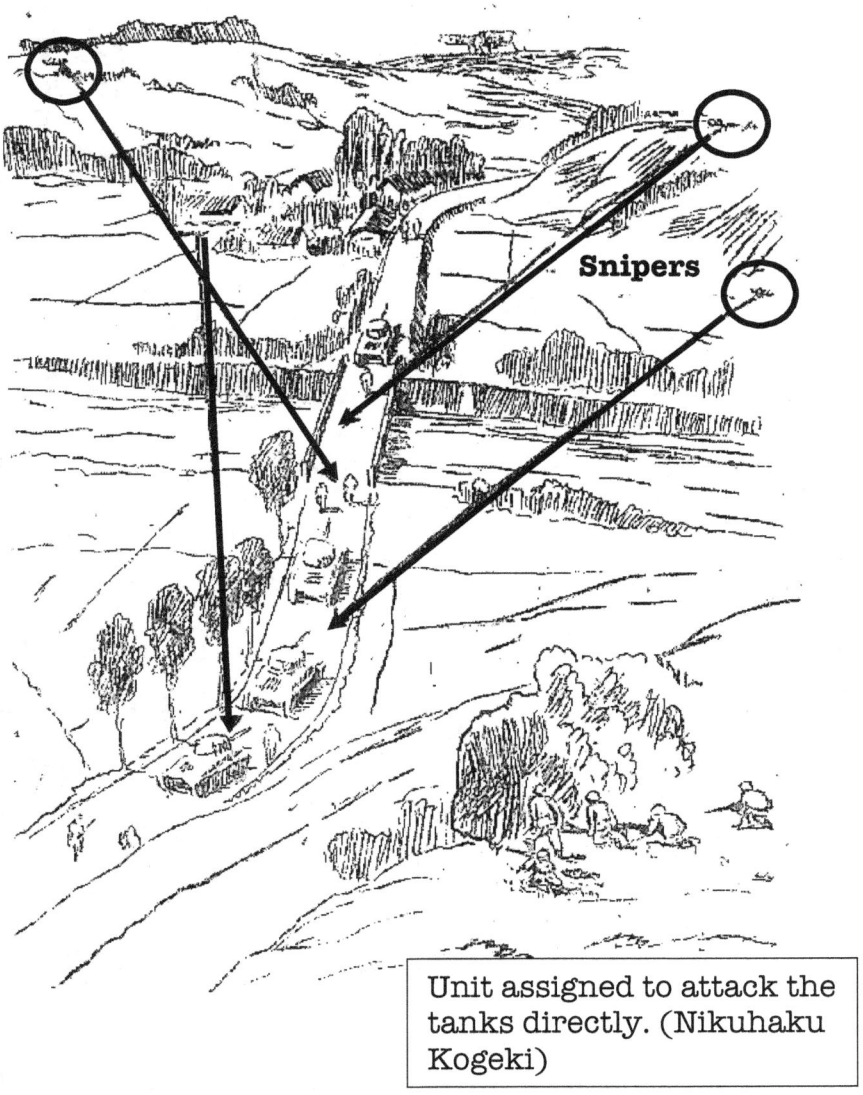

Snipers

Unit assigned to attack the tanks directly. (Nikuhaku Kogeki)

陣地ヲ作ル所
三、盆地

敵ノ前進ヲ待チ構ヘテ四方カラ一齊ニ攻撃スル

How to Position Your Unit
#3 Around a Valley

Wait for the enemy to advance on your position and then attack simultaneously from four directions.

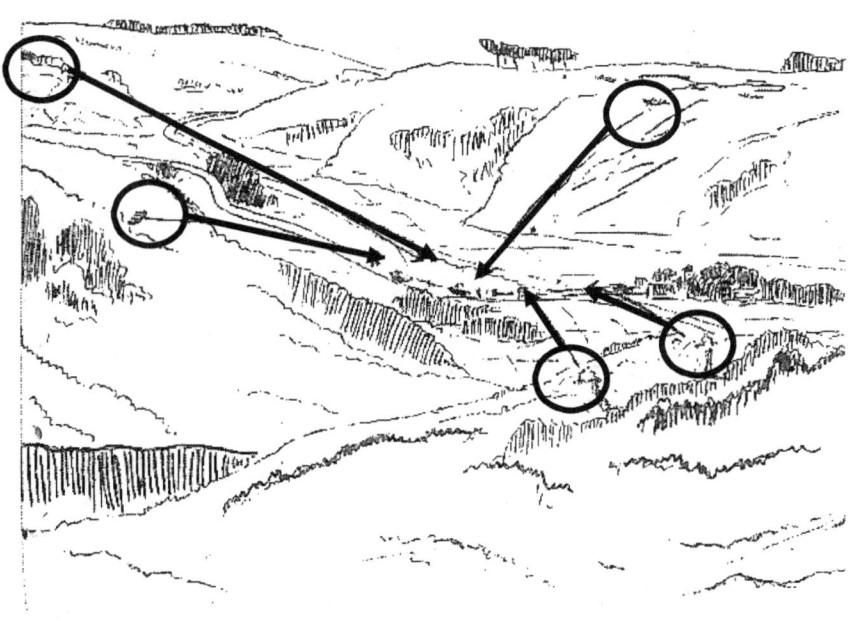

陣地ヲ作ル所
四、山道、森林

道ノ曲リ角ニ障碍物(石、防材等)ヲ設ケ又道路ヲ破壊スル

How to Position Your Unit
#4 On a Mountain Road or in the Forest

Place obstacles at the turns in the road. (Use rocks, lumber or other materials) You can also destroy the road at that spot.

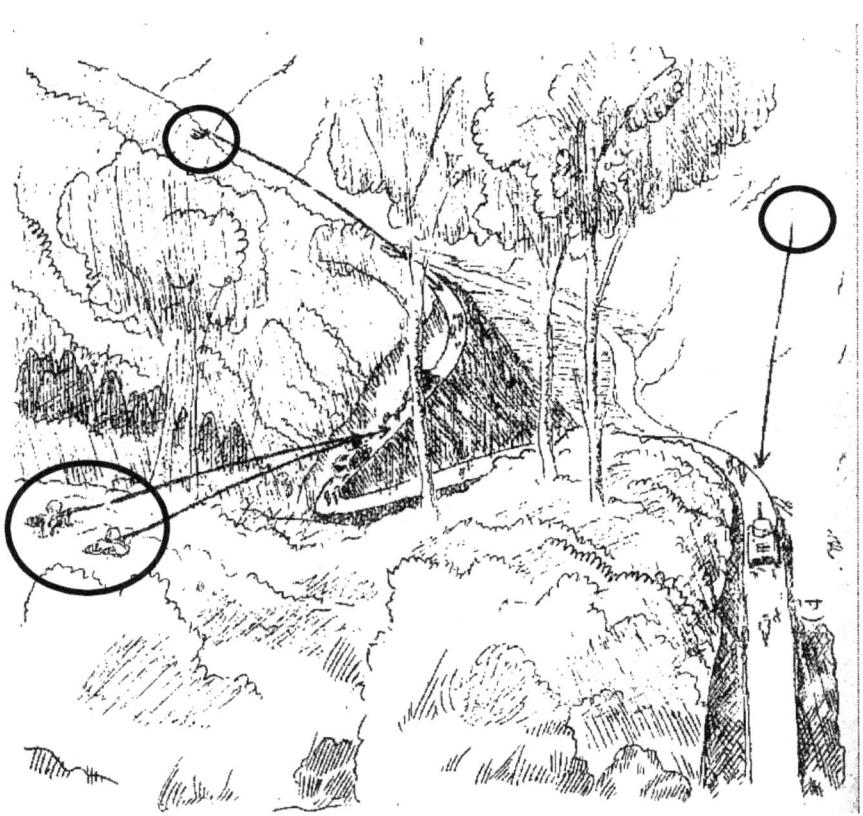

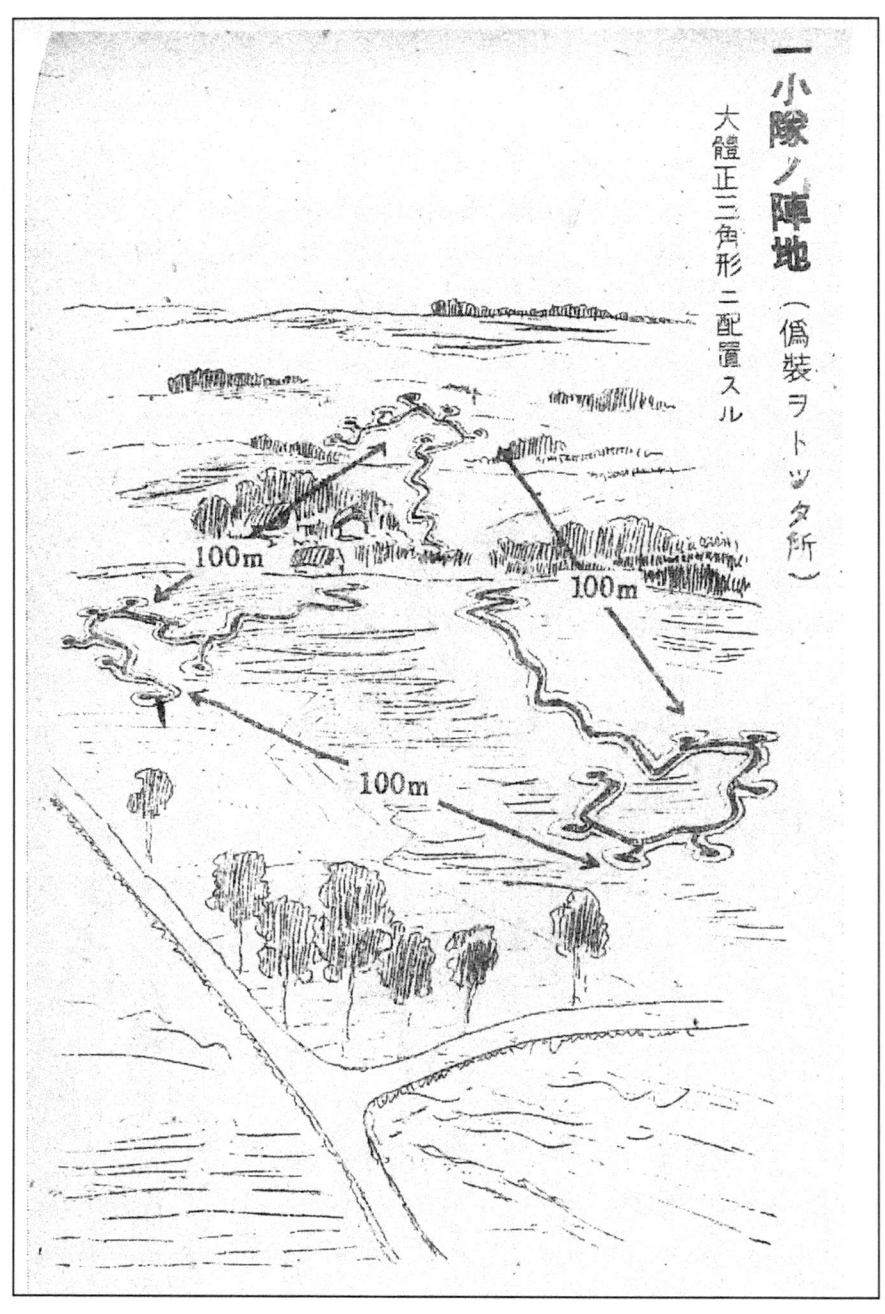

DEFENSE OF THE JAPANESE HOMELAND

How to Position One Small Unit
(A Camouflaged Position)
Your position should be laid out in a triangle.

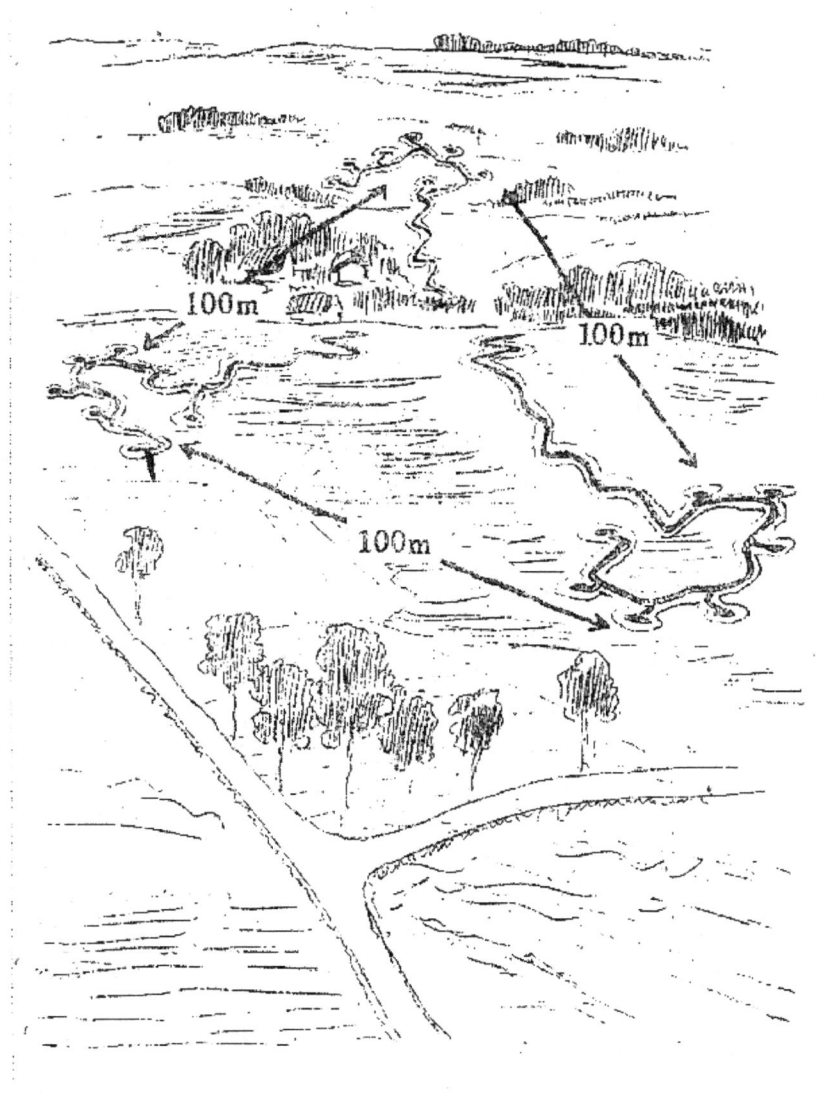

How One Unit Should Be Distributed
(A Camouflaged Position)

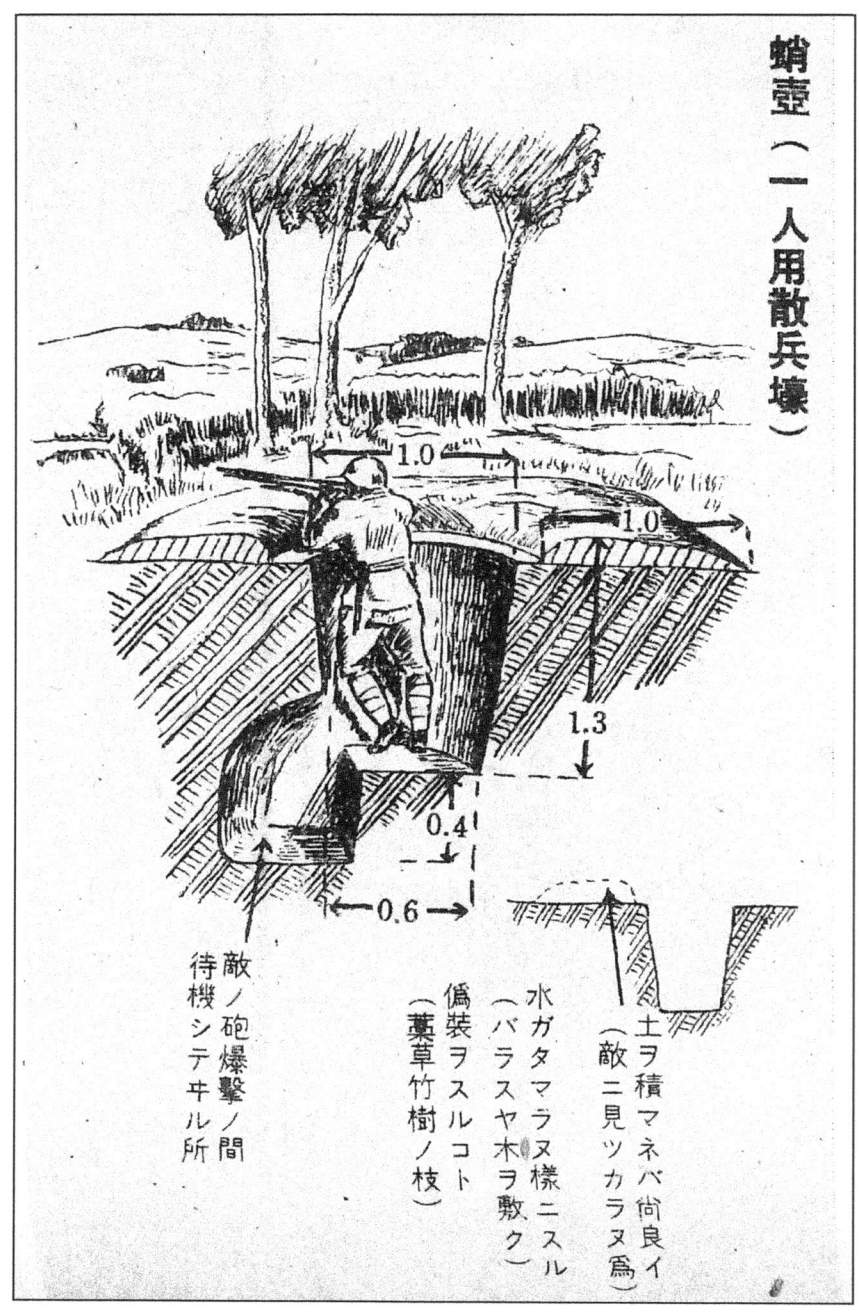

DEFENSE OF THE JAPANESE HOMELAND

Tako Tsubo[5] Foxhole
A One-Person Soldier's Air Raid Shelter

Be sure to prevent water from accumulating.
(Spread gravel or wood on the ground.)
Use camouflage.
(Rice straw, grass, bamboo or tree branches.)

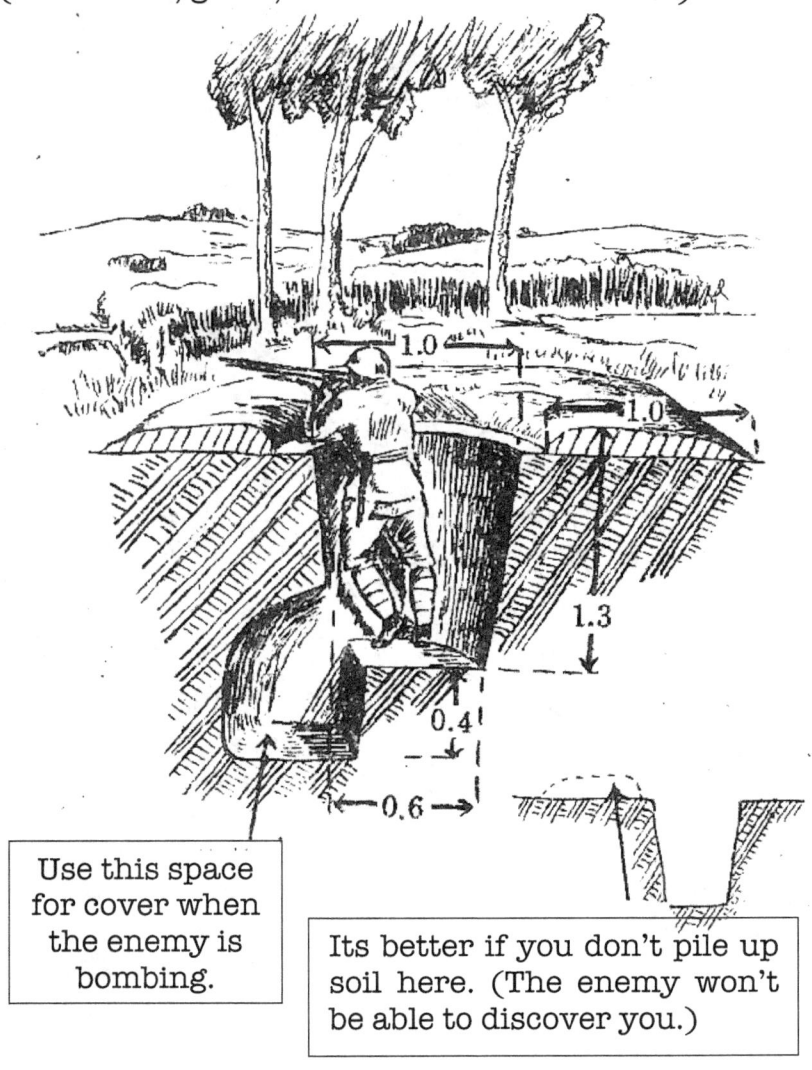

Use this space for cover when the enemy is bombing.

Its better if you don't pile up soil here. (The enemy won't be able to discover you.)

---

[5] Tako Tsubo is an "octopus pot" a tall earthenware pot submerged in the ocean to catch octopus.

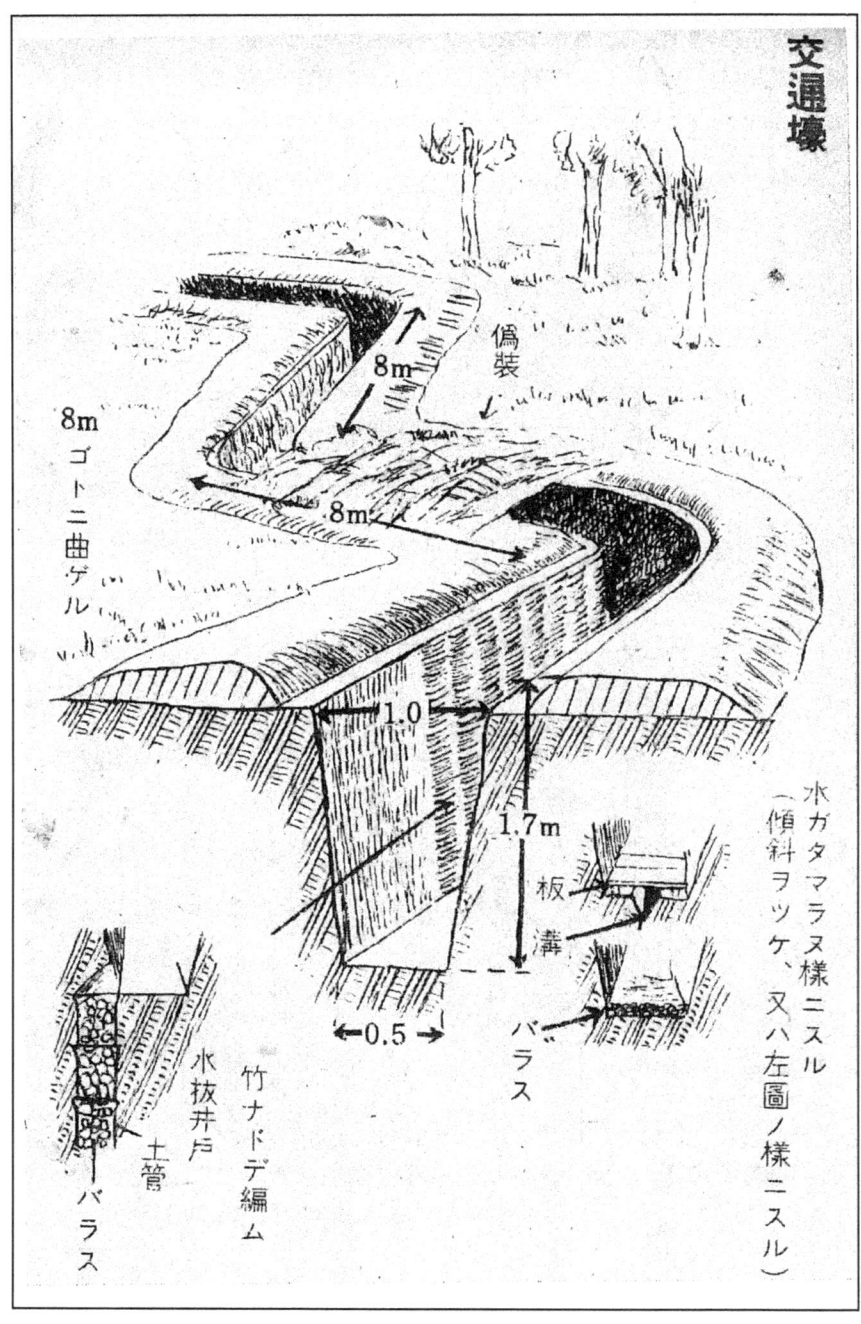

Interconnecting Trenches

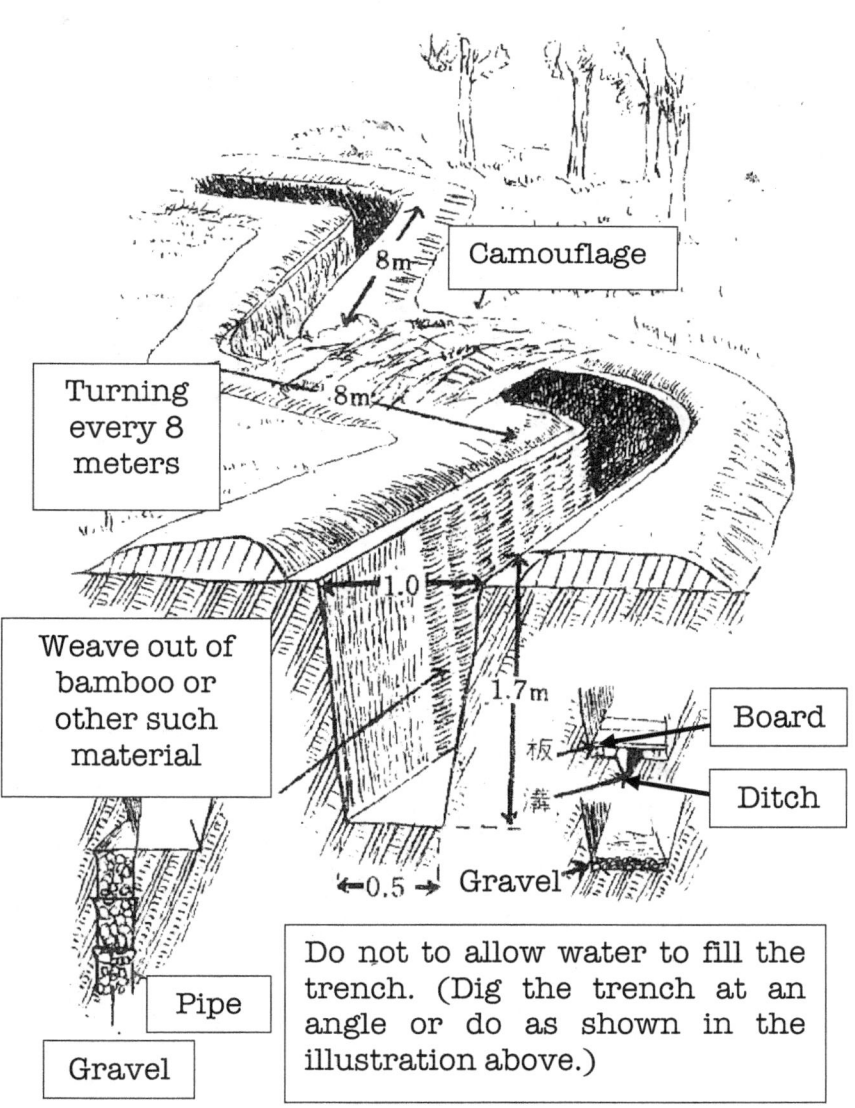

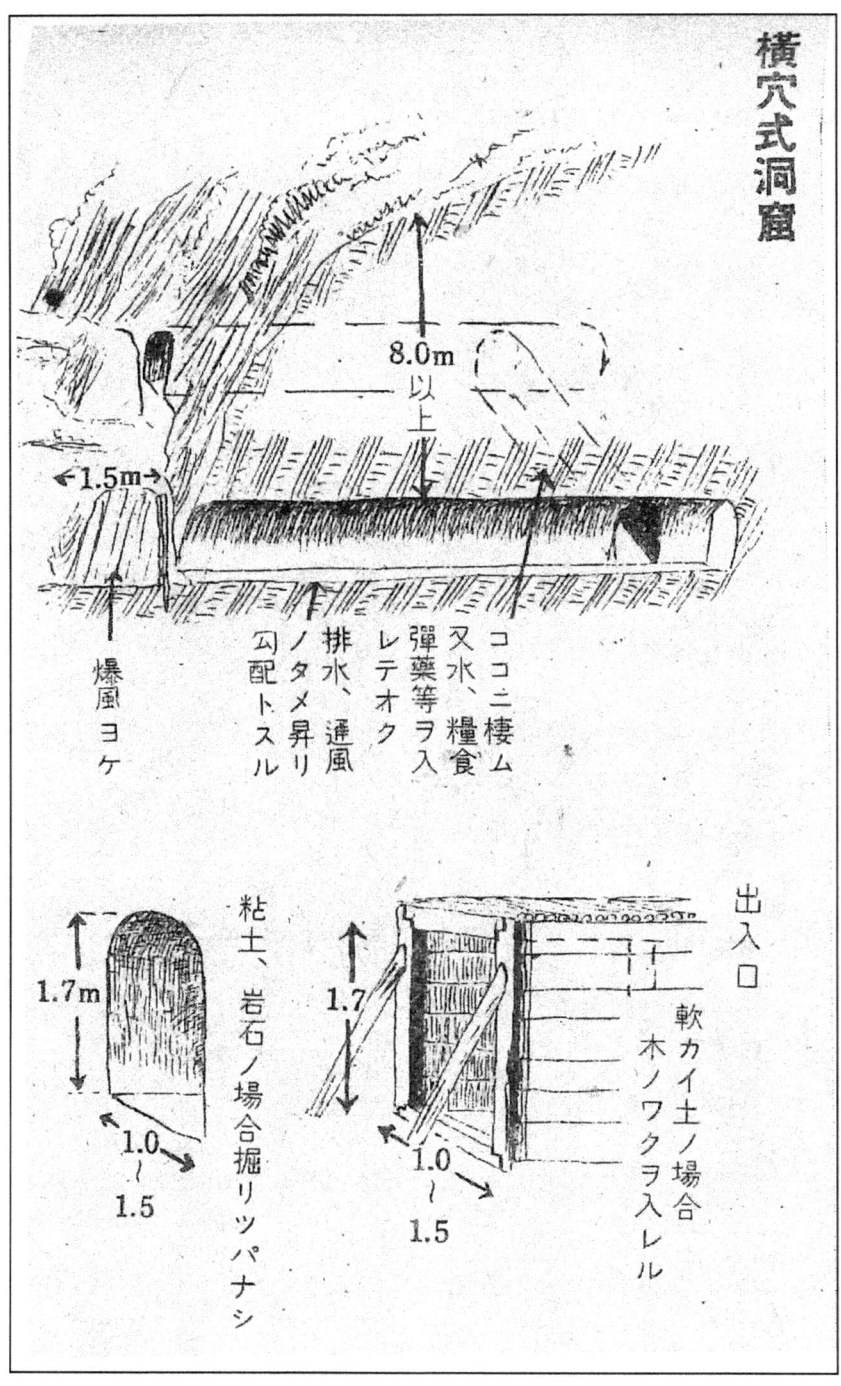

Horizontal Cave

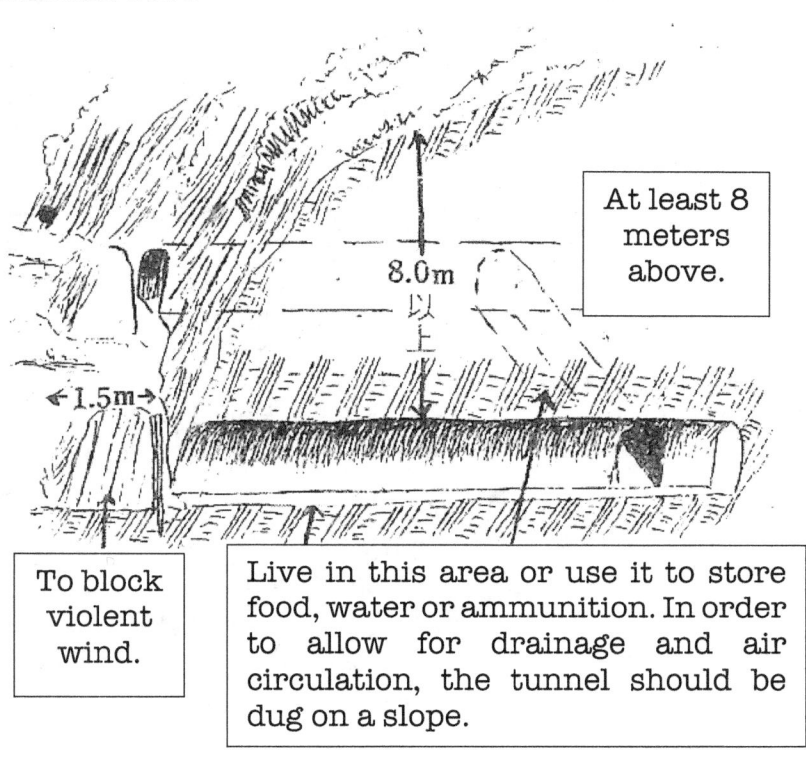

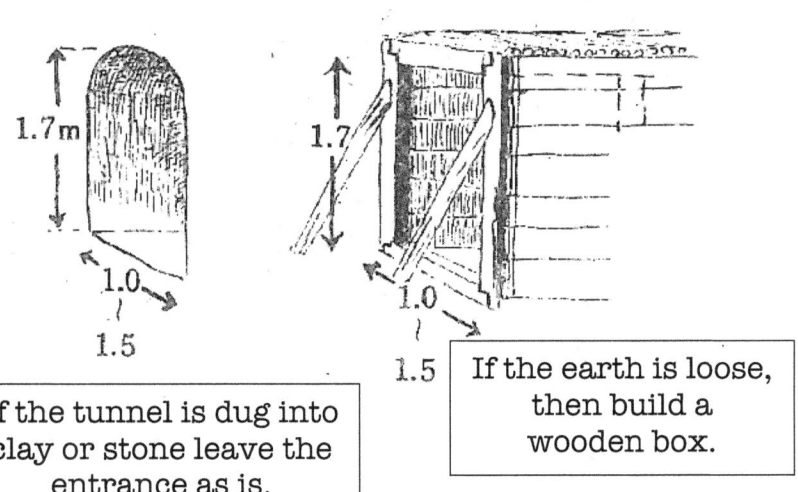

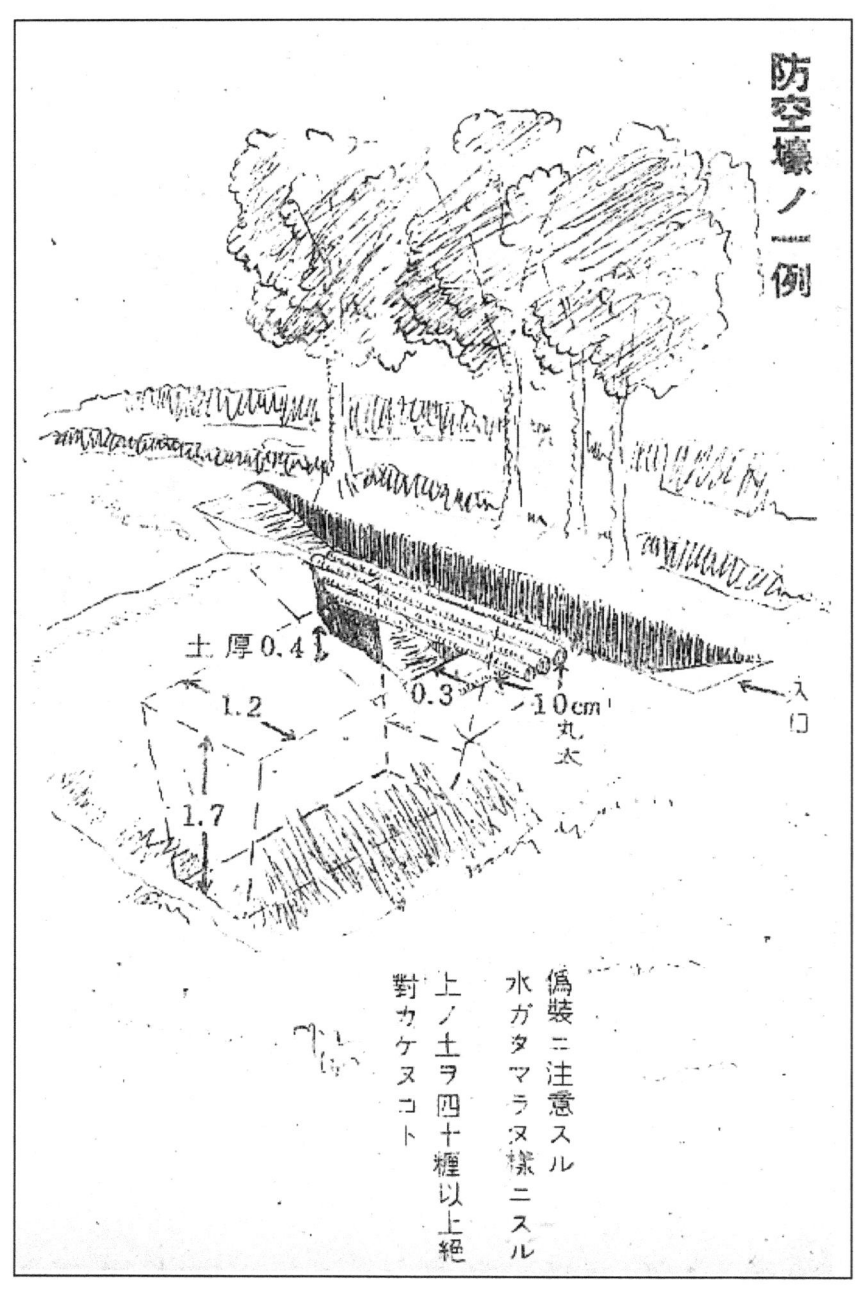

An Example of an Air Raid Shelter

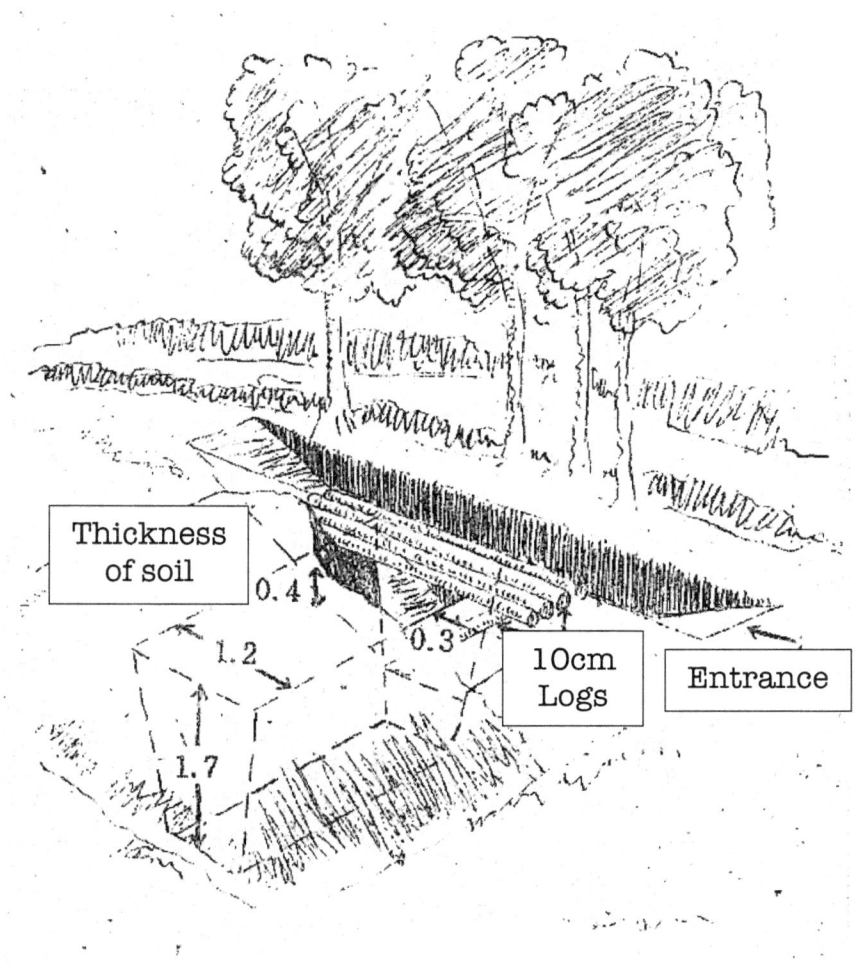

- Be careful how you camouflage the shelter.
- Do not allow water to pool at the bottom.
- Be absolutely certain there is at least 40 centimeters of soil above you.

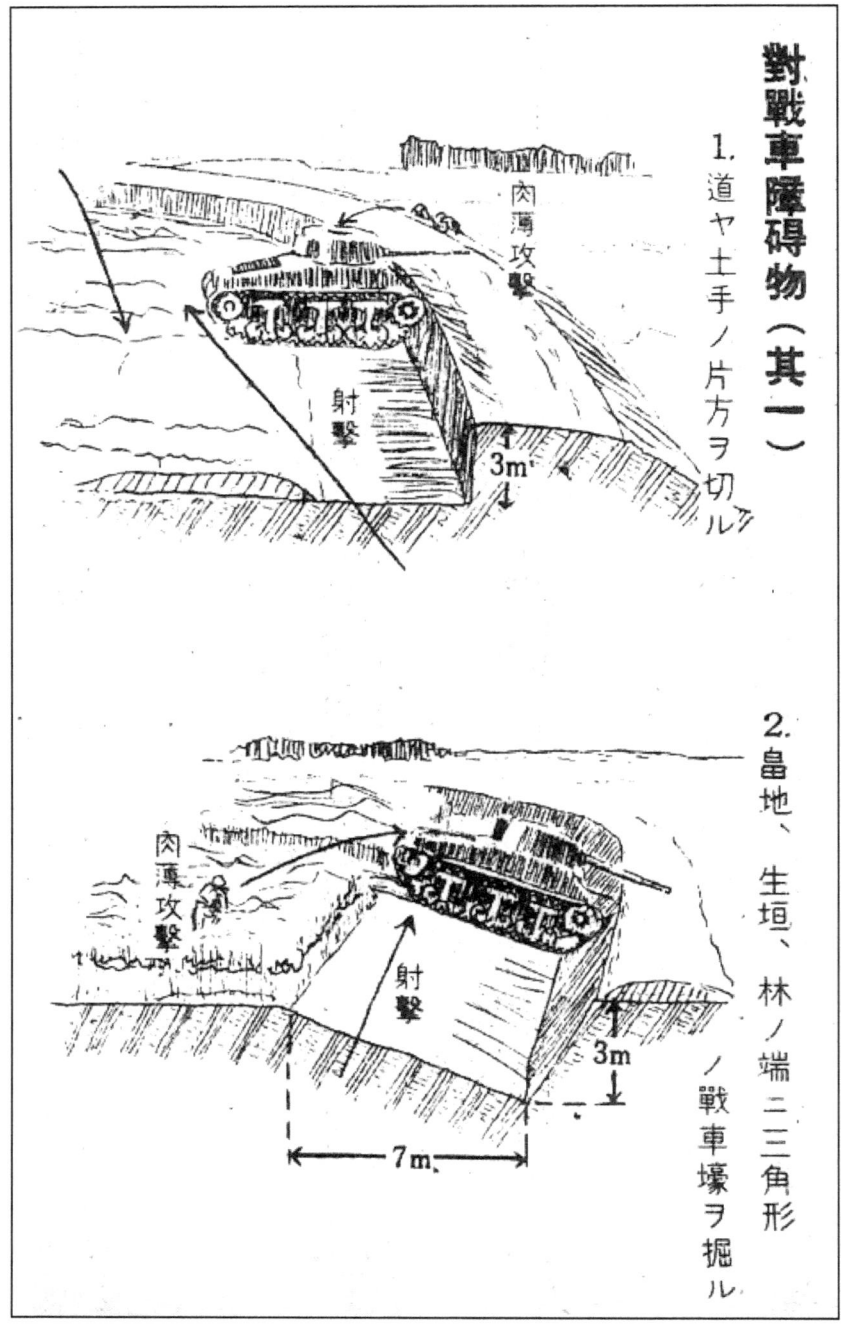

Building Tank Obstacles (Part 1)

1. Dig out a road or embankment on one side.

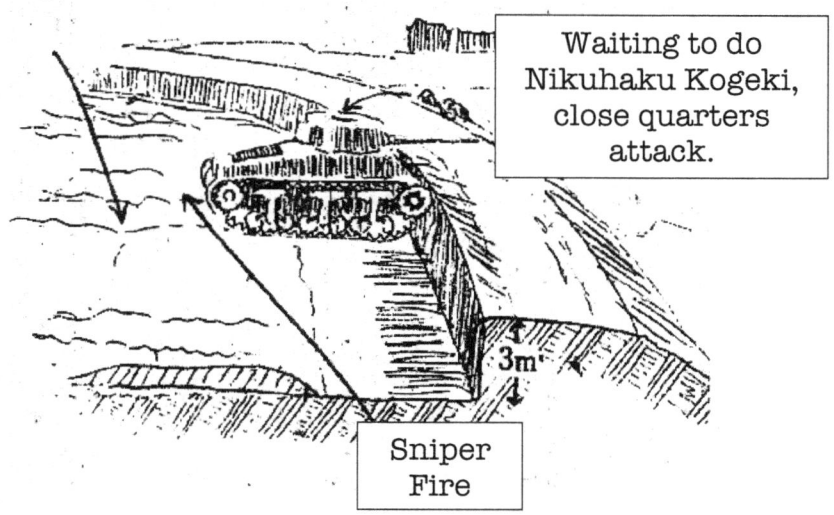

2. At the edge of a farm, section or undergrowth or wooded area, dig a triangular tank bunker.

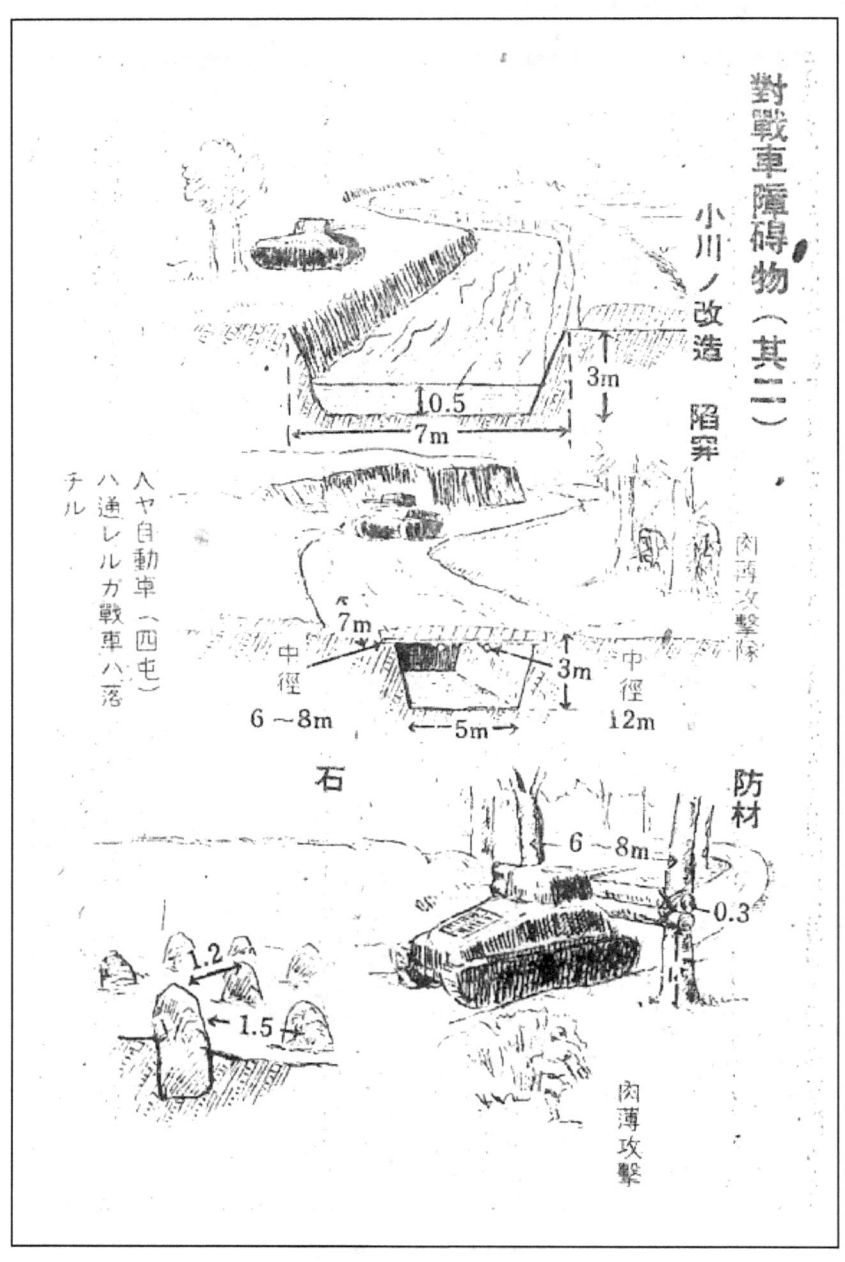

Building Tank Obstacles (Part 2)
Redirect a small river.

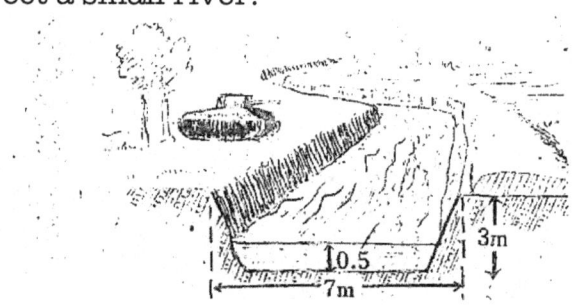

Make an Otoshi Ana, Deadfall
People or vehicles (up to 4 tons) can pass, but tanks will fall.

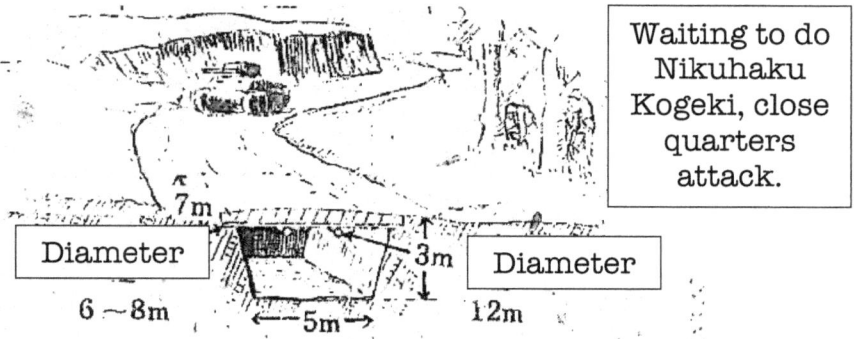

Waiting to do Nikuhaku Kogeki, close quarters attack.

Diameter 6 – 8m

Diameter 12m

Defensive materials

Rocks

Lumber

Waiting to do a close quarters attack.

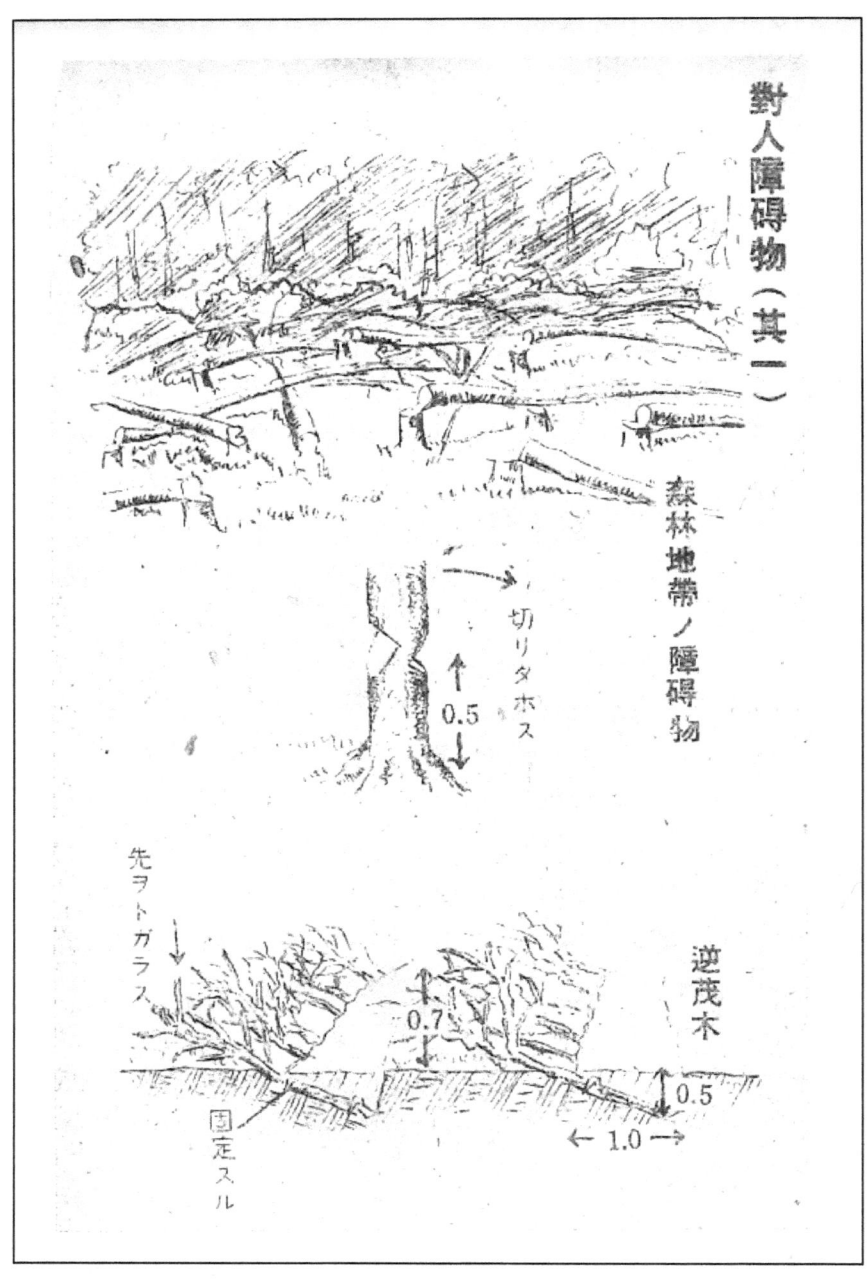

Anti-personnel Obstacles (Part 1)
How to make anti-personnel obstacles in the forest.

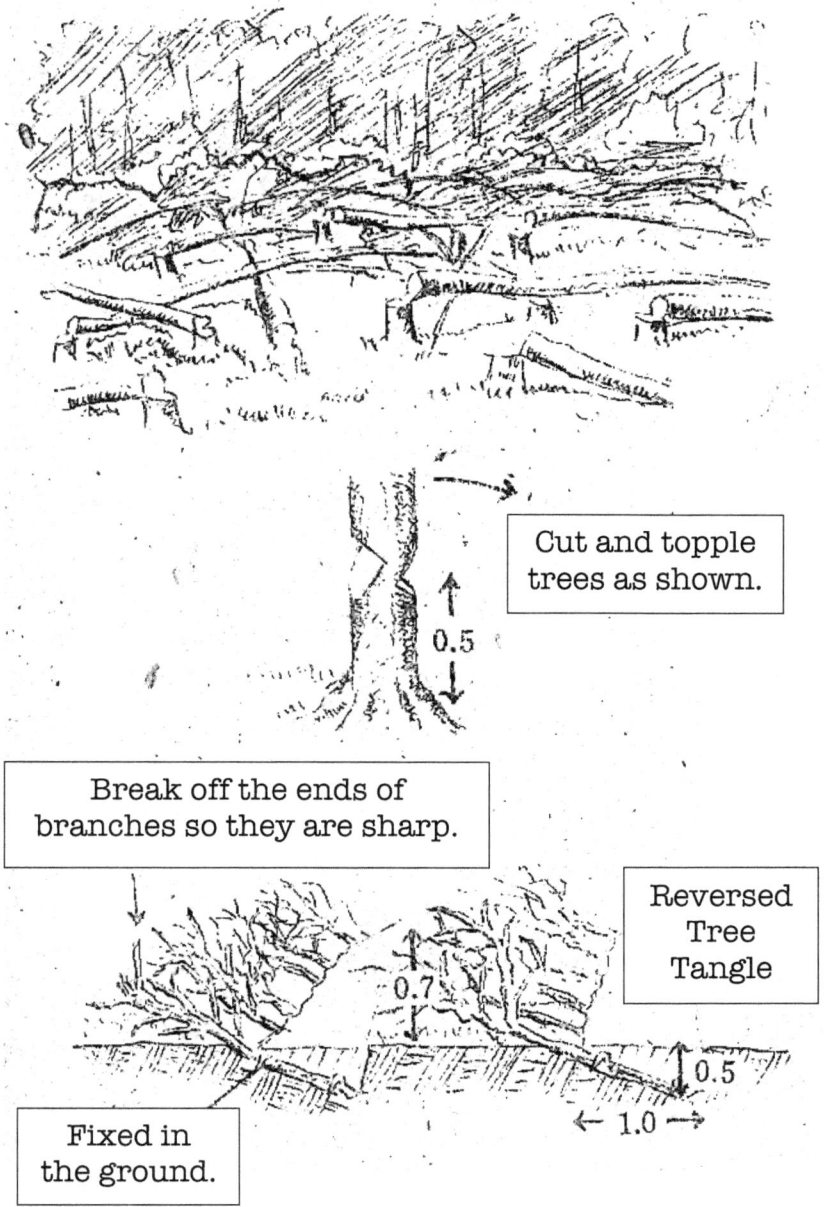

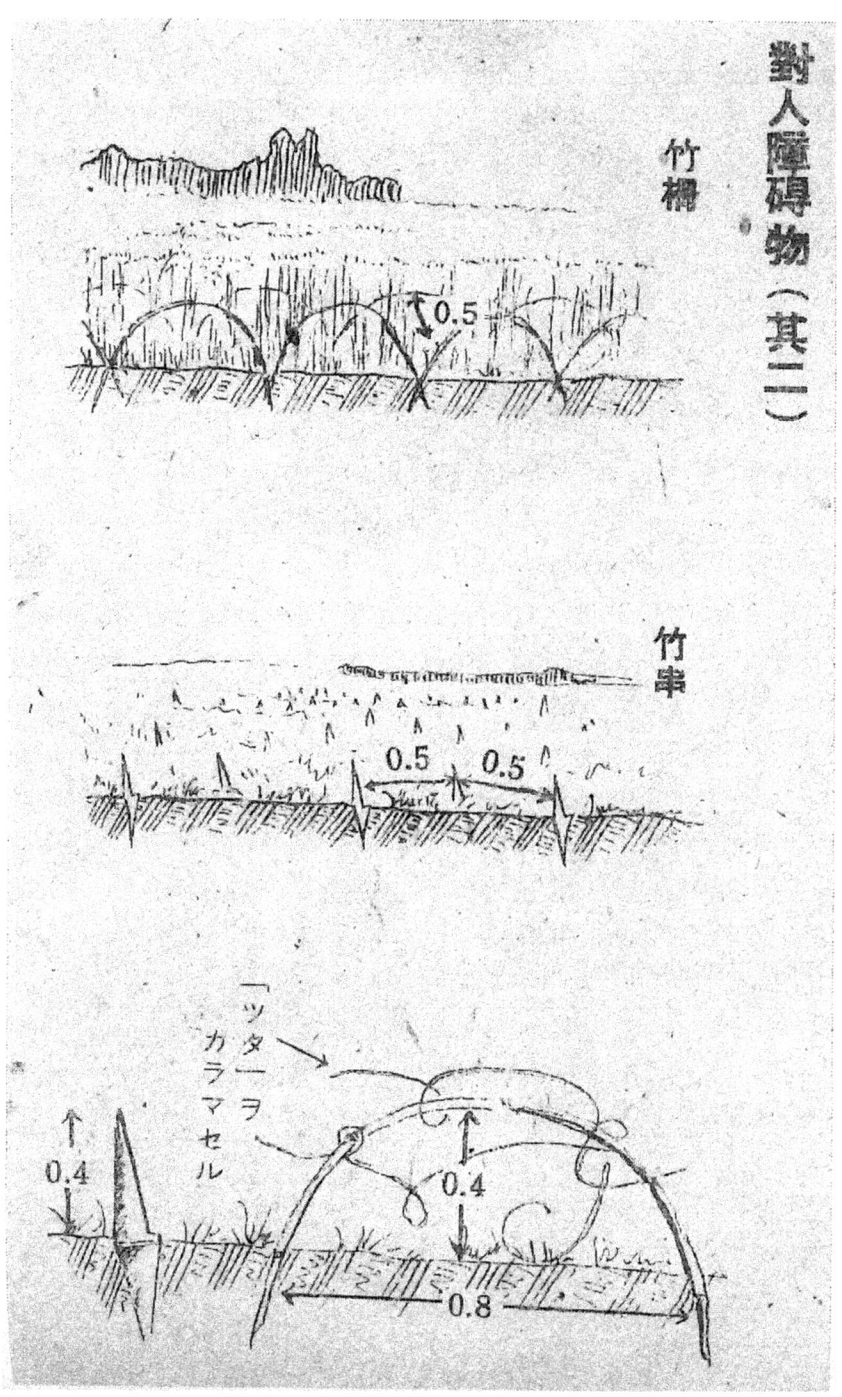

DEFENSE OF THE JAPANESE HOMELAND

Anti-personnel Obstacles (Part 2)

Bamboo Fence

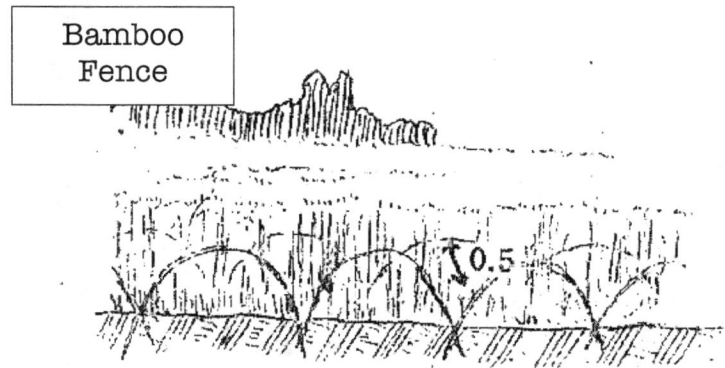

Bamboo Skewers

Conceal the fence with ivy.

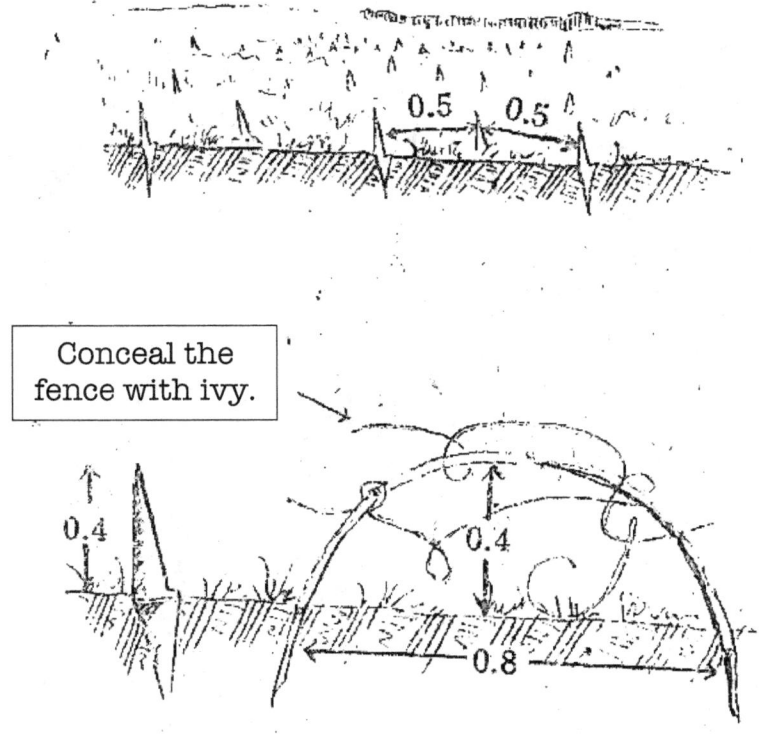

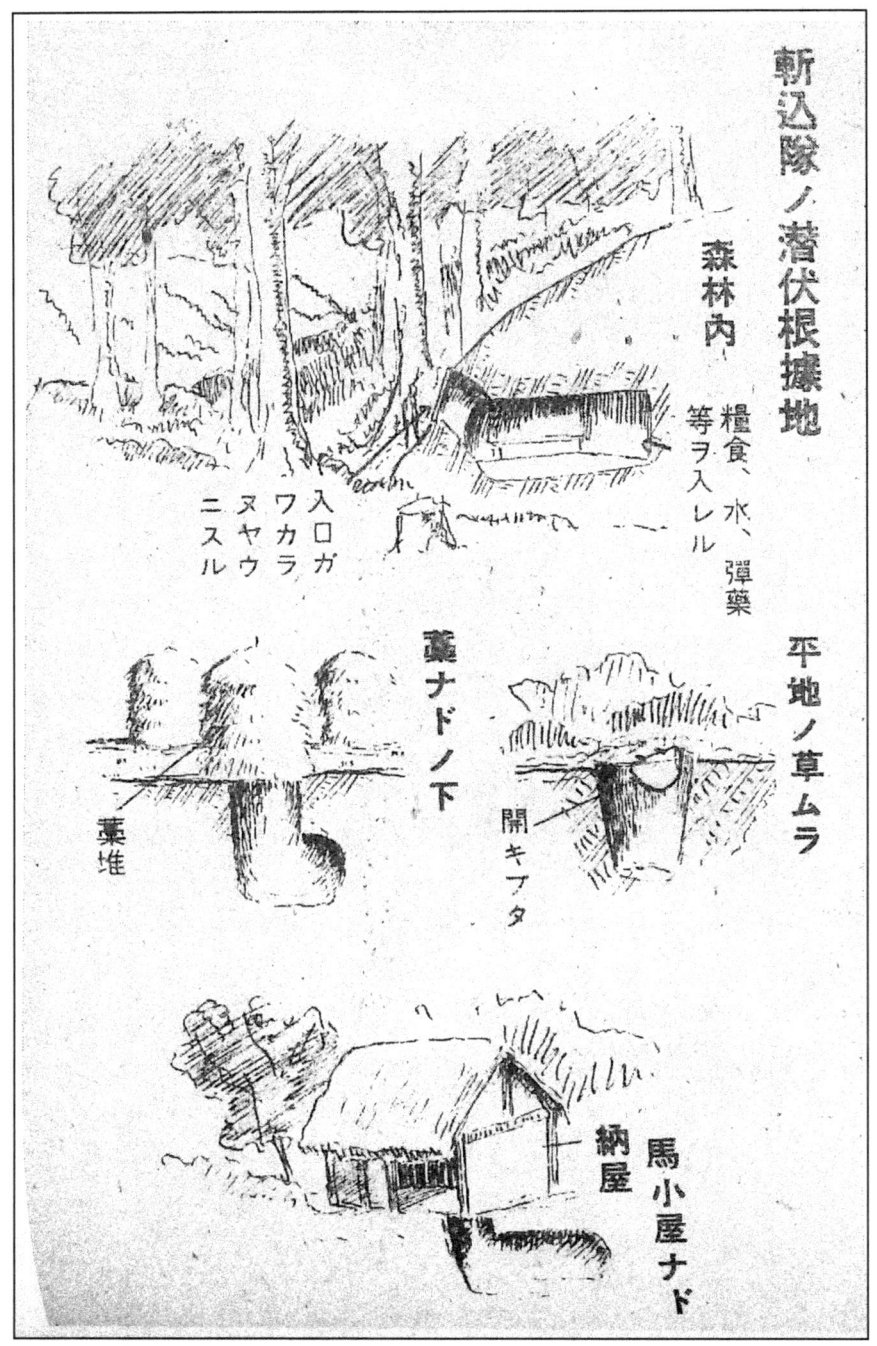

Undercover Base for the Kirikomitai, Cutting In Division/ Surprise Attack Division

In the forest.

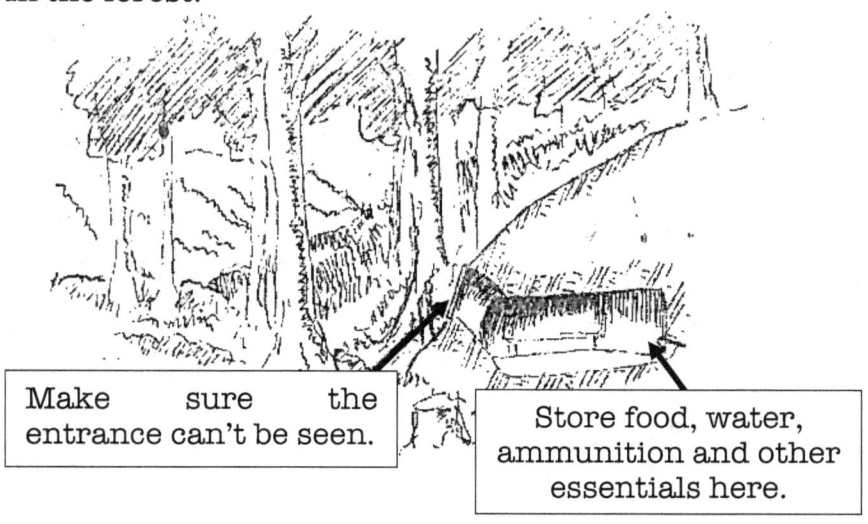

Make sure the entrance can't be seen.

Store food, water, ammunition and other essentials here.

Under a Haystack

In a Flat Grassy Area

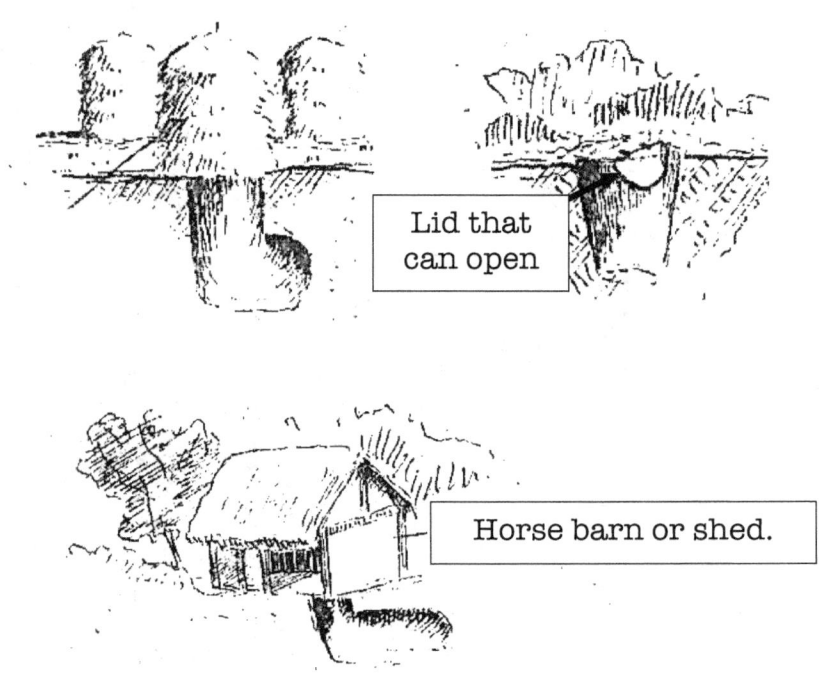

Lid that can open

Horse barn or shed.

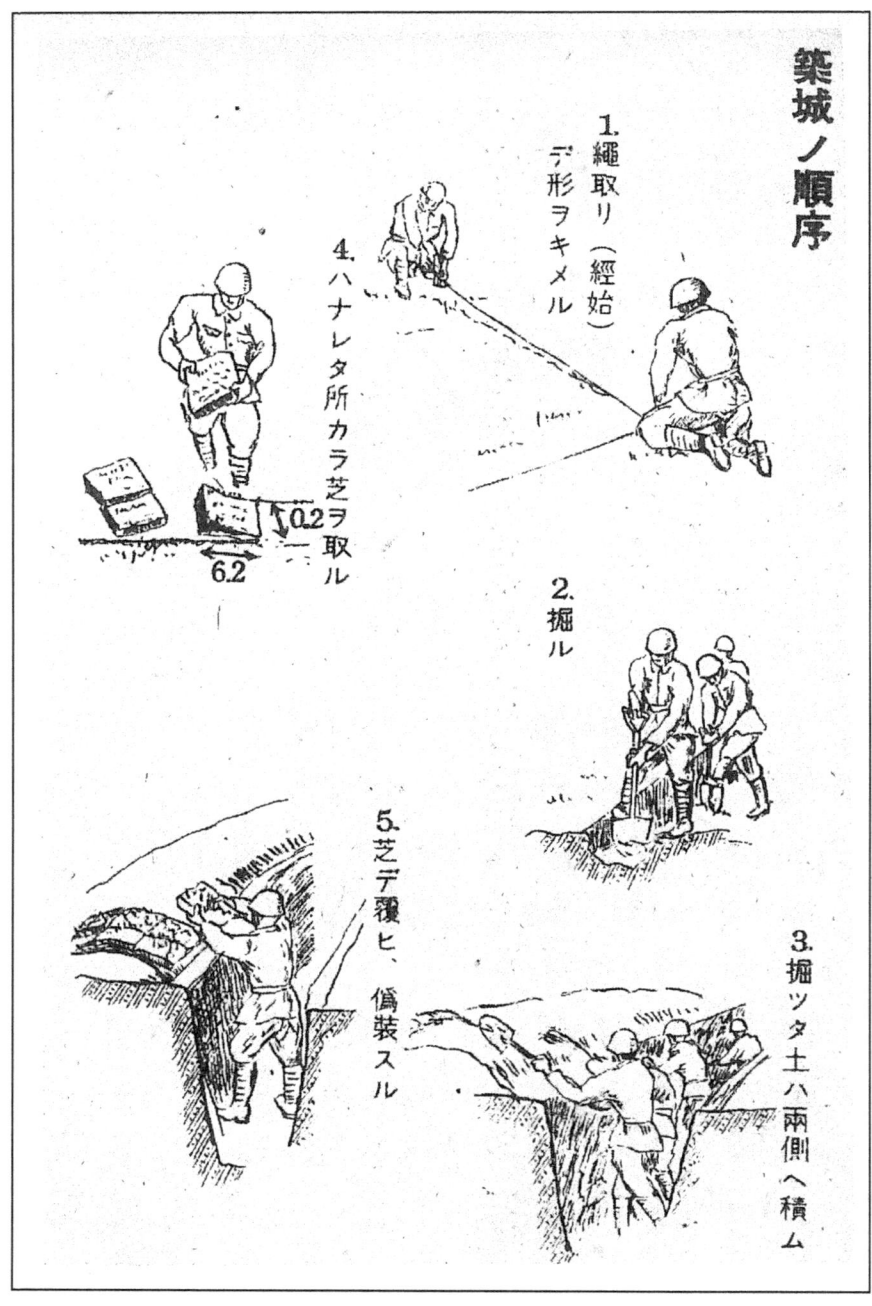

DEFENSE OF THE JAPANESE HOMELAND

The Proper Order for Building Fortifications

1. Roping Off The Area (Measuring)

4. Gather sod from an area some distance away.

2. Digging

5. Cover the mounded earth with sod to camouflage the area.

3. The soil you dig out should be piled towards the front.

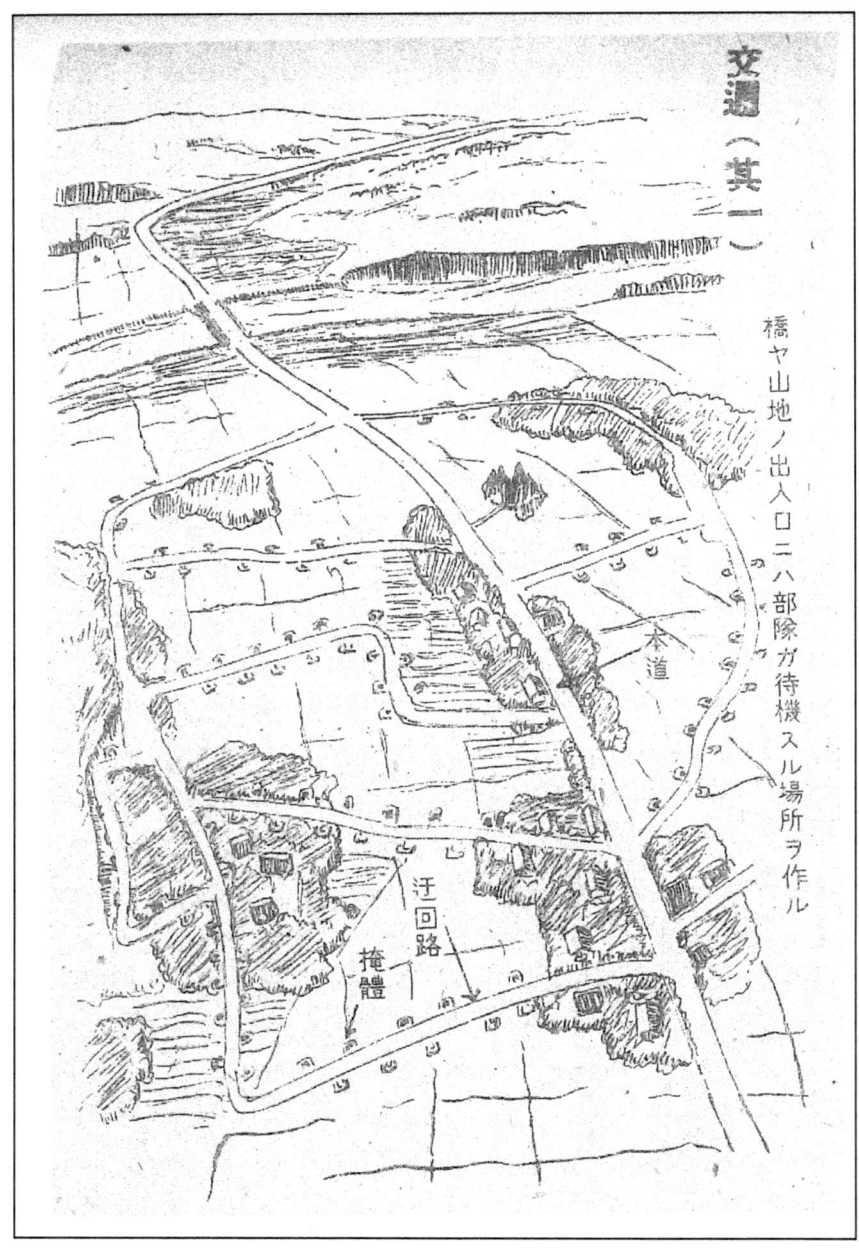

Transportation (Part 1)
Construct places for units to wait near bridges or the start of mountain roads.

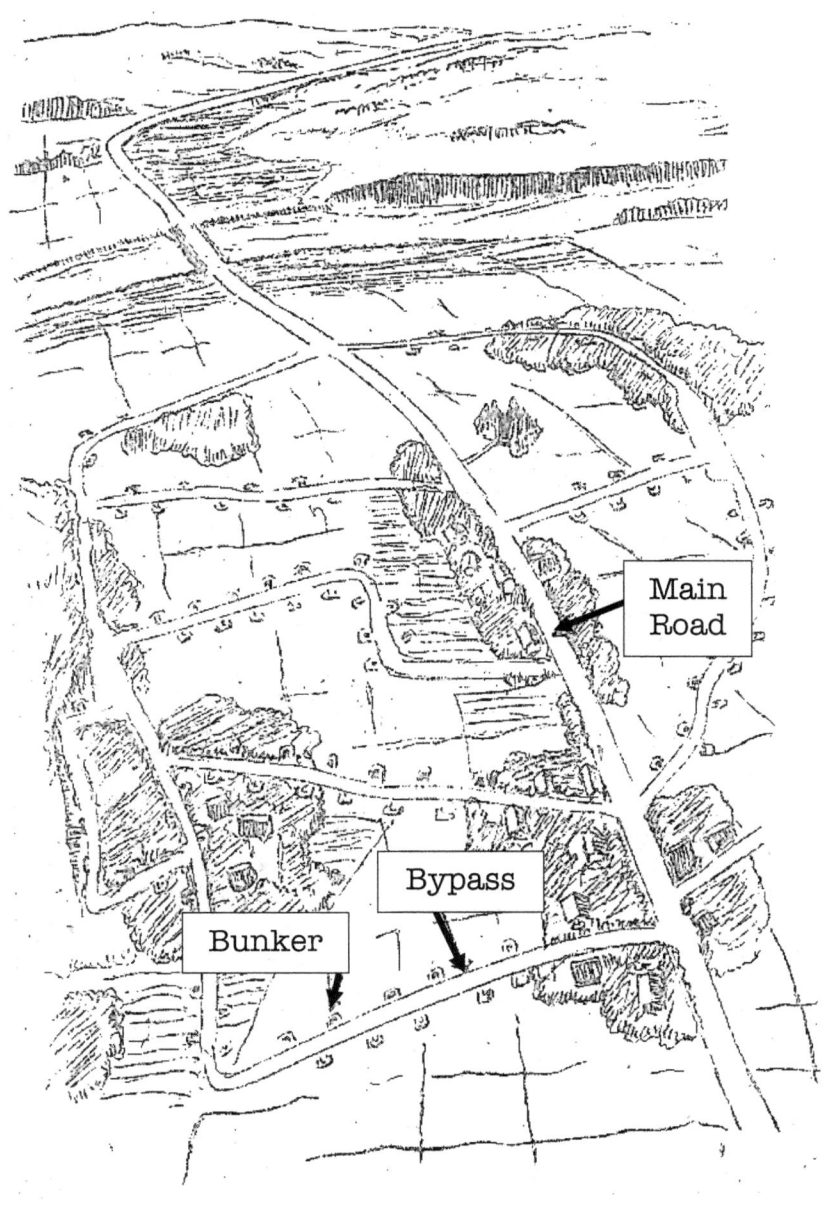

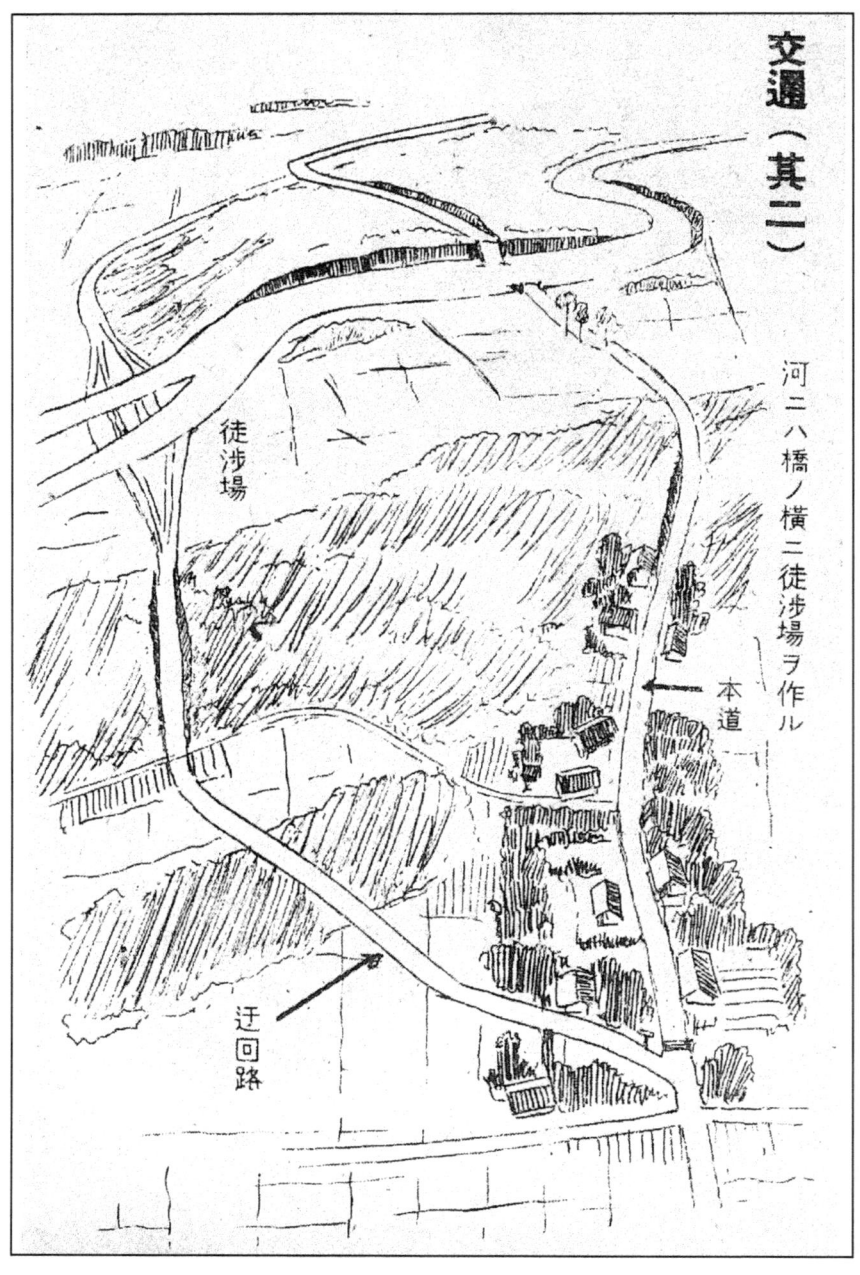

Transportation (Part 1)
Make a place next to a bridge where people can wade across.

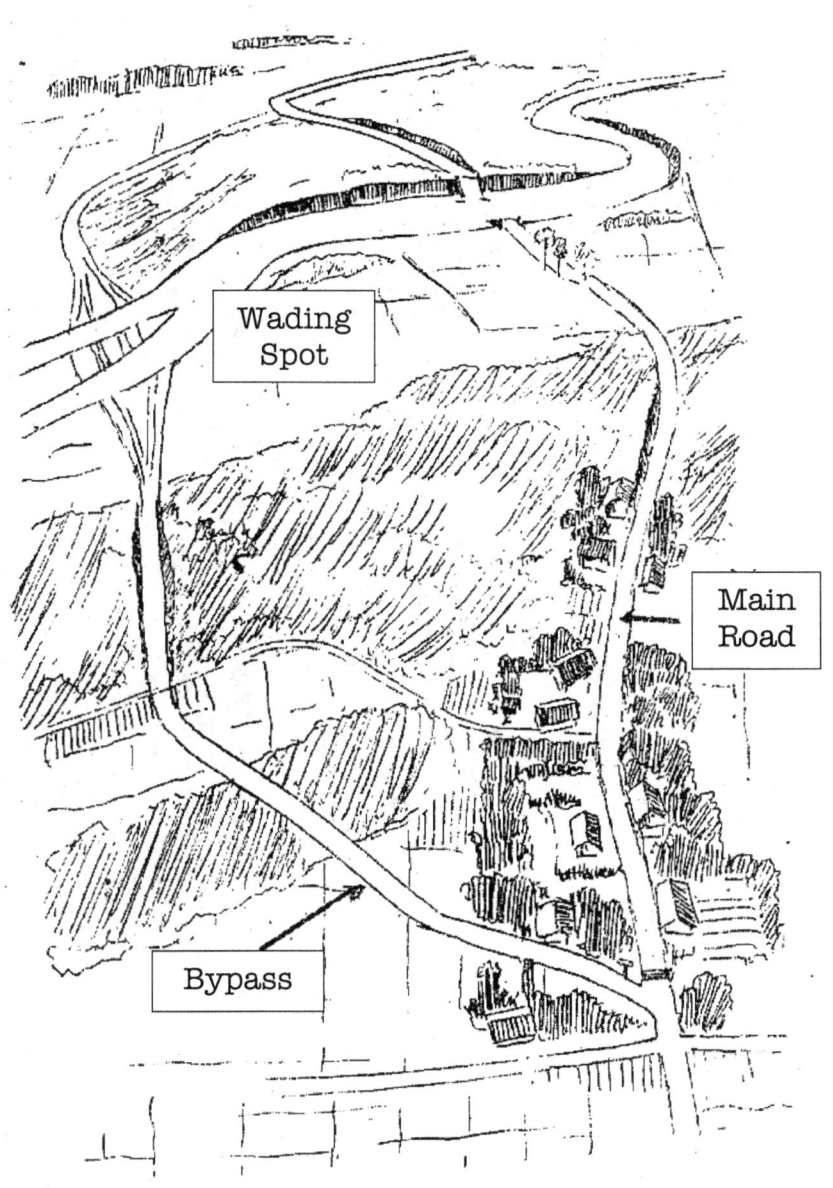

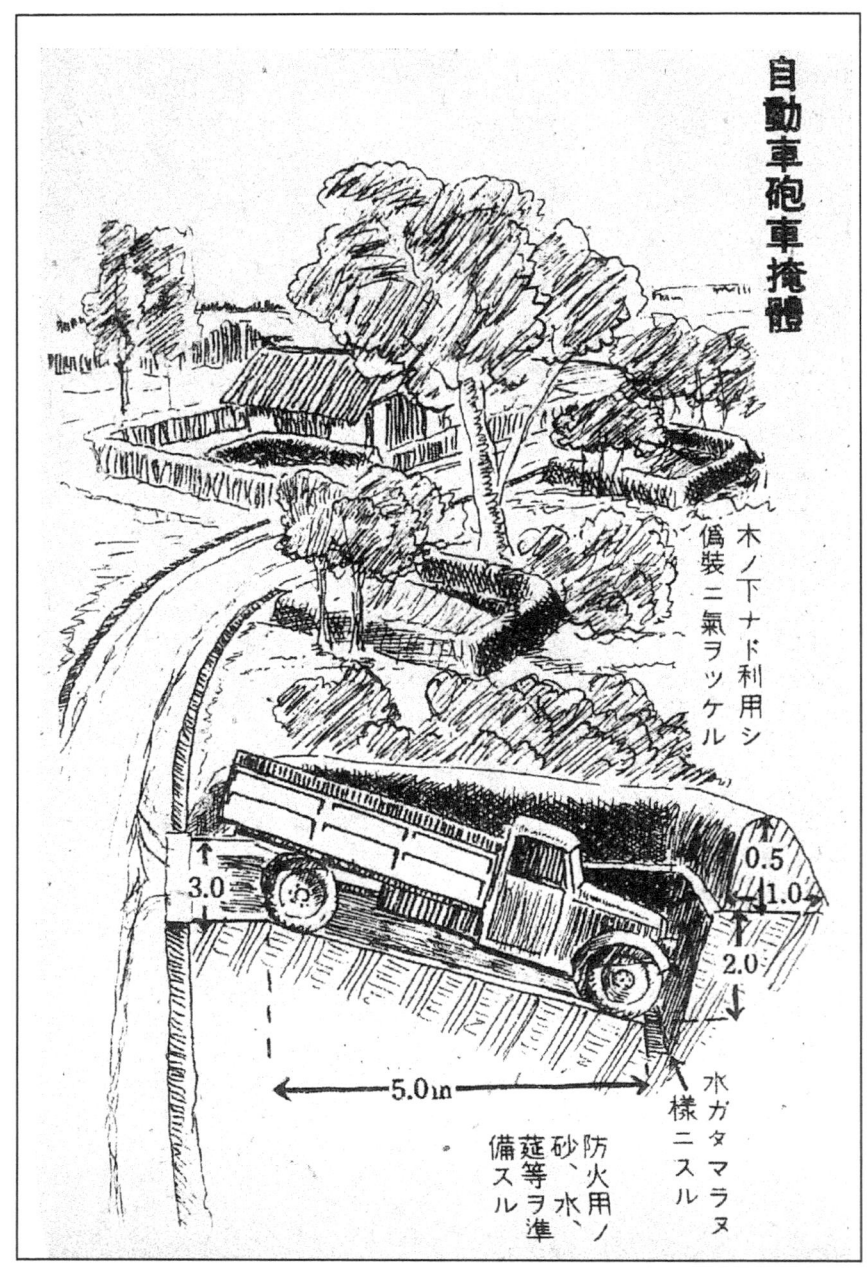

Bunker for Automobile or Gun Carriage

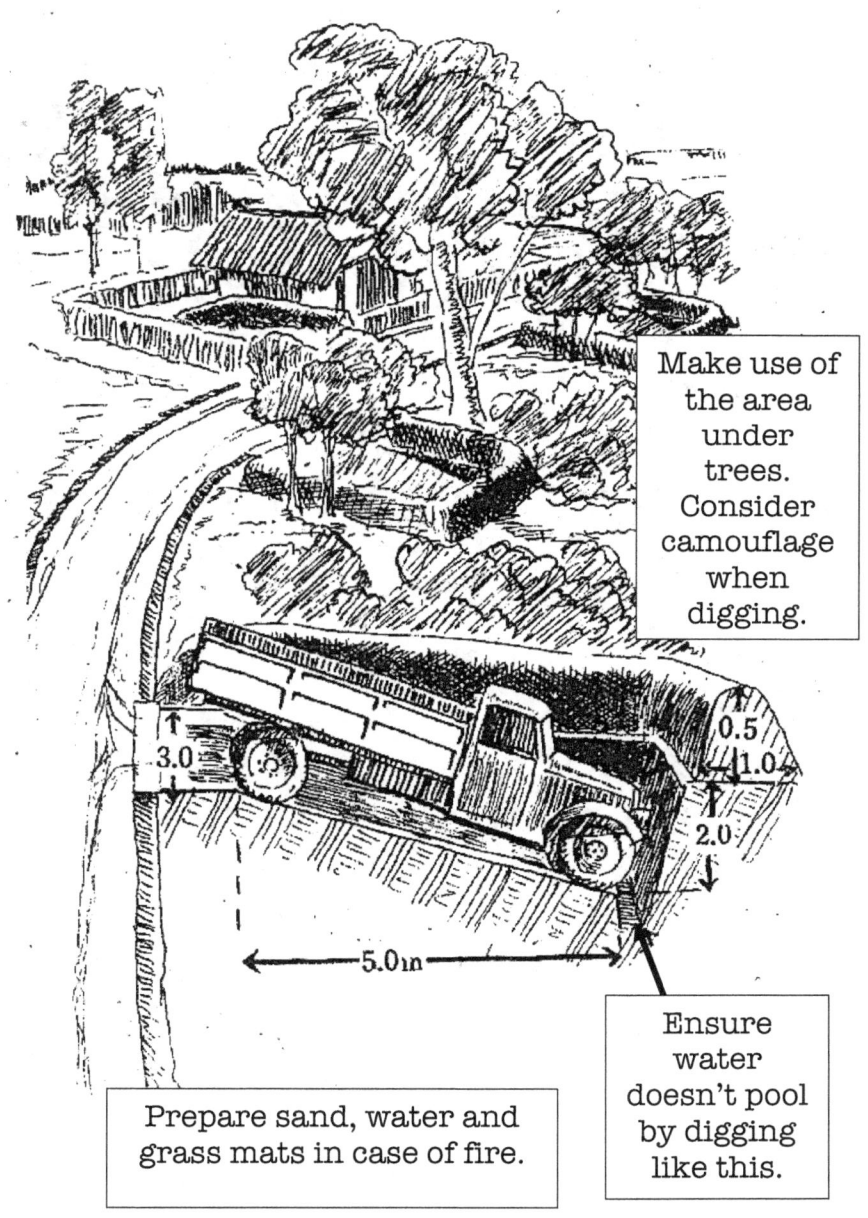

Tunnel-Style Gun Carriage Bunker

For automobiles the height should be 3 meters.

Be careful how you dispose of the soil taken from digging. Be sure to dispose of it in a way that it can't be seen from the air.

DEFENSE OF THE JAPANESE HOMELAND

Destroying a Bridge or Road
(This should only be done by order of the army.)

Sticks or grass.

Burning a bridge.

Building Fortifications:
The Citizen's Essential Guide

End

ERIC SHAHAN

DEFENSE OF THE JAPANESE HOMELAND

ERIC SHAHAN

DEFENSE OF THE JAPANESE HOMELAND

国民抗戦必携
National Resistance Manual

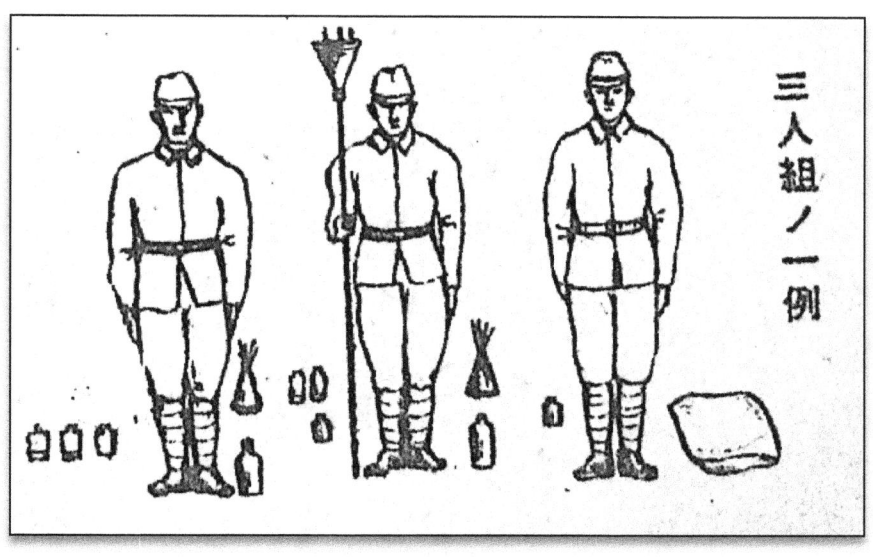

JAPANESE ARMY MANUAL

Published 1945

DEFENSE OF THE JAPANESE HOMELAND

Translator's Introduction

This is a reprint and translation the *Kokumin Kosen Hikkei* 国民抗戦必携 *National Resistance Manual* published by the Army Section of the Imperial General Headquarters on the 25th of April 1945. The manual contains 26 illustrated pages. Newspapers in Japan such as the Yomiuri and Asahi also published additional information to supplement this manual. However the Chubu Nihon Newspaper published the entire *National Resistance Manual* over the course of eight issues and included the additional information as well.
This translation will include the complete *National Resistance Manual* as well as the information included in the eight Chubu Nihon newspaper articles which ran from June 19th ~ 26th 1945.

Left: A June 10th 1945 Yomiuri Newspaper article announcing the forthcoming publication of the *National Resistance Manual* as well as *The People's Guide to Building Fortifications*. The article is titled, *100 Million Special Attack Soldiers : A Guide to the Final Battle in the Homeland.*

How the Chubu Newspaper articles were organized. This is article #3 from June 21st 1945.

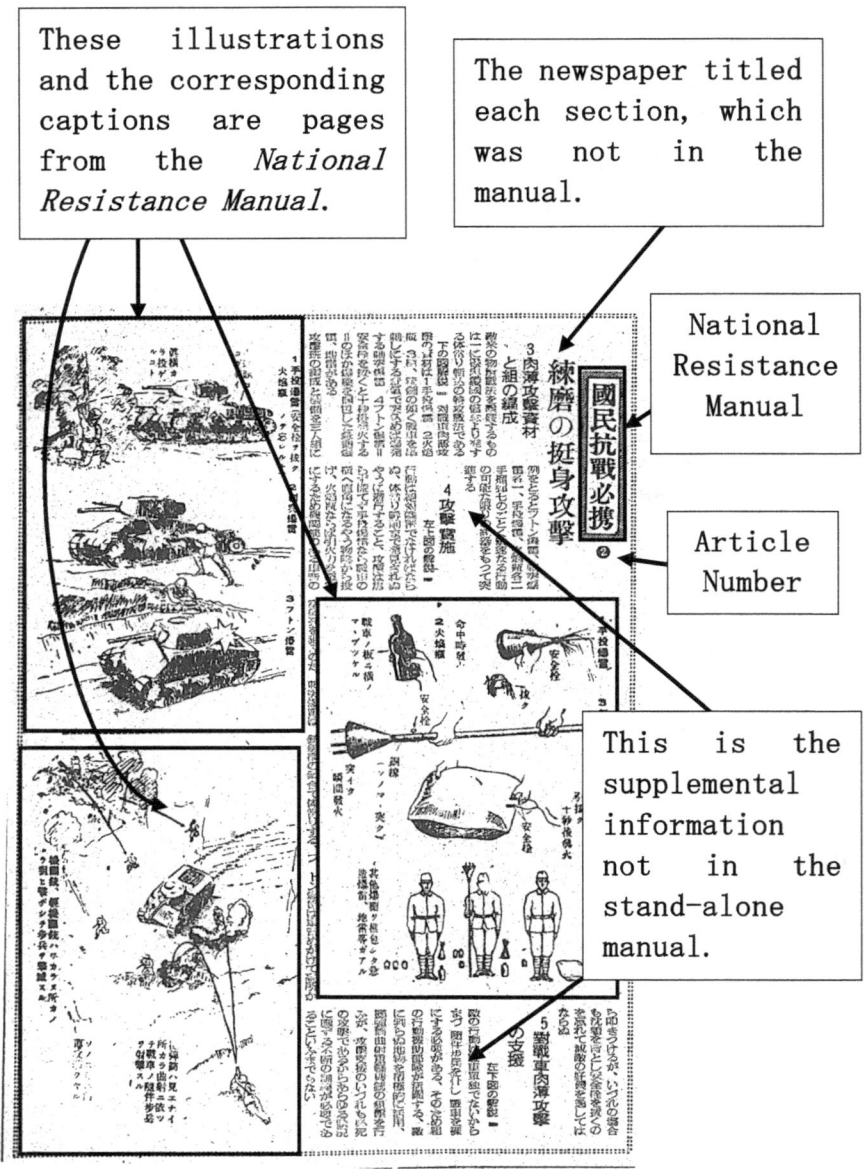

These illustrations and the corresponding captions are pages from the *National Resistance Manual*.

The newspaper titled each section, which was not in the manual.

National Resistance Manual

Article Number

This is the supplemental information not in the stand-alone manual.

ERIC SHAHAN

National Resistance Manual

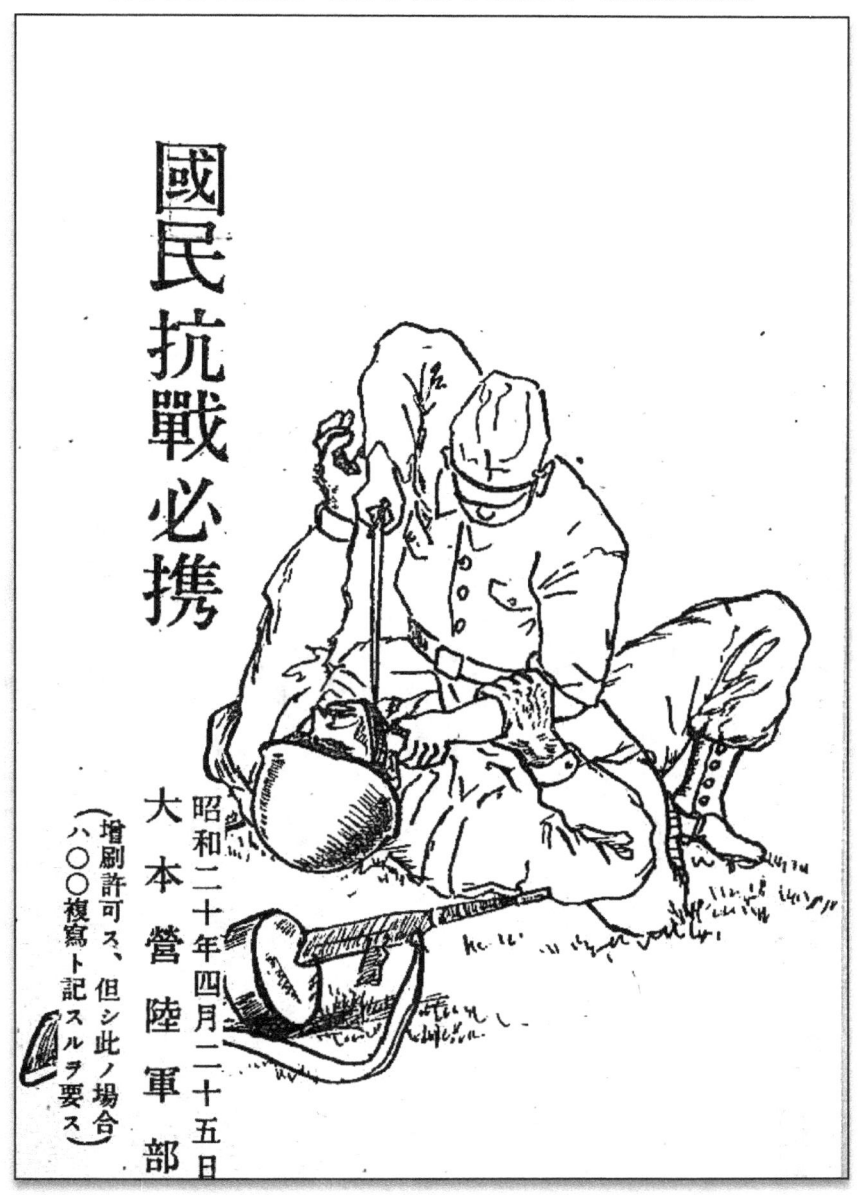

Published April 25th 1945
Newspaper Articles June 19th ~ 26th 1945

ERIC SHAHAN

Newspaper Article 1
Directly Attacking Enemy Tanks Without Fear
A. Outline

DEFENSE OF THE JAPANESE HOMELAND

A. Outline
If the enemy choses to attack the mainland, a combined force of 100,000,000 Tokko, Special Attack Soldiers, will obliterate them. They will, with absolute certainty defend this imperial land.
B. The *Kokumin Giyutai*, People's Honorable and Brave Unit, also known as Volunteer Fighting Corps, will conduct the training, build fortifications and teach everyone how to defend their locality. This will include how to advance on the enemy undercover and kill them. It is essential that all cooperate with the military's strategy.
C. This is the training necessary for the final battle and will cover the following topics:
    a. How directives will be issued from command
    b. How to be a sniper, throw grenades, cut down enemies with a sword and do close quarters attacks on tanks.

ERIC SHAHAN

Newspaper Article 1
Directly Attacking Enemy Tanks Without Fear

Chapter 1
How to Do a Close-Quarters Attack on a Tank

How to Do a Close-Quarters Attack on a Tank

1. Essential data regarding enemy tanks and striking points.

The enemy tanks should be attacked in vital areas. The enemy Americans primarily use two types of tanks, the M4 Mid-sized tank and the M1 Heavy tank.

The best way to attack an M4 tank is to detonate a futon-bomb on the dome or on the back. The back of the tank can also be attacked with Molotov cocktails. The front of a tank as well as the turret are vulnerable to bomb-tipped spears as well as hand-thrown explosives. Hand-thrown explosives can shatter a tank's treads
Charging at the advancing tank while holding a 7 kilogram quick-made bomb is also an effective method.

For the heavily armored M1 tank, attack the dome or back with a futon-bomb. Molotov cocktails can also be thrown at the back. Stab into the sides of the tank with bomb-tipped spears. Attacks to the front of the tank should be done with a 10 kilogram quick-made bomb.

M4 Mid-Sized Tank

6.1 meters long
2.9 meters wide
2.8 meters tall

The armor on the prime areas such as the front and turret is 85 millimeters thick. The weakest points are 60 millimeters thick. It is armed with a 76 mm cannon and 3 heavy machine guns.

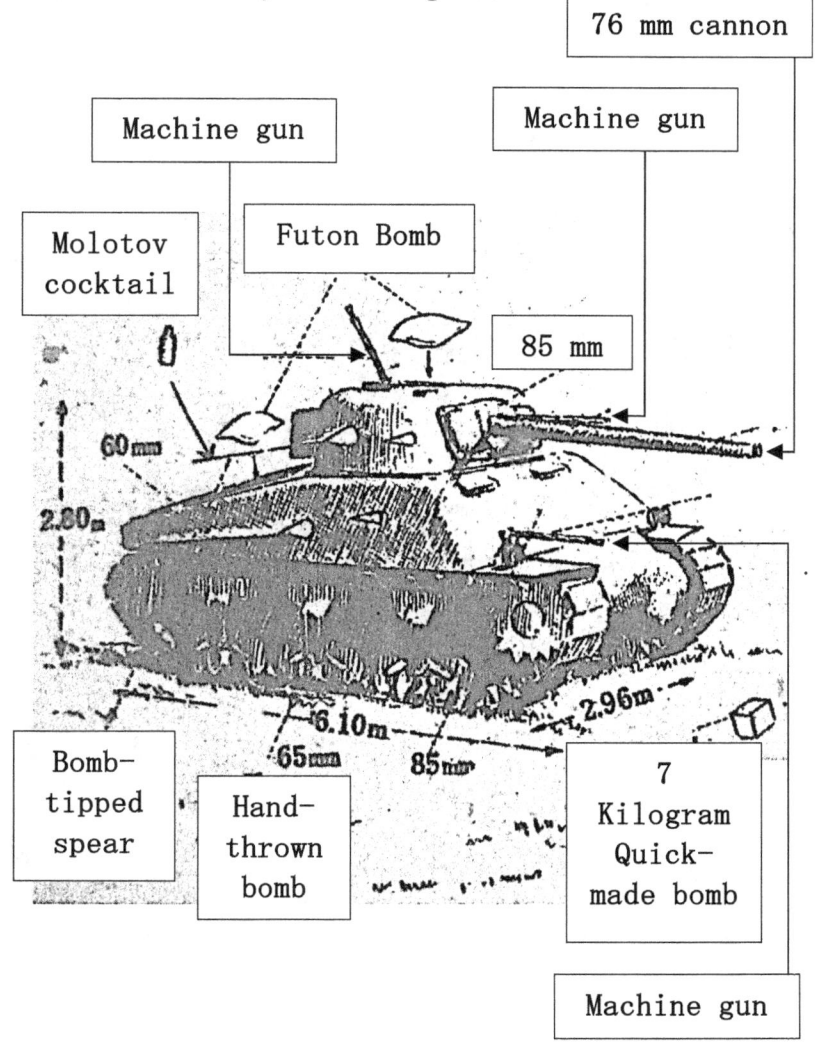

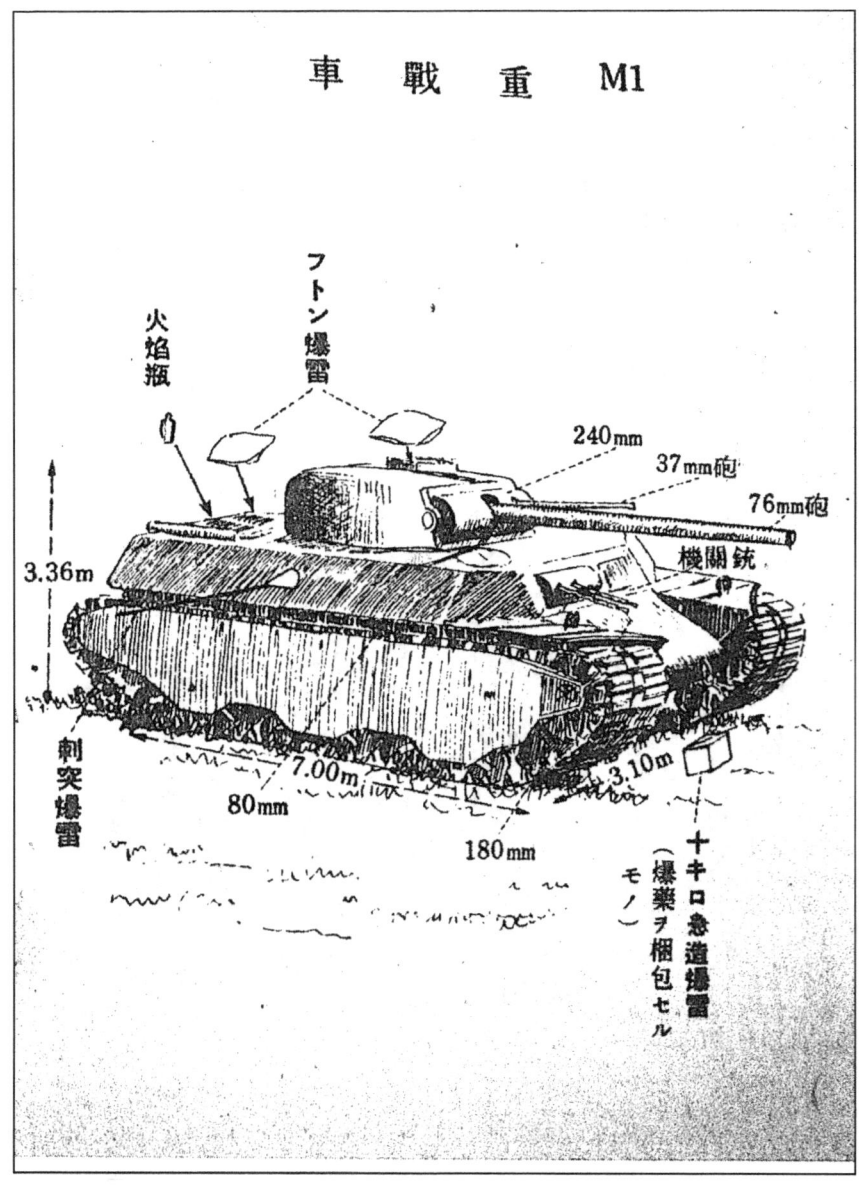

M1 Heavy Tank

7 meters long
3.1 meters wide
3.36 meters tall
Armor is 24-80 millimeters thick.
It is armed with one 76 millimeter cannon and 1 37 mm cannon and carries two heavy machine guns.

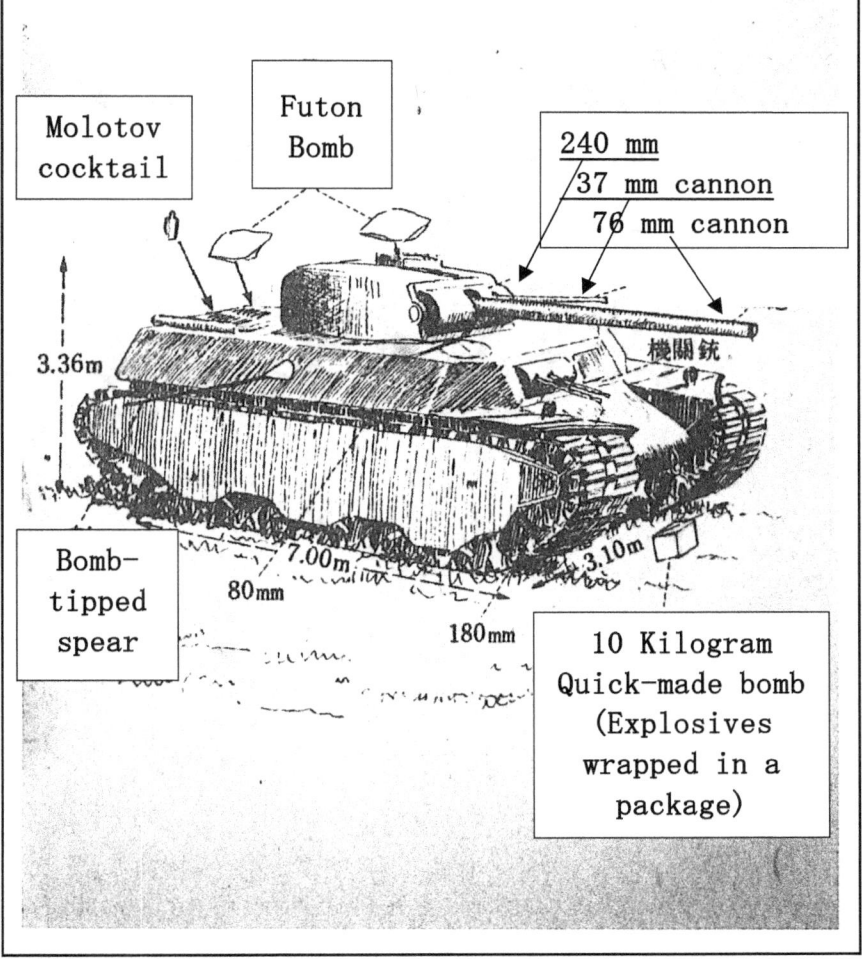

- Molotov cocktail
- Futon Bomb
- 240 mm
- 37 mm cannon
- 76 mm cannon
- Bomb-tipped spear
- 10 Kilogram Quick-made bomb (Explosives wrapped in a package)

Newspaper Article 1
Directly Attacking Enemy Tanks Without Fear
2. The Strategy Used by Enemy Tanks: Advancing

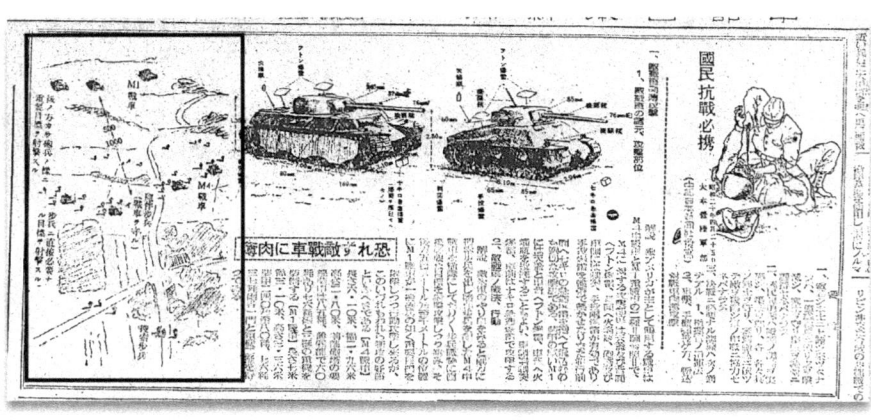

2. The Strategy Used by Enemy Tanks: Advancing

Looking at the standard operating procedure of the enemy American military, tank units tend to send scout troops ahead. The foot-soldiers assigned to accompany an M4 tank will form in ranks to the sides and advance forward slowly, firing at any essential target they come in contact with.

Stationed behind that unit, the M1 tanks continually fire on the essential targets similar to how the soldiers that are assigned to stationary artillery operate. Either of these targets are delicious treats for us.

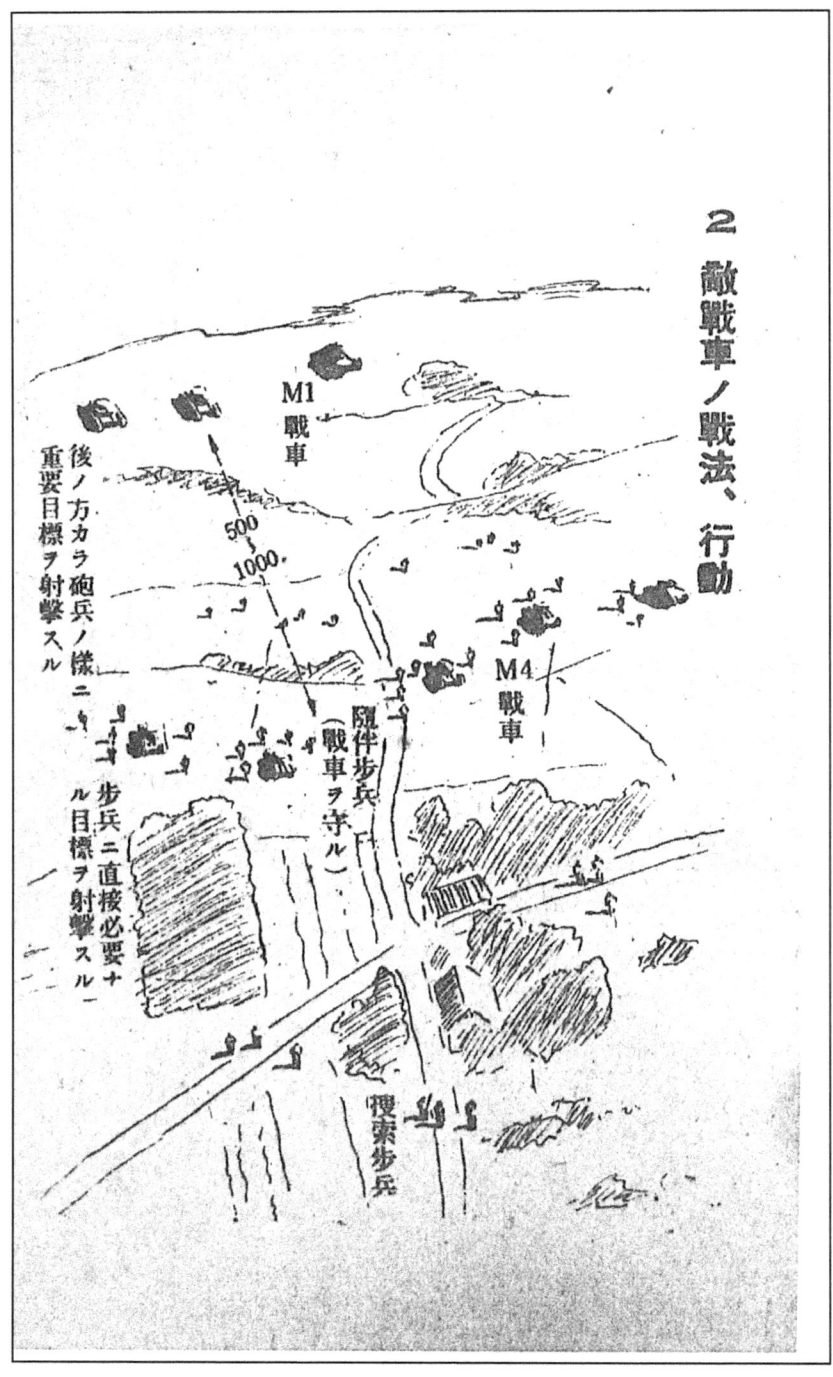

2. The Strategy of Enemy Tank Units and How They Move.

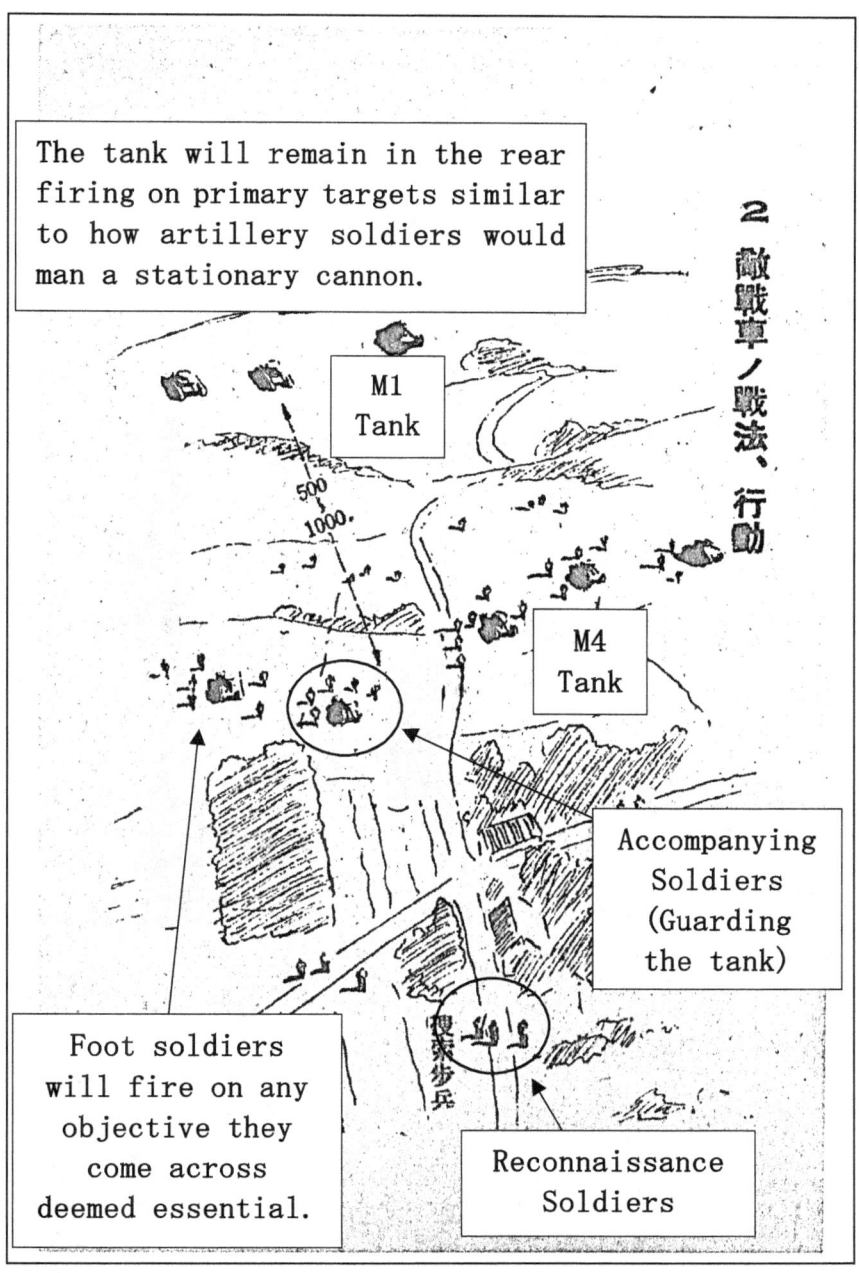

Newspaper Article 2
Well-Practiced Volunteer Attack Units
3. Information on How to Conduct Close Quarters Attacks and How to Form Units

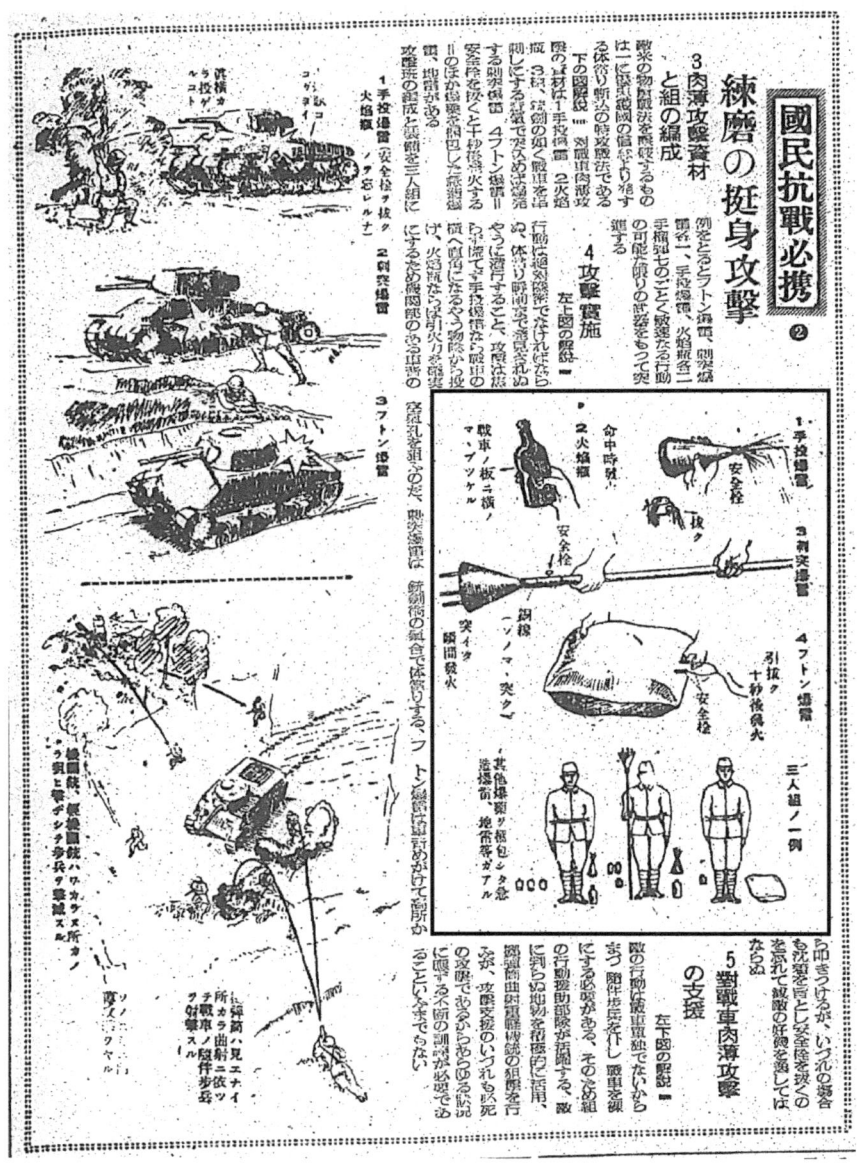

3. Information on How to Conduct Close Quarters Attacks and How to Form Units

One method we have for attacking and destroying the American supply chain strategy that provides material resources their military is our willingness to throw our bodies at them and cut our enemy down. This is due to our utter devotion to defending our country. This is our *Tokko Senpo*, Special-Attack War Strategy.

The resources for a close-quarters assault on tanks are as follows:
1. *Tenage Bakurai* : Hand-Thrown Explosives
2. *Kaenbin* : Fire Bottles (Molotov Cocktails)
3. *Shitotsu Bakurai* : Bomb-Tipped Spears. A bomb that explodes on impact when you charge a tank and stab it like you are attacking with a spear or bayonet.
4. *Futon Bakurai* : Pillow Bomb. A device that will ignite 10 seconds after you pull the safety pin. Another version is a parcel of explosives called a *Kyuzo Bakurai*, Ready-Made Bomb. Also known as a Jirai, Mine.

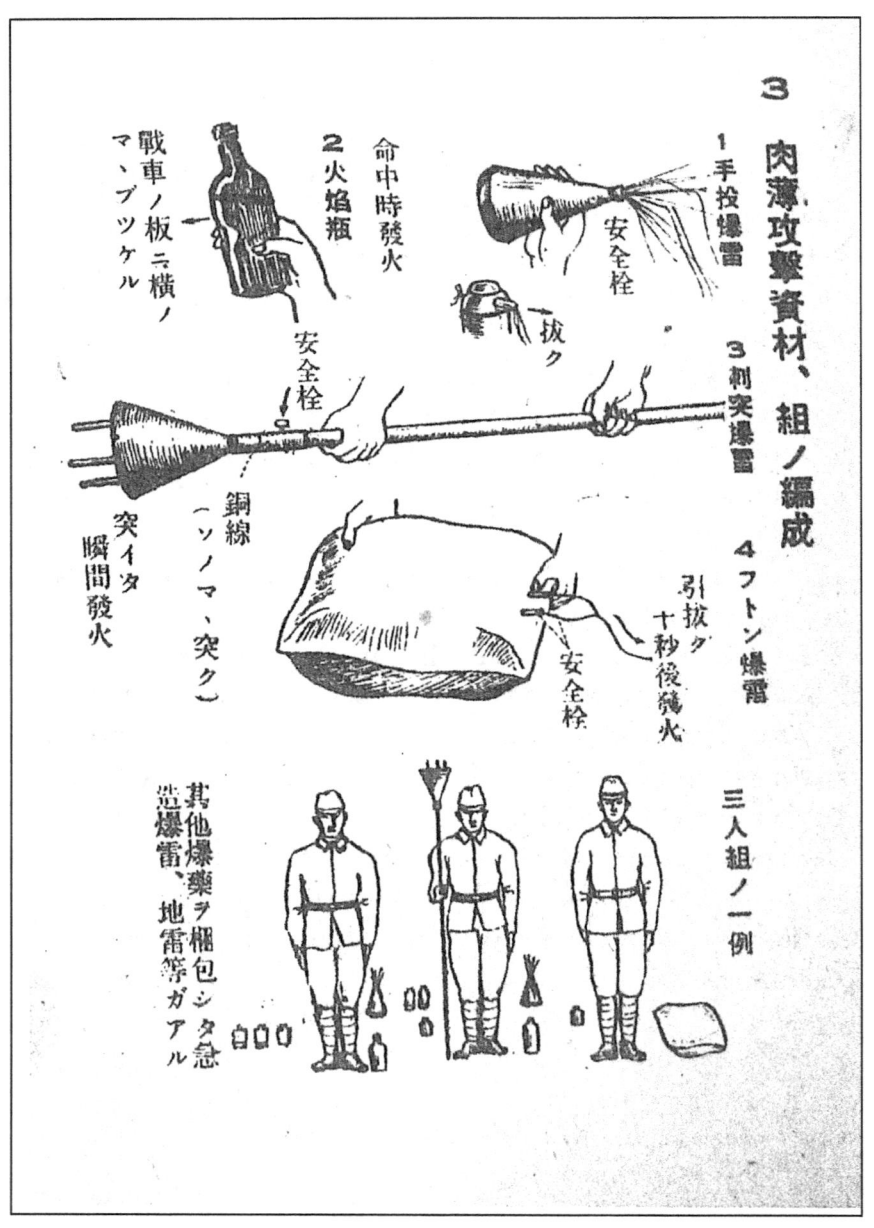

3. Information on How to Conduct Close Quarters Attacks and How to Form Units

2. Molotov Cocktail	1. Hand-thrown Explosive
Throw it sideways like this onto the tank's armor plate.	Ignites when it strikes the target.

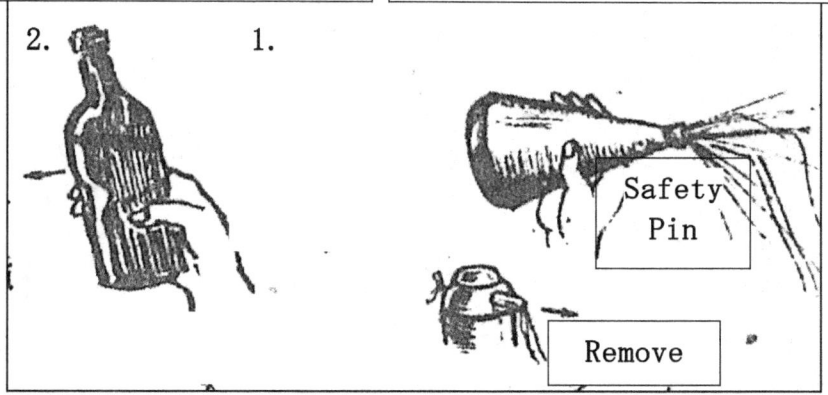

3. Bomb-Tipped Spear

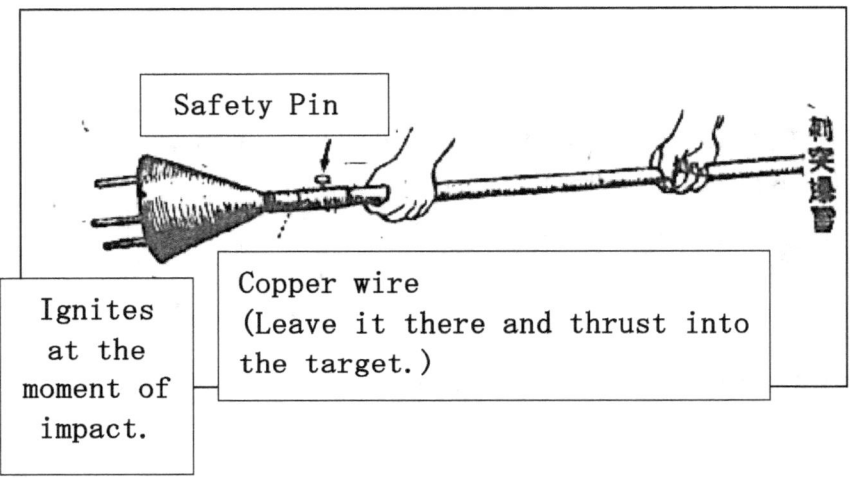

Safety Pin

Ignites at the moment of impact.

Copper wire
(Leave it there and thrust into the target.)

4. Futon "Pillow" Bomb

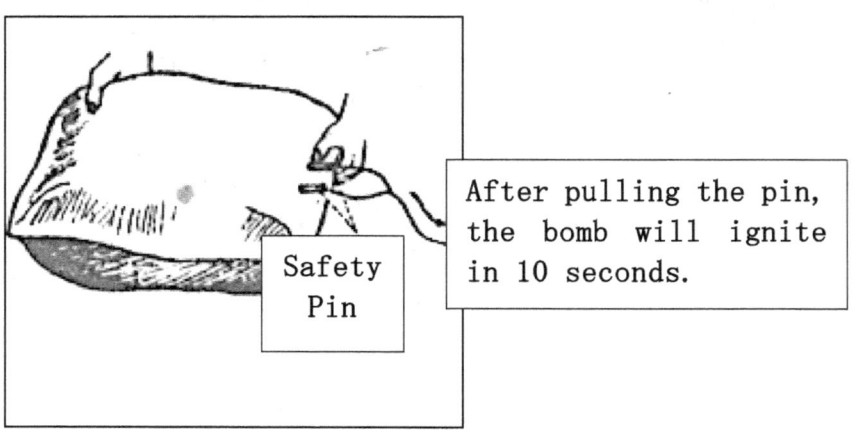

Safety Pin

After pulling the pin, the bomb will ignite in 10 seconds.

Example of a 3-Person Unit

Each team would have one Futon "pillow" bomb, one bomb-tipped spear, two hand-thrown explosives, two Molotov cocktails and seven hand grenades.
In addition, they would be equipped with wrapped explosives to use as a Quick-Made bomb or mine.

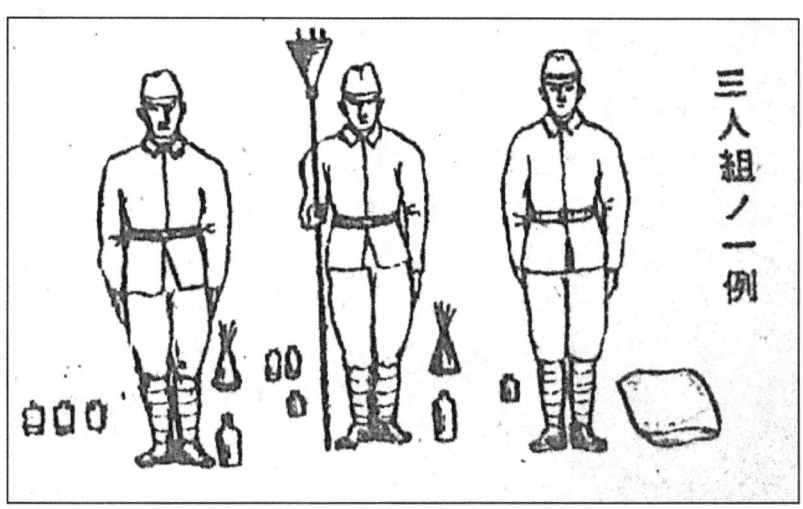

Newspaper Article 2
Well-Practiced Volunteer Attack Units
4. How to Carry Out an Attack

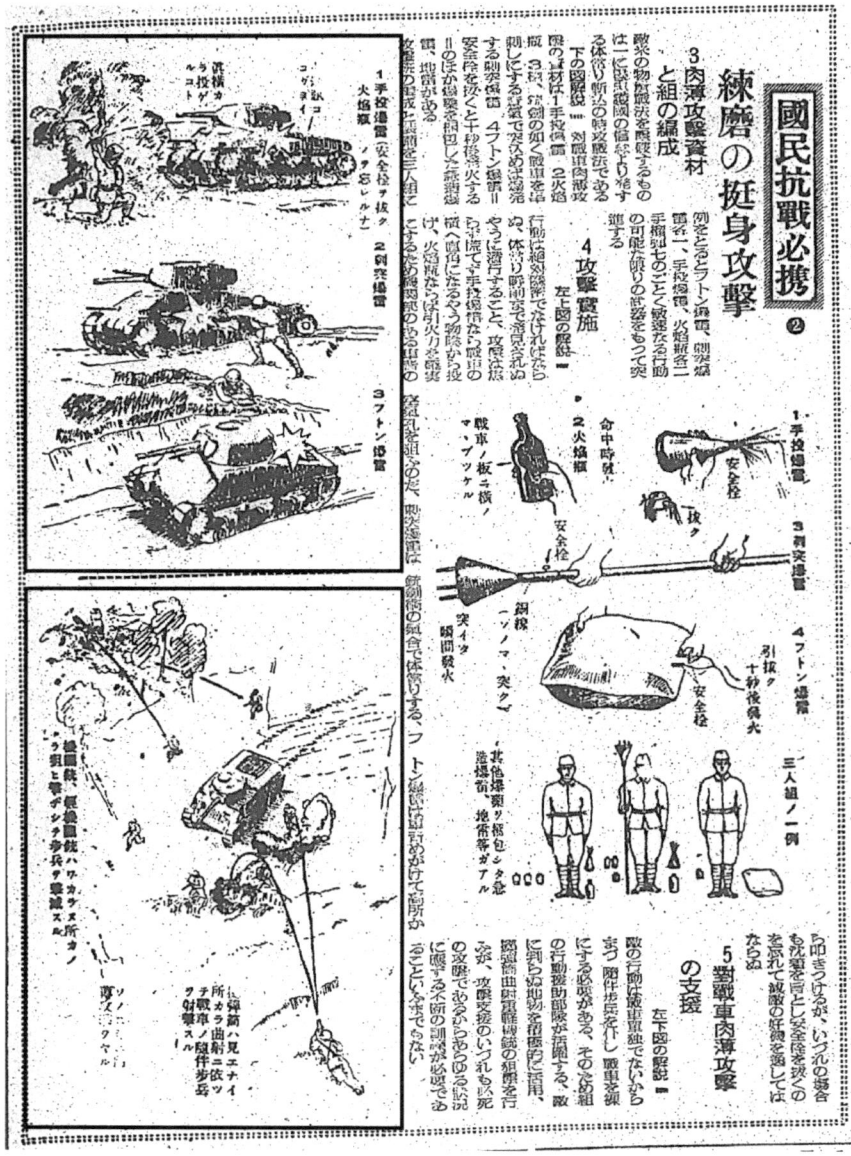

4. How to Carry Out an Attack

Your movements must be completely covert, thus it is imperative you remain concealed and not be discovered until the moment of your attack. When attacking do not rush and do not get flustered.

- If using a hand-thrown bomb, be sure to wait in a concealed place, perpendicular to your target, so you can throw at the side of the tank.
- When throwing a Molotov cocktail, to ensure it ignites with maximum power. Target the exhaust port near the engine on the back of the tank.
- When attacking with a bomb-tipped spear, use the same Kiai, shout unifying body and action, as you slam into your target with your whole body.
- When using a Futon "pillow" bomb, aim for the back of the tank and throw it down hard from a high place.

No matter which way you attack, remain calm and be certain to pull the safely pin. Do not lose a great chance to destroy the enemy.

DEFENSE OF THE JAPANESE HOMELAND

4. How to Carry Out an Attack
   1. Hand-Thrown Bombs (Do not forget to pull the safety pin)
   2. Molotov Cocktail
   3. Futon Bomb

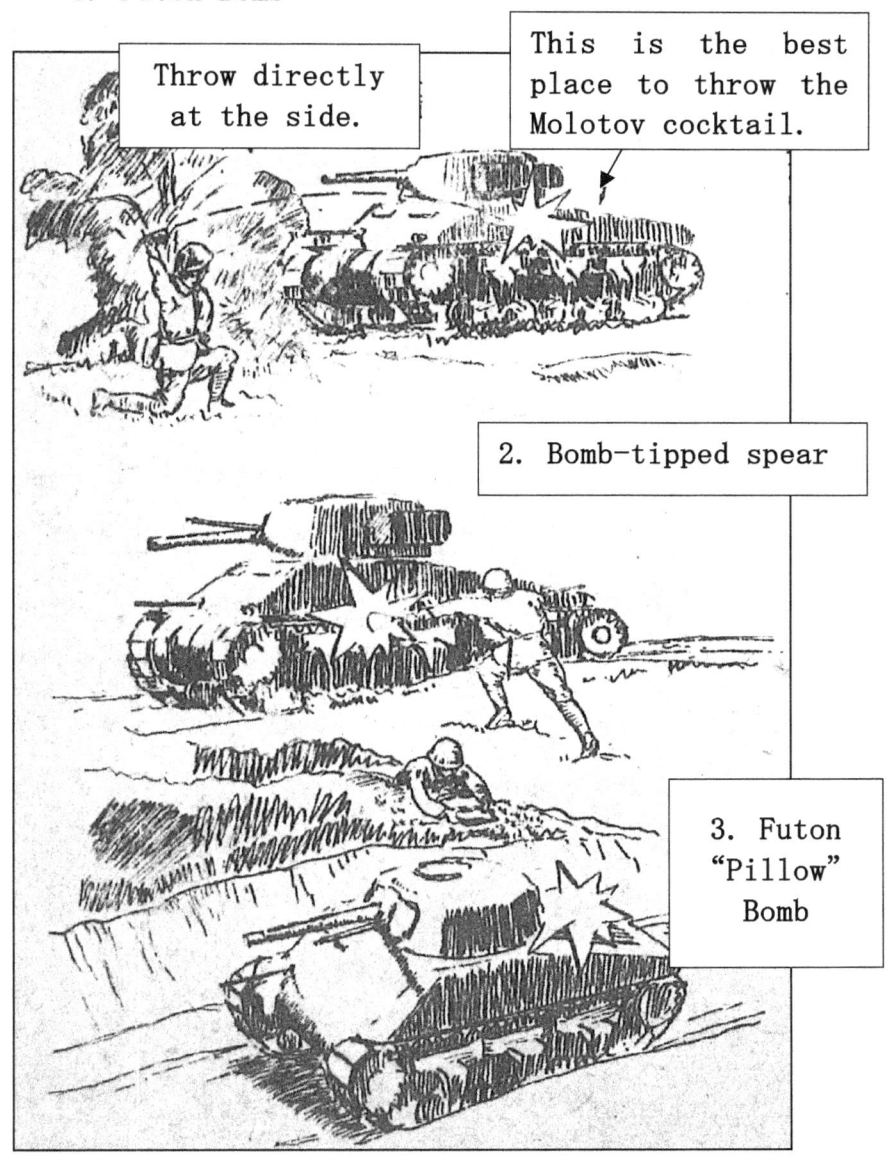

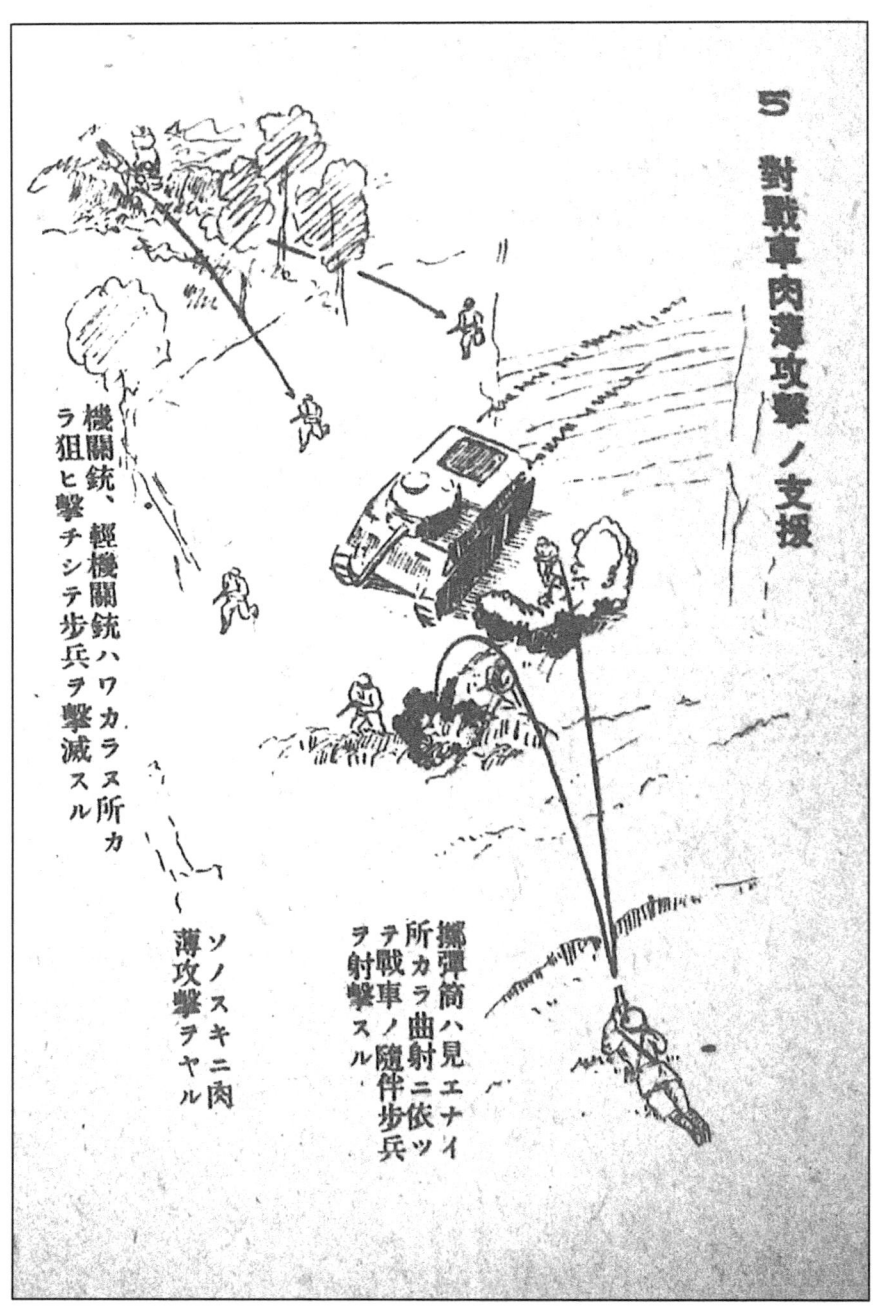

DEFENSE OF THE JAPANESE HOMELAND

5. How to Support a Close Quarter Attack on a Tank

Look for places that will allow you to hide yourself from the machineguns and submachineguns and shoot at the foot soldiers, eliminating them.

Use that opportunity to launch a close quarters attack.

Fire the grenade launcher from a place that cannot be seen. The grenades should arch down onto the foot soldiers accompanying the tank.

Newspaper Article 3
Our Ever-Victorious Military Strategy

1. *Teishin Kirikomi*
Volunteer Attack Units

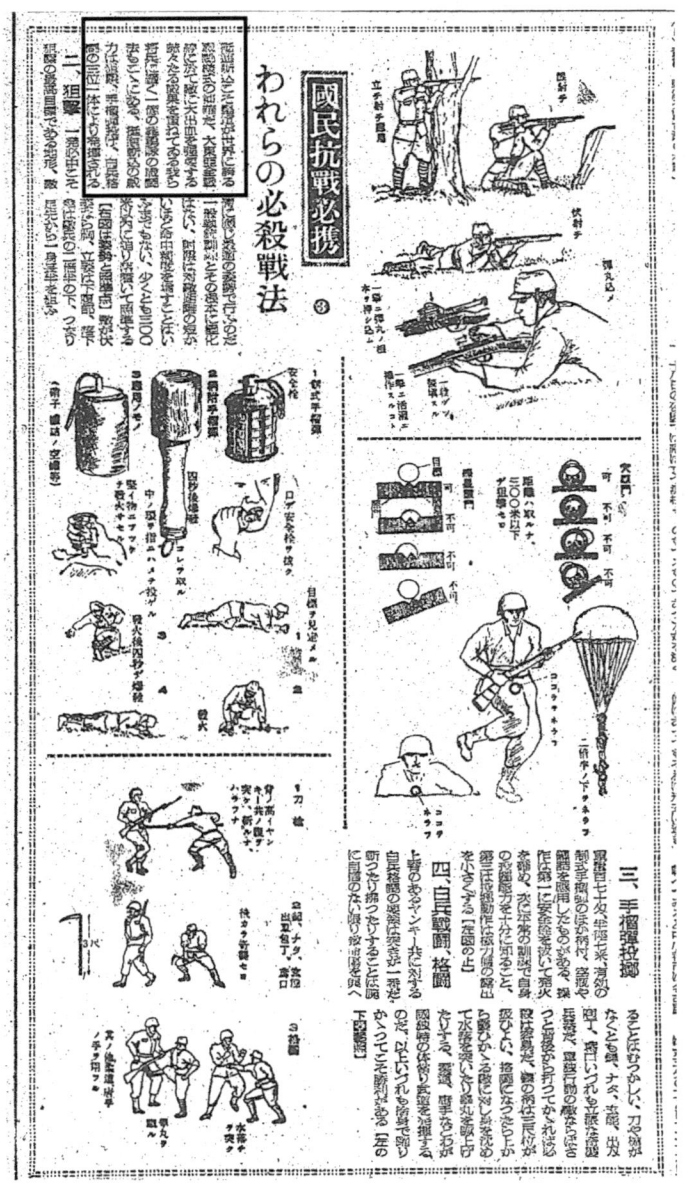

1. *Teishin Kirikomi*
Volunteer Attack Units

The *Teishin Kirikomi*, Volunteer Attack Units, are a glorious reflection of the Imperial Army, which is renowned all over the world for its style of fighting. Our officers and men, have spread the blazing red fires of war and caused the blood of our enemies to hemorrhage all over the battlefields throughout Asia. The threat of our Volunteer Attack Units will be demonstrated with the unification of the triple threat of sniper fire, throwing hand grenades and close-quarters combat.

Newspaper Article 3
Our Ever-Victorious Military Strategy

2. *Sogeki* A Sniper

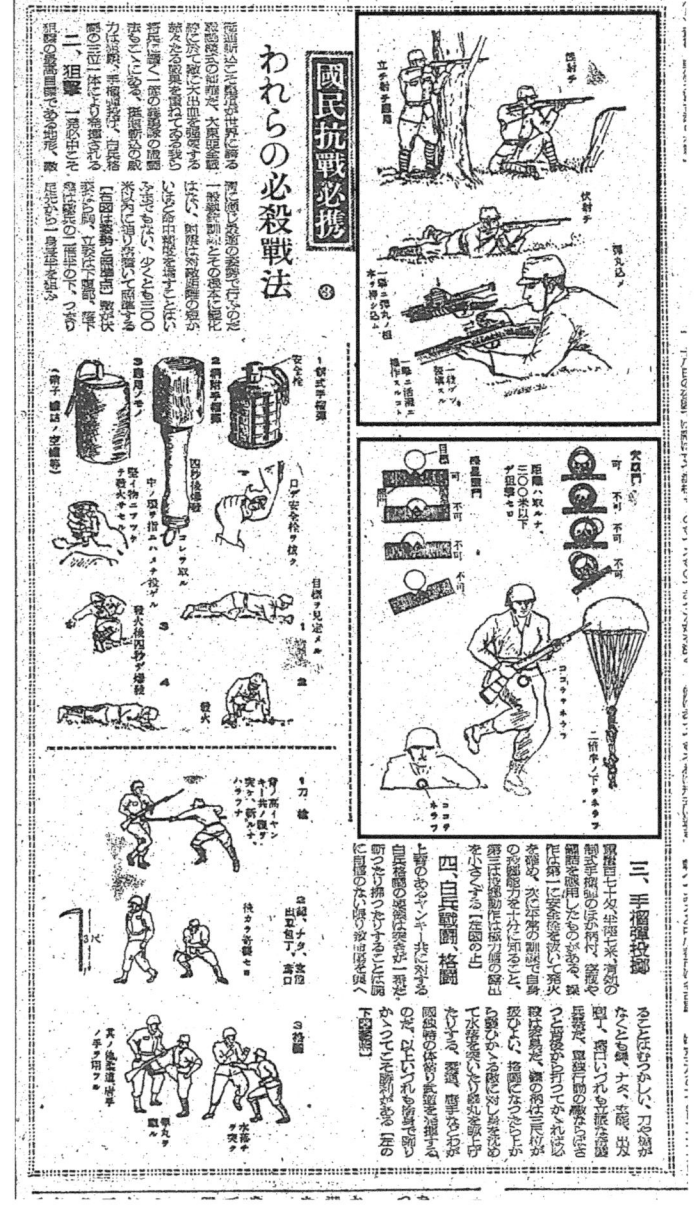

2. *Sogeki* A Sniper

The highest goal of a sniper is to always hit your target with the first shot. It requires that you adapt to the terrain and the disposition of the enemy when shooting. This is no different from the fundamentals taught during basic rifle training.

It goes without saying that your likelihood of hitting your target increases the closer you are to the enemy. Thus, you need to advance closer than 300 meters from your target before calmly sighting in.

If the enemy is prone, then aim for the chest. If standing then aim for the lower abdomen. If your target is a soldier parachuting, aim 2.5 body lengths below. This means to sight in one and a half body lengths below his legs.

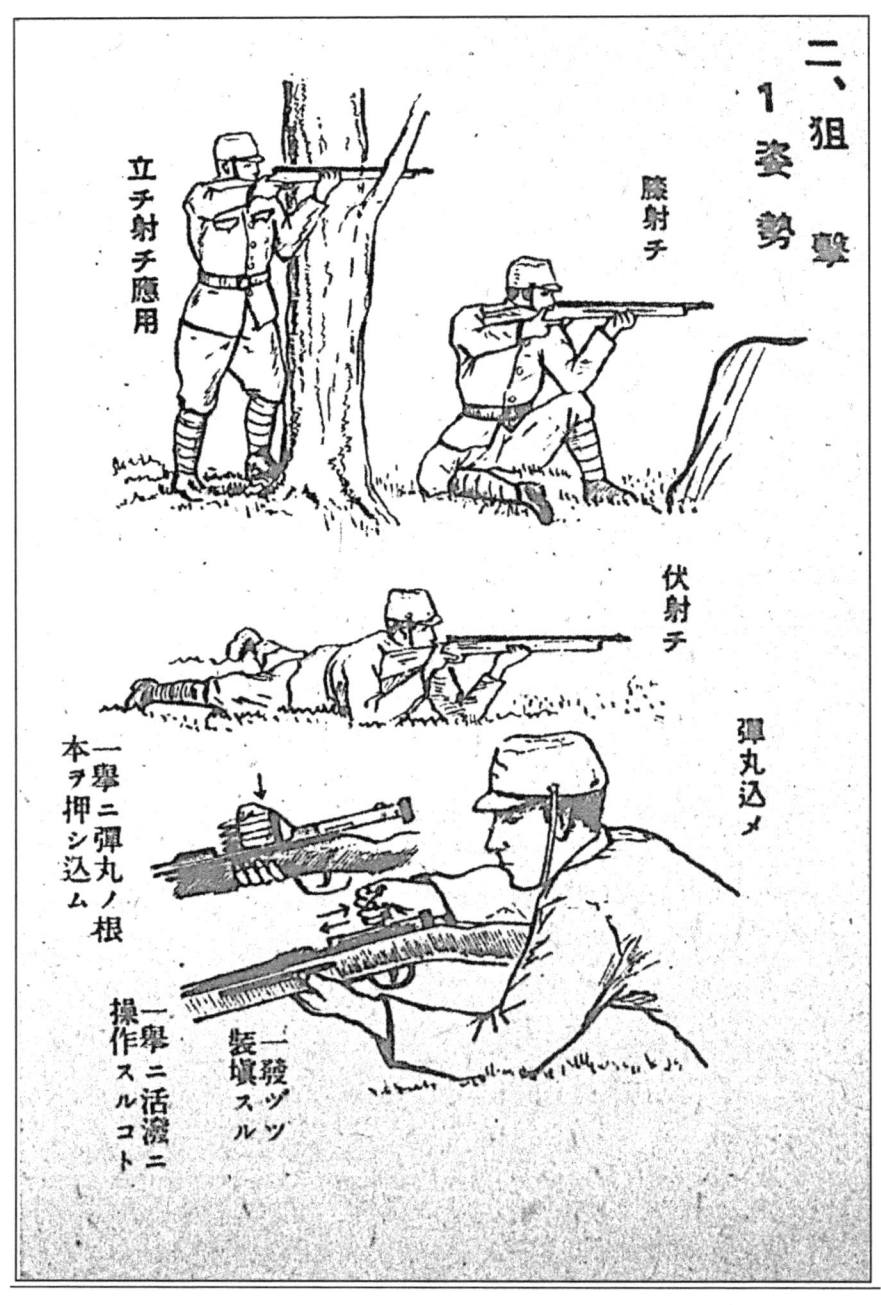

2. *Sogeki*
A Sniper

Shooting Postures

Useful when shooting while standing

Knee Shooting

Shooting While Lying Prone

Loading Bullets

Push the clip of bullets entirely into the rifle.

Chamber Each Round
·
Make Every Round in the Clip Count

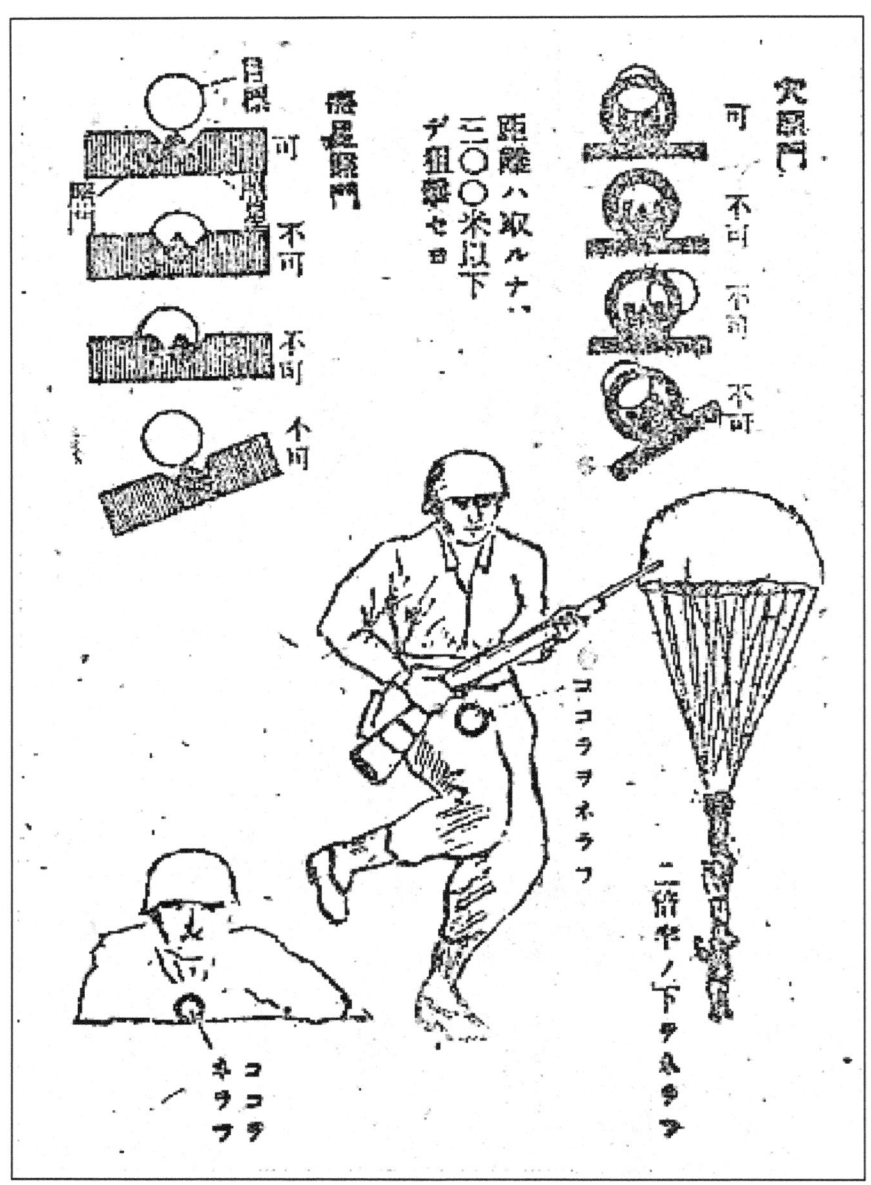

Using an 穴照門 Aperture Sight

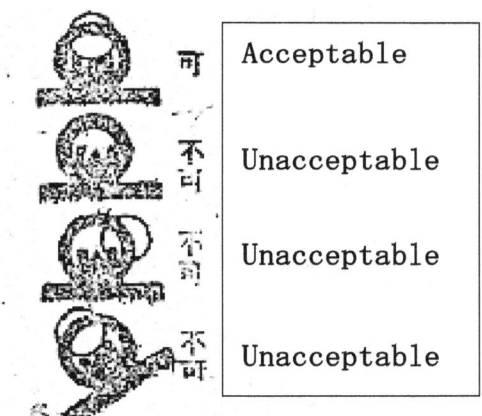

Comparing the Star, Comparing the Gate :
Using a Notch Sight

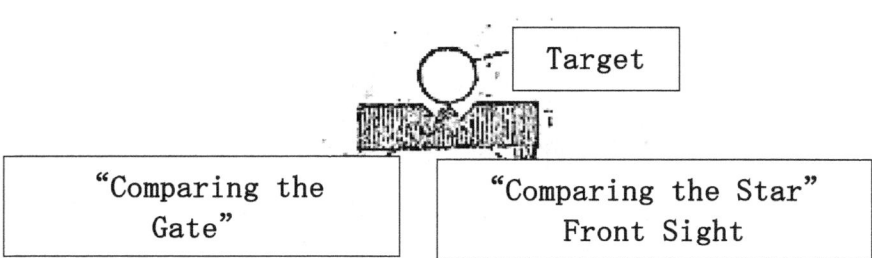

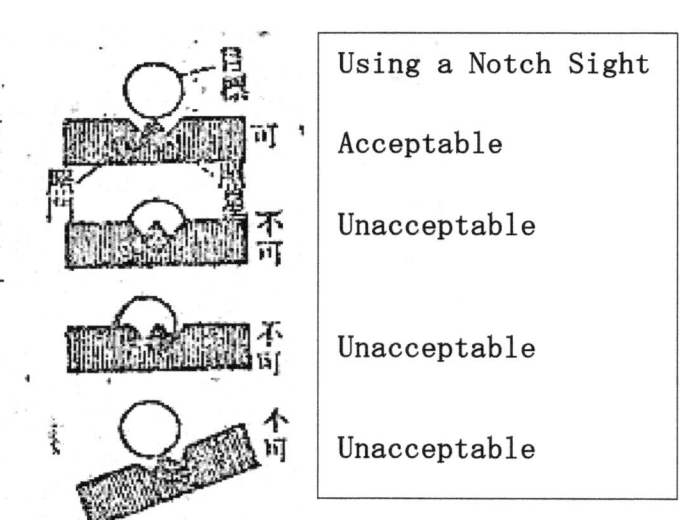

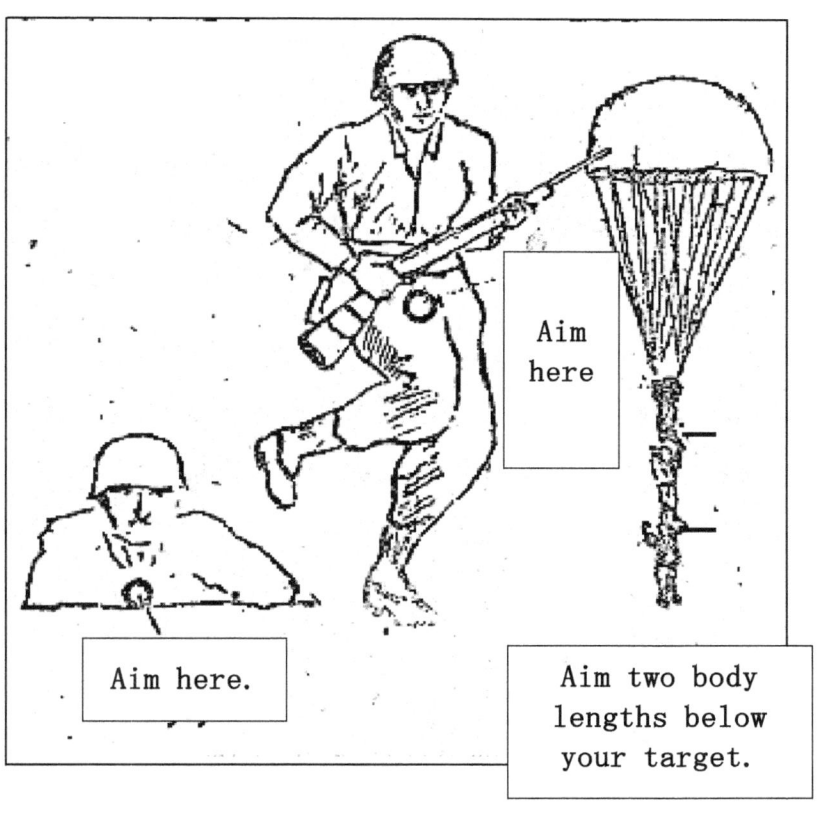

Newspaper Article 3
Our Ever-Victorious Military Strategy

3. *Shuryudan Toteki*
Throwing Grenades

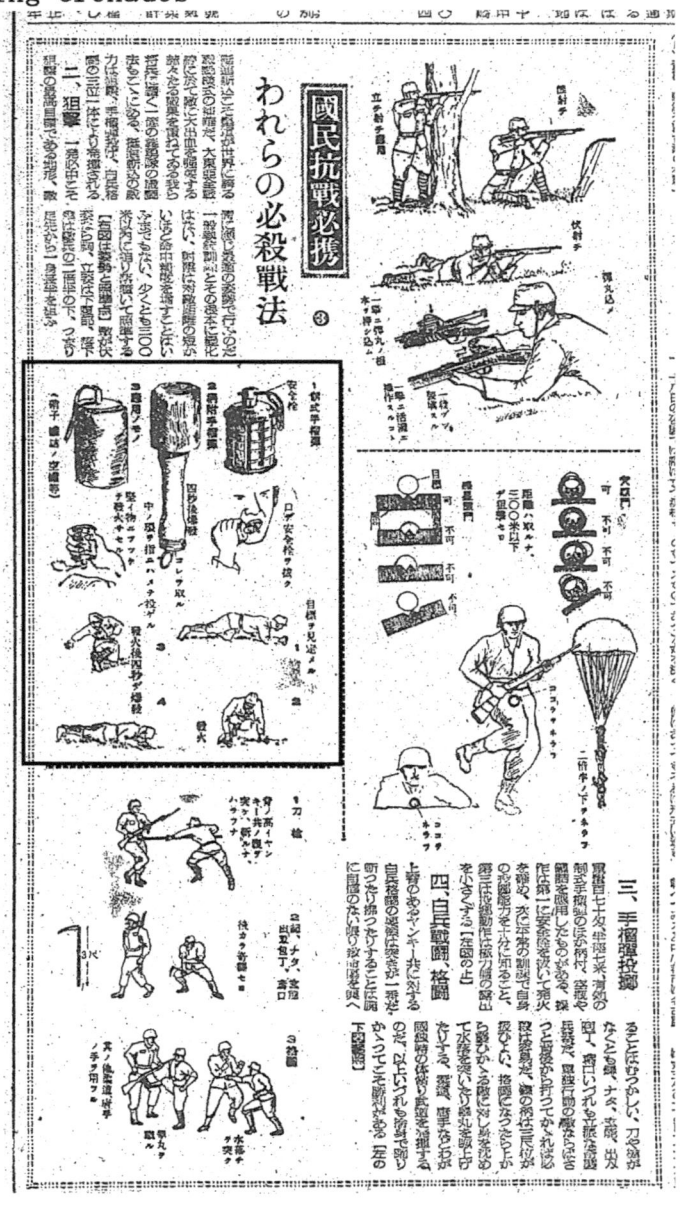

3. *Shuryudan Toteki*
Throwing Grenades

A grenade weighs 170 Monme, 637 grams. The standard grenade is effective up to 7 meters and there are also ones with handles. Empty bottles and cans can also be adapted.
To operate a grenade, first pull the safety pin and confirm the fuse is lit. Next, consider your throwing ability based on your everyday training. Third, throw while focusing all your power on one small point.

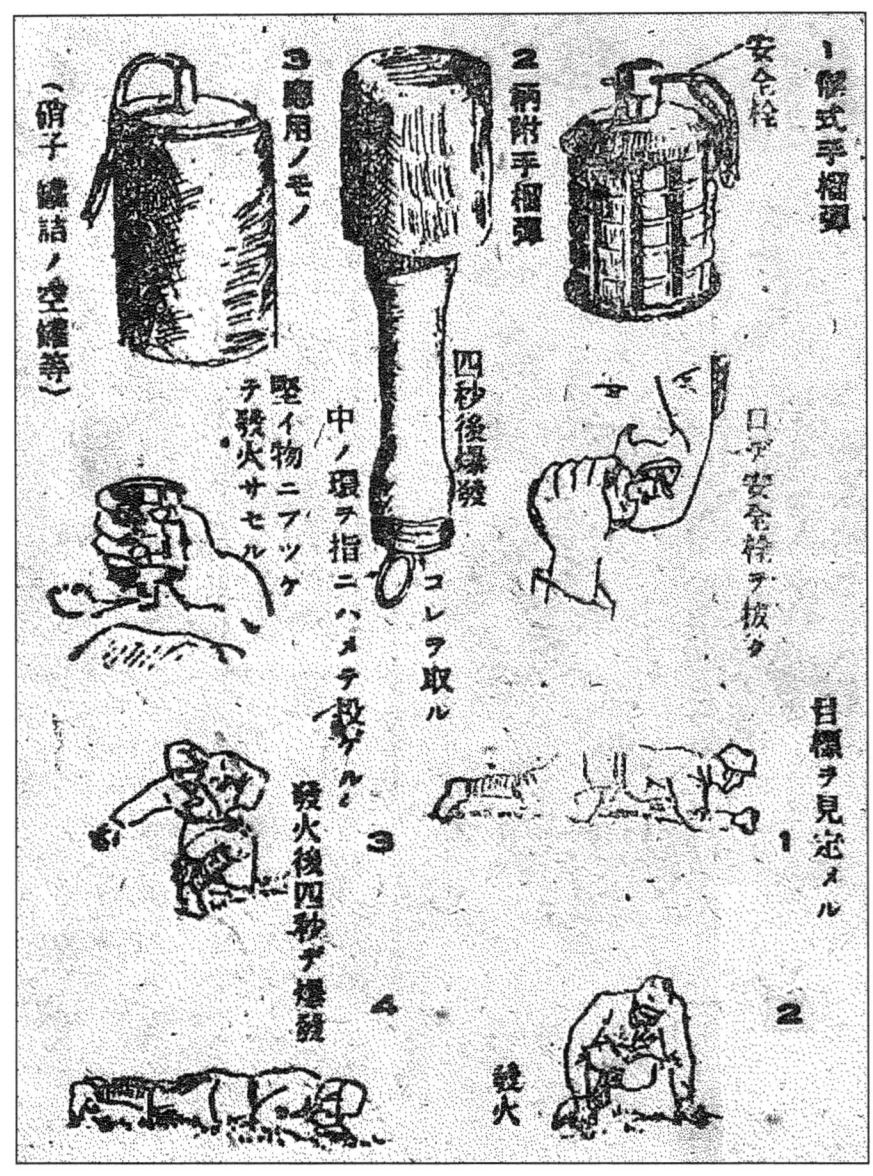

1. 九七式手榴弾 *Kyunana-shiki Shuryudan*
Type 97 Hand Grenade

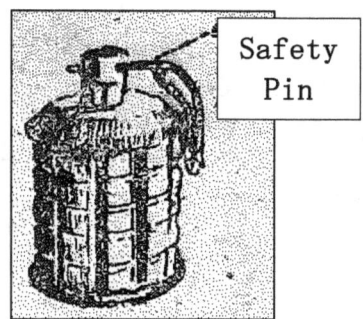

Safety Pin

Pull the safety pin out with your teeth.

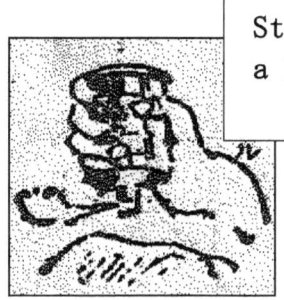

Strike against a hard surface to ignite.

2. Grenade with Handle

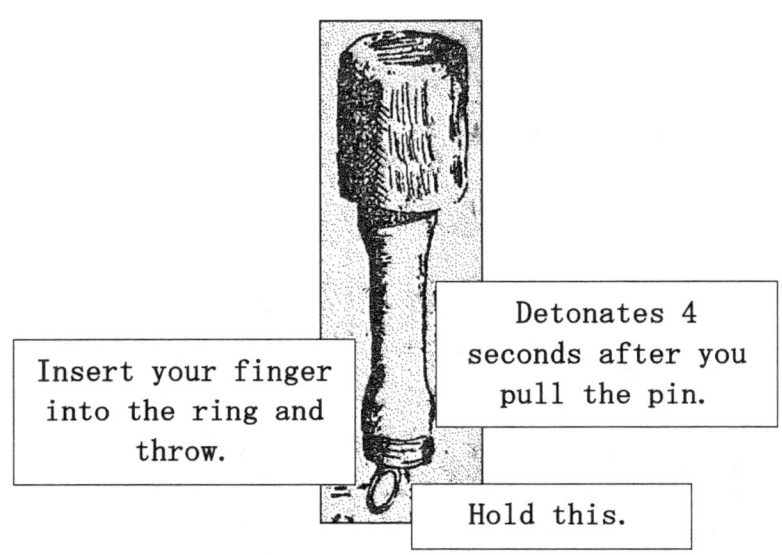

Insert your finger into the ring and throw.

Detonates 4 seconds after you pull the pin.

Hold this.

3. Adapted Object
(These can be glass bottles or cans filled [with explosives])

Newspaper Article 3
Our Ever-Victorious Military Strategy
4. *Hakuhei Sento, Kakuto*
Close-Quarters Combat, Unarmed Fighting

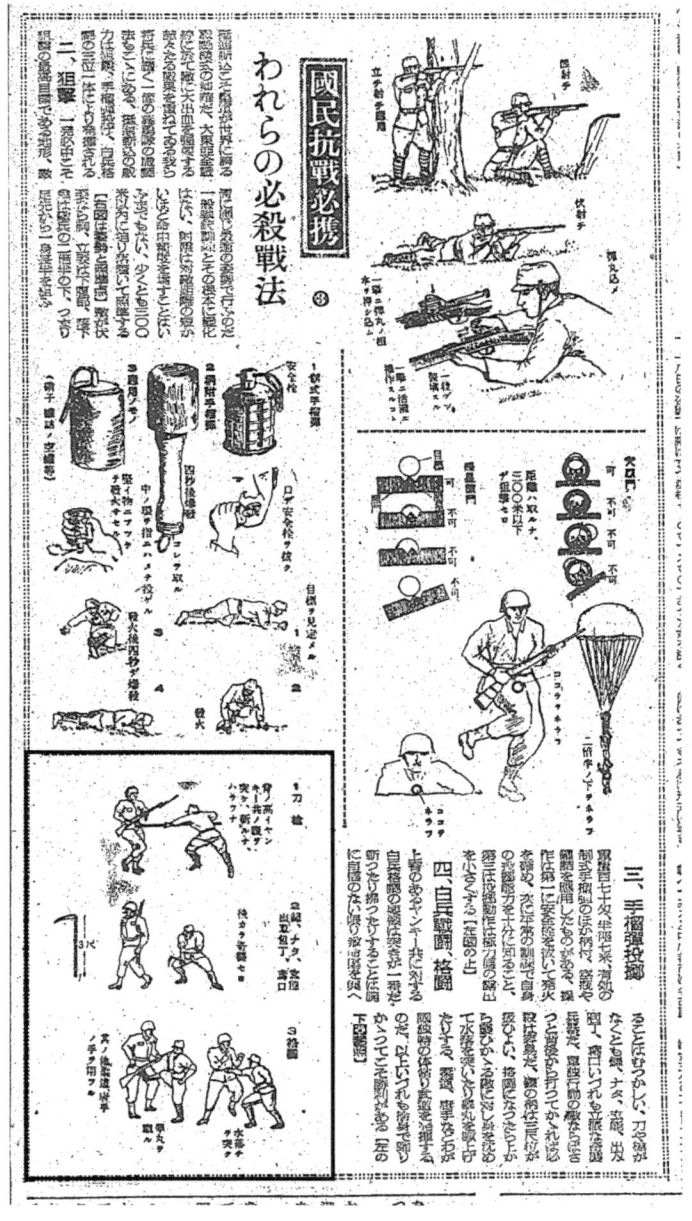

4. *Hakuhei Sento, Kakuto*
Close-Quarters Combat, Unarmed Fighting

The best way to attack the tall Yankees in close-quarters combat with a sword is to use Tsuki, a straight thrust. Unless you are particularly skilled with a sword, cutting straight down from above or using a sweeping cut will not deliver a fatal blow.
Even if you don't have a Katana or spear, a sickle, hatchet, hammer, kitchen knife or picaroon, can all be used as a military weapon for a surprise attack.
If you come across an enemy moving about on his own, it will be easy to approach him from behind and then strike a fatal blow. It is best to use a sickle with a handle 3 Shaku, 90 centimeters long.
If you become engaged in hand to hand combat, the enemy will be attacking from above, so drop your hips down and strike to Mizo Ochi, the solar plexus, or kick to Kogan, the groin. In this situation make use of the striking and grappling techniques particular to the martial arts of Japan, such as those found in Judo or Karate.
No matter what you do, leaping in and sacrificing your body will result in victory.

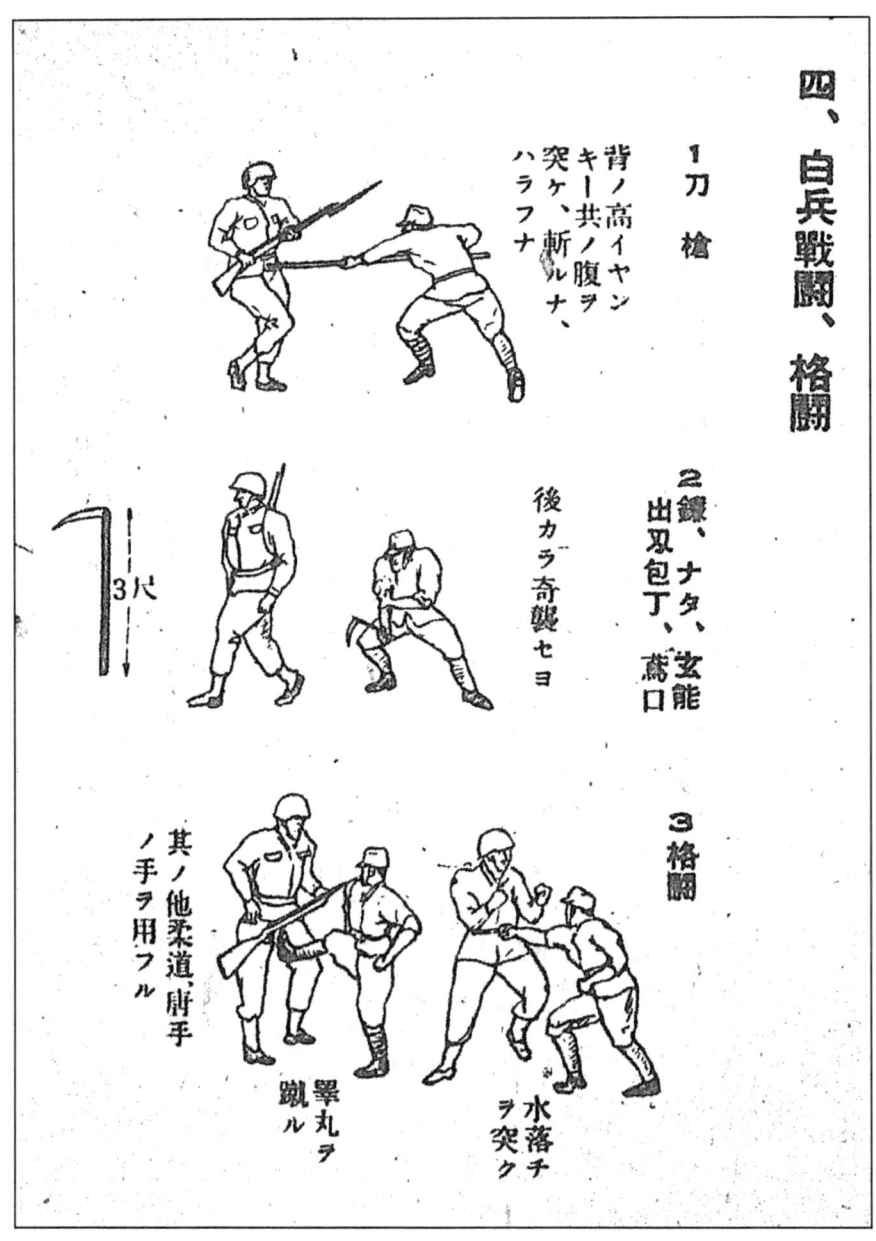

Our Ever-Victorious Military Strategy
4. *Hakuhei Sento, Kakuto*
Close-Quarters Combat, Unarmed Fighting

1. Using a Katana or Spear
Stab the Yankees, who tend to be tall, in the stomach. Don't try to cut, don't try to attack with a sweeping cut.

2. You should sneak up from behind and attack unexpectedly using any of the following:

Kama Sickle
Nata Chopping hatchet
Genno Hammer
Deba-bocho Japanese-style Kitchen Knife
Tobiguchi Picaroon

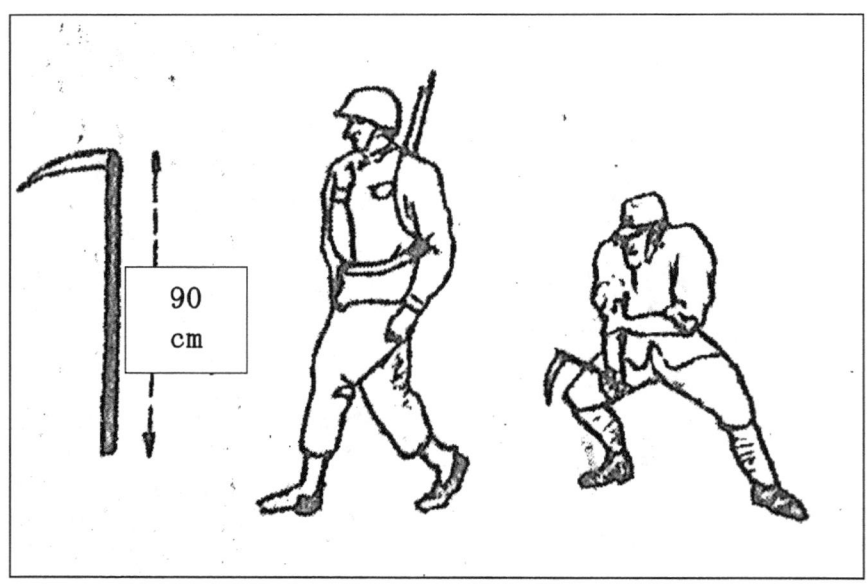

DEFENSE OF THE JAPANESE HOMELAND

3. Hand to Hand Fighting
Punch to Mizo-uchi "Water Drop" or the solar plexus.

Kick to Kogan, the testicles. In addition you can use Judo or Karate techniques.

Newspaper Article 4
Completely Committed to Operating Covertly

5. *Teishin Kirikomi*
Volunteer Attack Units

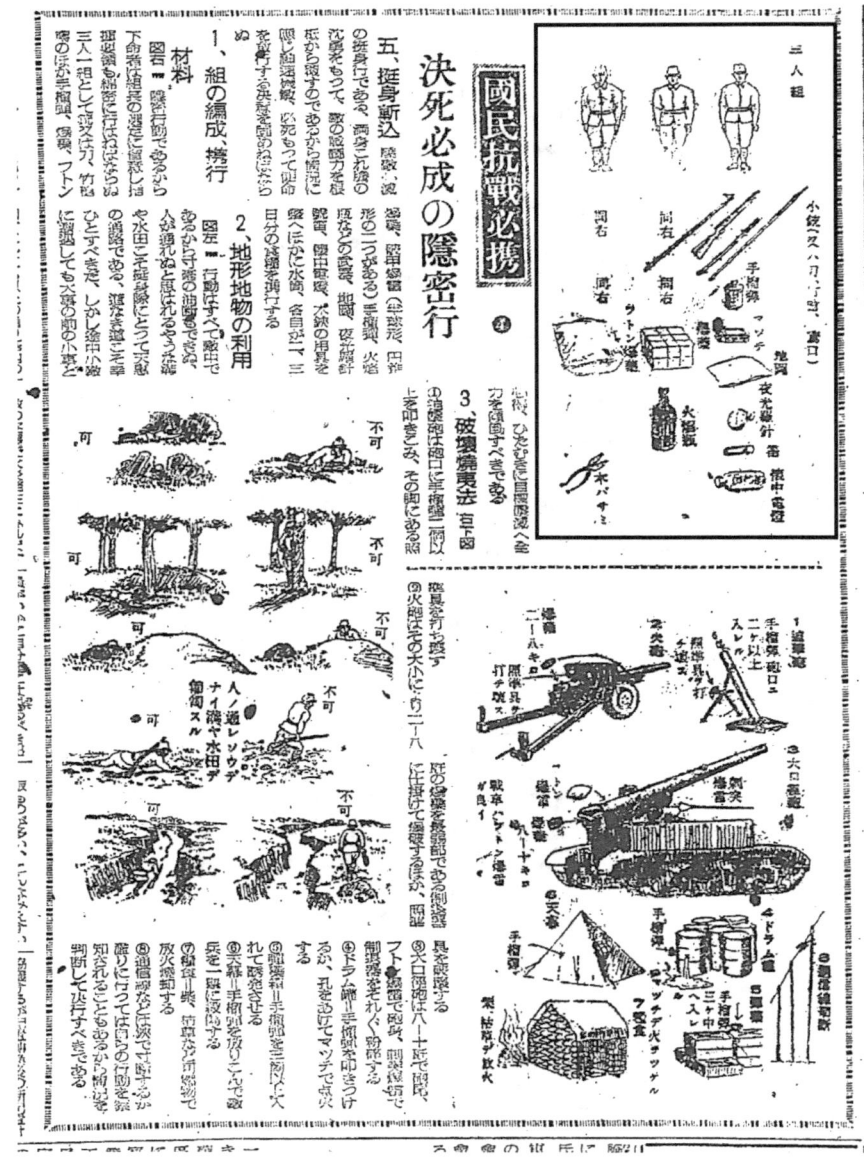

5. *Teishin Kirikomi*
Volunteer Attack Units

This describes how those that have become *Teishin Kirikomi,* Volunteer Attack Units, will advance on and invariably kill the arrogant enemy. Your entire body should be brimming with determination and composed courage, which you will use to uproot the enemy's military power. Thus, depending on the situation, you will have to respond quickly and deftly. You must be prepared to strive with all your might and take decisive action in order to achieve your mission.

1. How to Form a Unit, Items to be Carried

When you receive orders from your area leader, bear in mind that you have been selected to carry out a particular mission covertly and in complete secrecy. The members of the 3-person team should carry the following:

A gun or Katana, bamboo spear, picaroon or other such weapon.

In addition, grenades, Futon "pillow" bombs, explosives and armor piercing explosives (These come in two shapes, half-sphere and cone-shaped,) in addition to Molotov cocktails and other such weapons. You should also carry a map, a glow-in-the-dark compass, a whistle, a flashlight and a pair of pruning shears. In addition, each person should carry a water bottle and 2 or 3 days' worth of food.

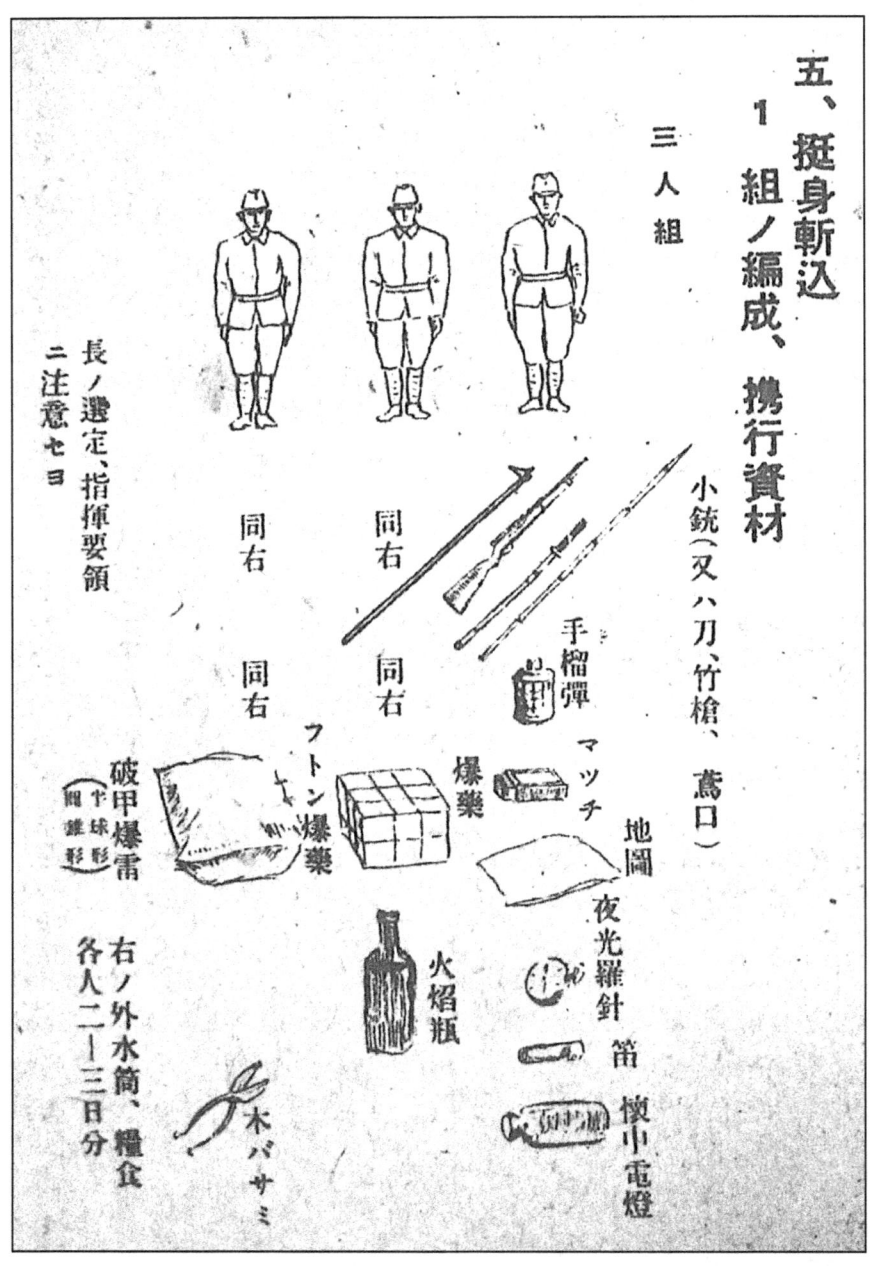

A 3-Person Unit

Be sure to follow the selection and operational parameters dictated by the overall leader.

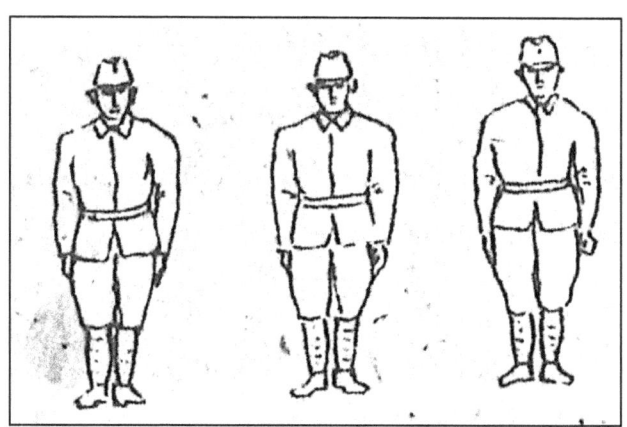

Each person should be armed with a small gun.

(Other options are a Katana,

Takeyari Bamboo Spear,

or a *Tobiguchi* Picaroon.)

手榴彈	*Shuryudan* Grenade
マッチ	*Macchi* Matches
爆藥	*Bakuyaku* Explosives
フトン爆藥	*Futon Bakuyaku* Futon Explosive
破甲爆雷	*Hakou Bakurai* Armor shattering bomb. (Can be half-sphere or cone-shaped.)
地圖	*Chizu* Map
夜光羅針	*Yakorashin* Glow-in-the-dark compass

	Fue Whistle
	Kaichu Dento Pocket Flashlight
	Kaenbin Molotov Cocktail
	Kibasami Pruning Shears
	In addition to the items listed on this page, each person should have a water bottle and two or three days' worth of food.

Newspaper Article 4
Completely Committed to Operating Covertly
2. *Chikei Chibutsu no Riyo*
How to Use the Terrain and Man-made or Natural Features

DEFENSE OF THE JAPANESE HOMELAND

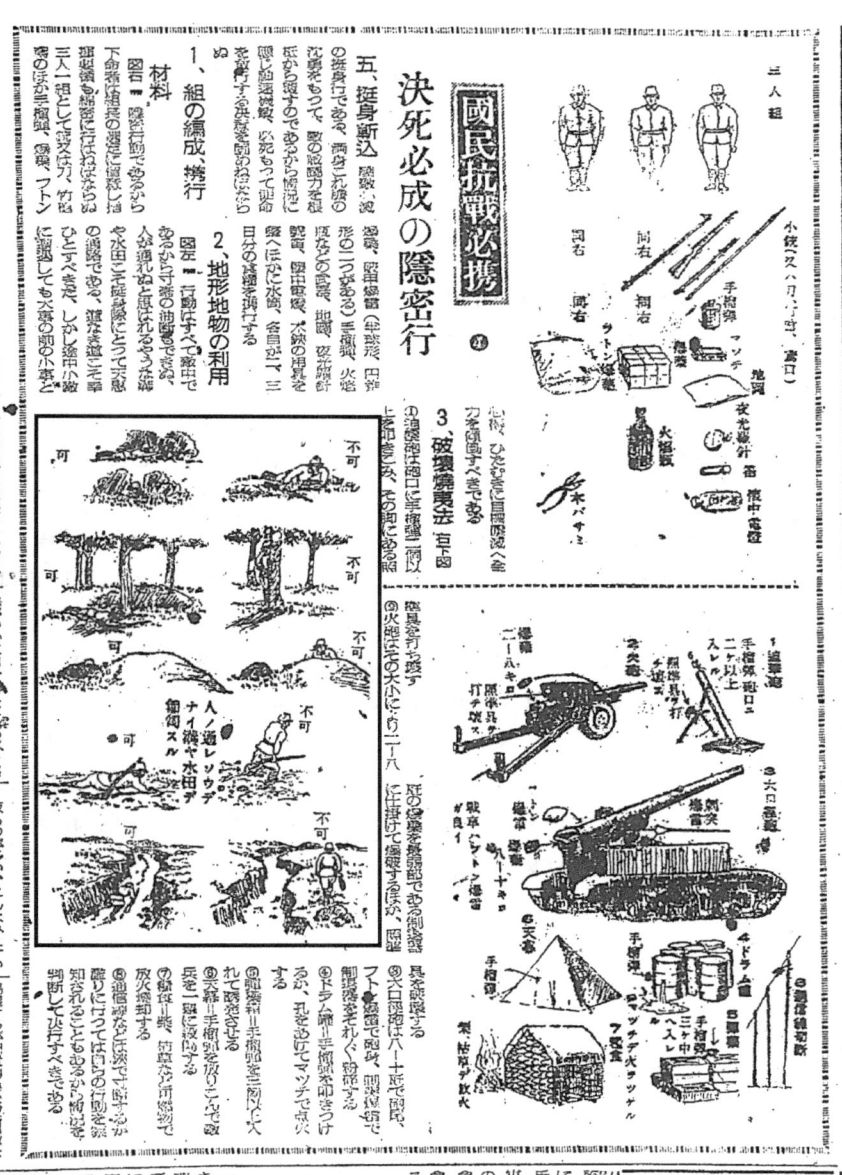

2. *Chikei Chibutsu no Riyo*
How to Use the Terrain and Man-made or Natural Features

All of your activities will be done amongst the enemy, so you cannot allow even the slightest error.

A drainage ditch or flooded rice field that no one is likely to pass by is a road that is heaven sent for volunteer attack units. Finding a road that is not actually a road is a great boon, however if you encounter a smaller enemy unit that is not your primary target, remember to not allow a minor distraction to derail your main objective. You need to be single-minded in your determination to obliterate your target.

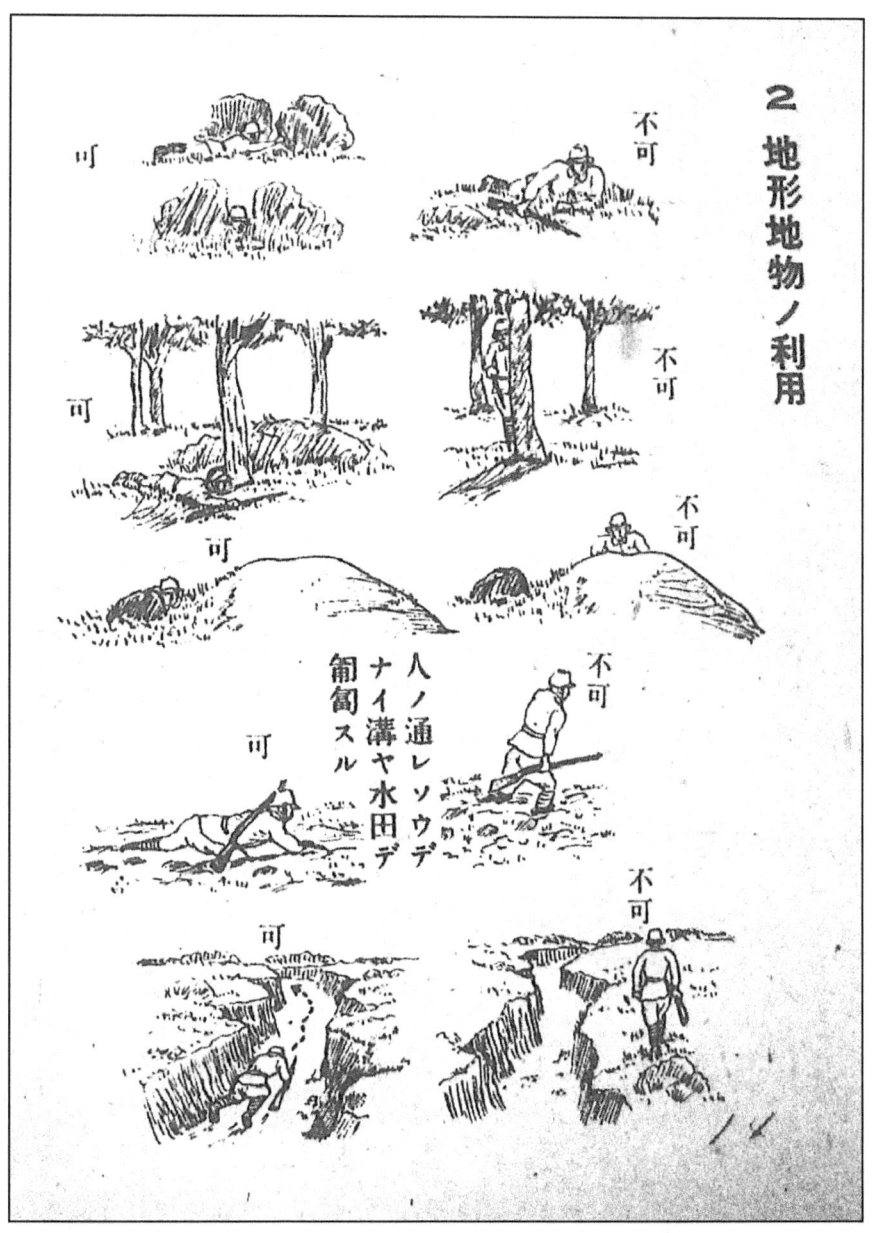

Crawl through a water-filled rice field or drainage ditch that people are unlikely to pass near.

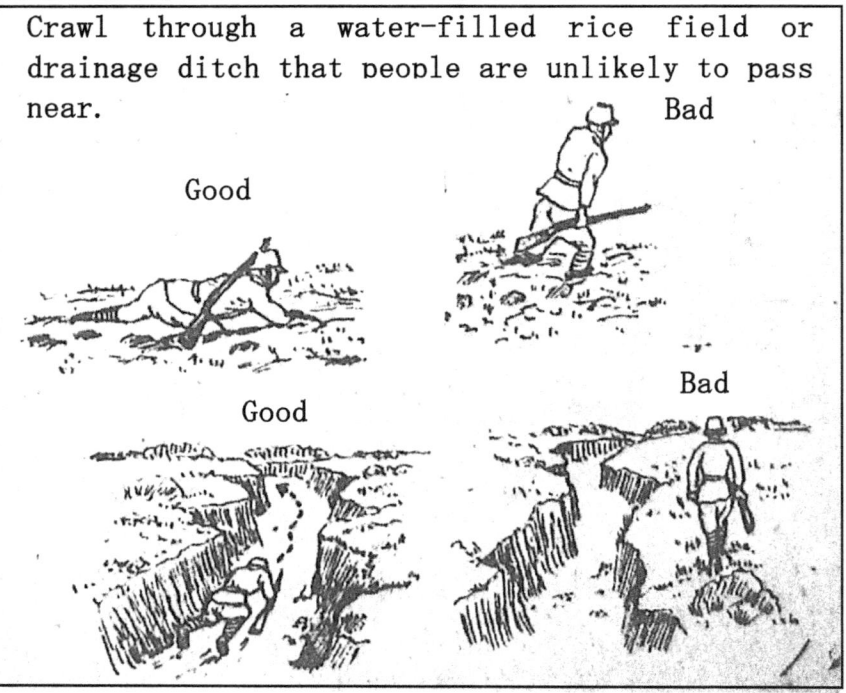

Newspaper Article 4
Completely Committed to Operating Covertly

3. *Hakai Shoiho*
How to Destroy or Incinerate

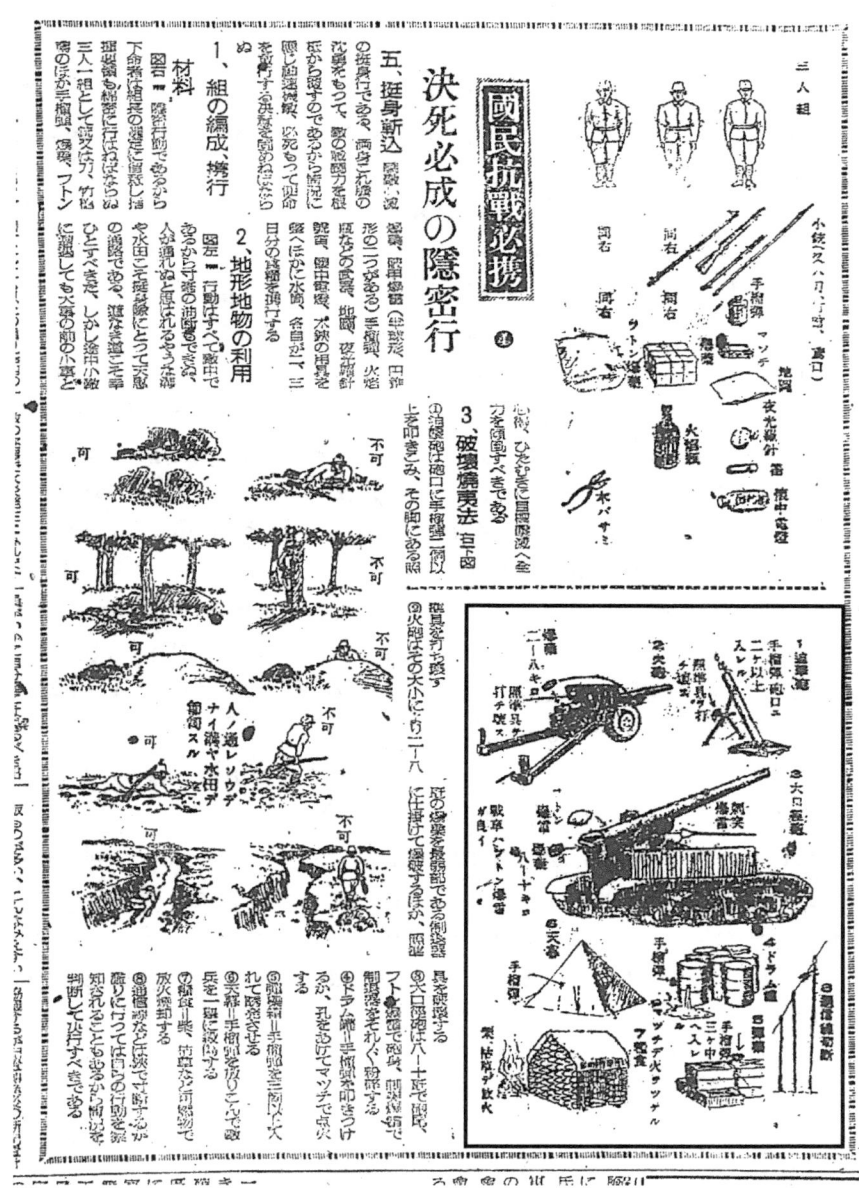

3. *Hakai Shoiho*
How to Destroy or Incinerate

1. To destroy mortars, throw two or more grenades down the barrel. Also break the sighting mechanism located on the legs.
2. To destroy artillery you will need between 2-8 kilograms of explosives depending on the size of the weapon. Blow up the most fragile part, the barrel. Also destroy the sighting mechanism.
3. When attacking a large bore cannon, pack between 8-10 kilograms of explosives into the tail end, place a Futon bomb on the body and use a bomb-tipped spear on the barrel to destroy each part of the weapon.
4. To destroy fuel barrels, throw a grenade or start a fire with a match after opening a hole.
5. For boxes of explosives, use three or more grenades to start an explosion that will spread to the rest.
6. Throw a grenade into a tent to kill all the enemy soldiers inside at once.
7. Incinerate military provisions by igniting sticks, dry grass or other flammable material.
8. Use scissors to cut communication and other wires. However, if you continue this activity for too long, you are likely to be discovered. You should judge the situation carefully before deciding on a course of action.

DEFENSE OF THE JAPANESE HOMELAND

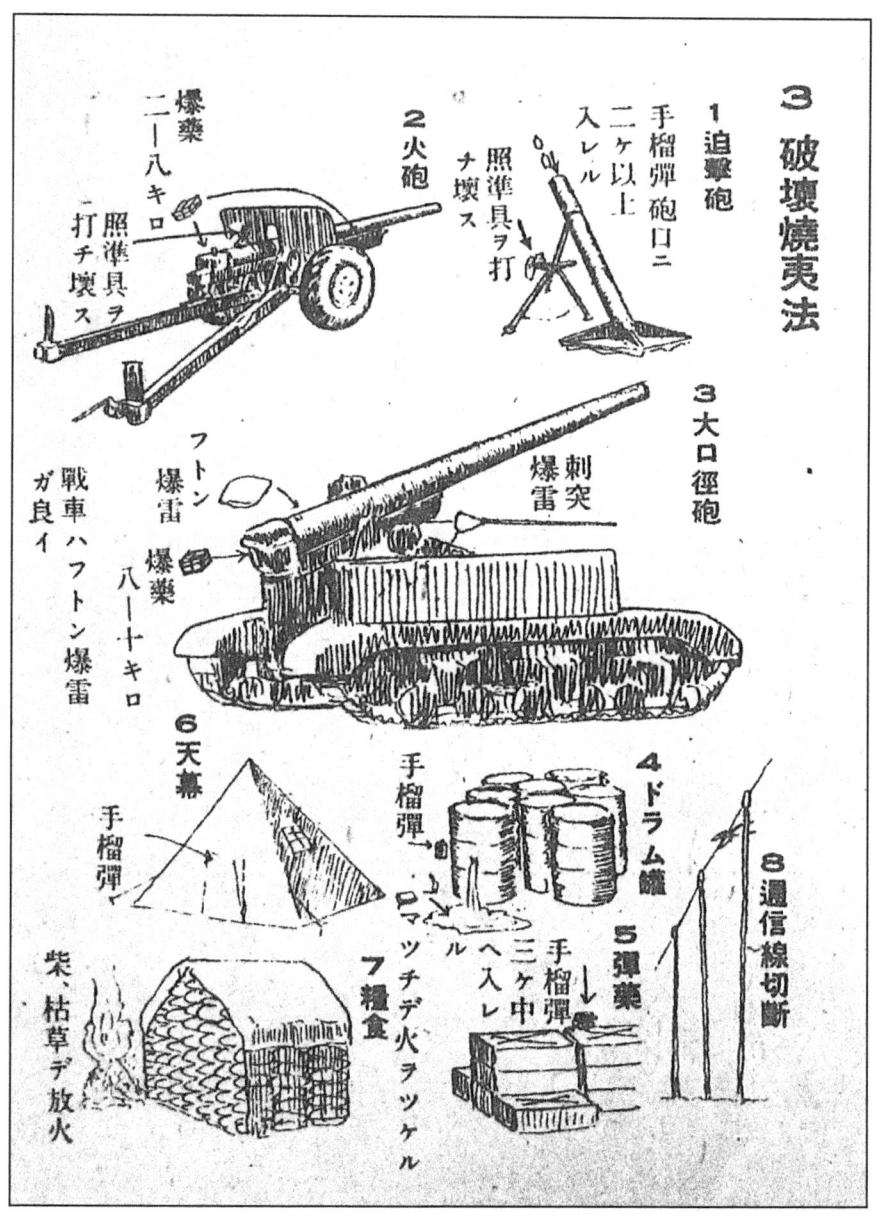

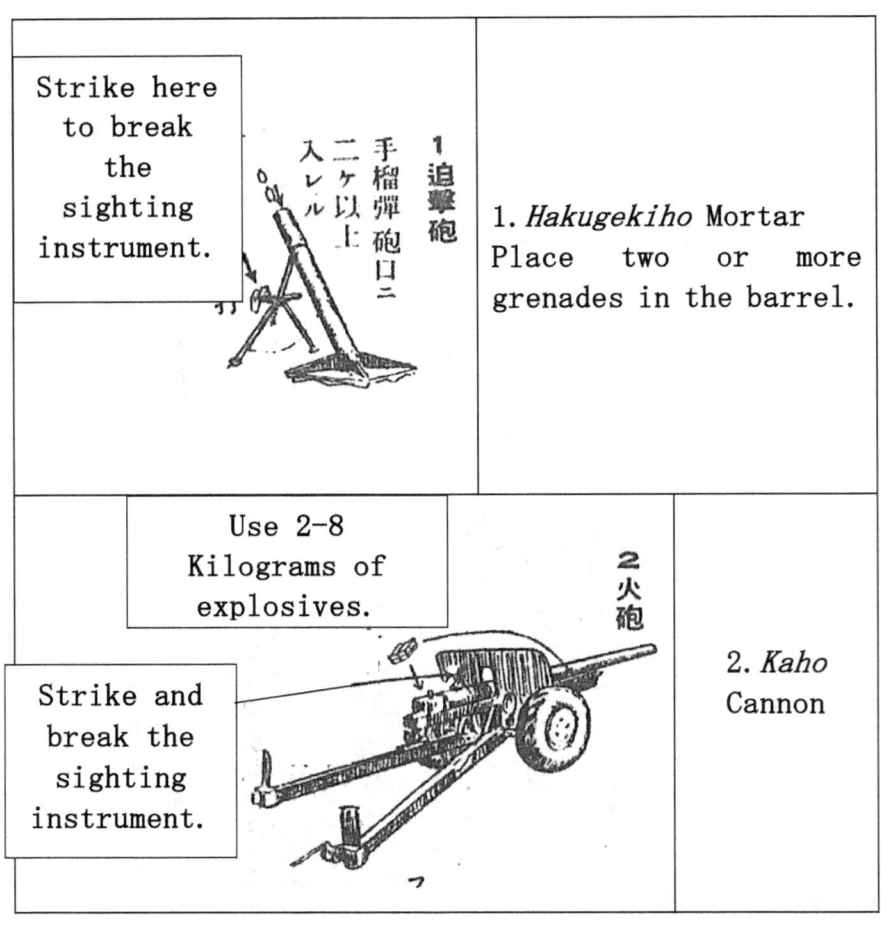

Strike here to break the sighting instrument.

1. *Hakugekiho* Mortar
Place two or more grenades in the barrel.

Use 2-8 Kilograms of explosives.

Strike and break the sighting instrument.

2. *Kaho* Cannon

DEFENSE OF THE JAPANESE HOMELAND

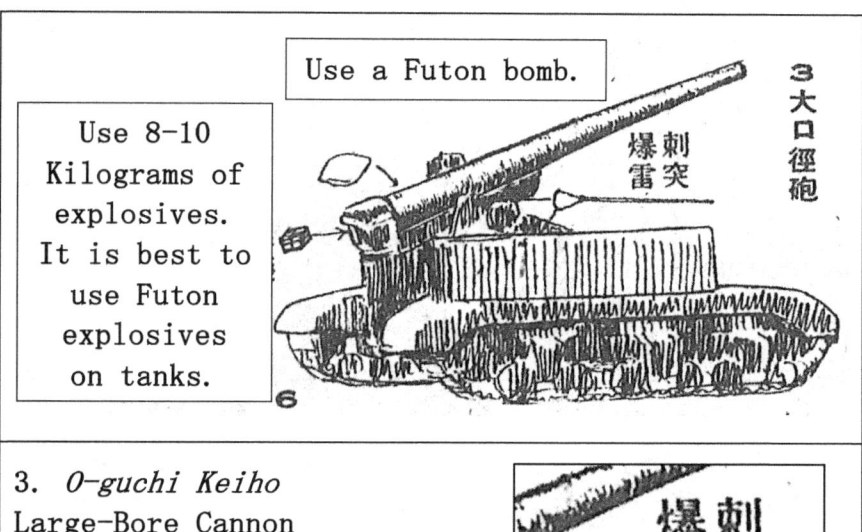

Use a Futon bomb.

Use 8-10 Kilograms of explosives. It is best to use Futon explosives on tanks.

3. *O-guchi Keiho* Large-Bore Cannon

Use a bomb-tipped spear.

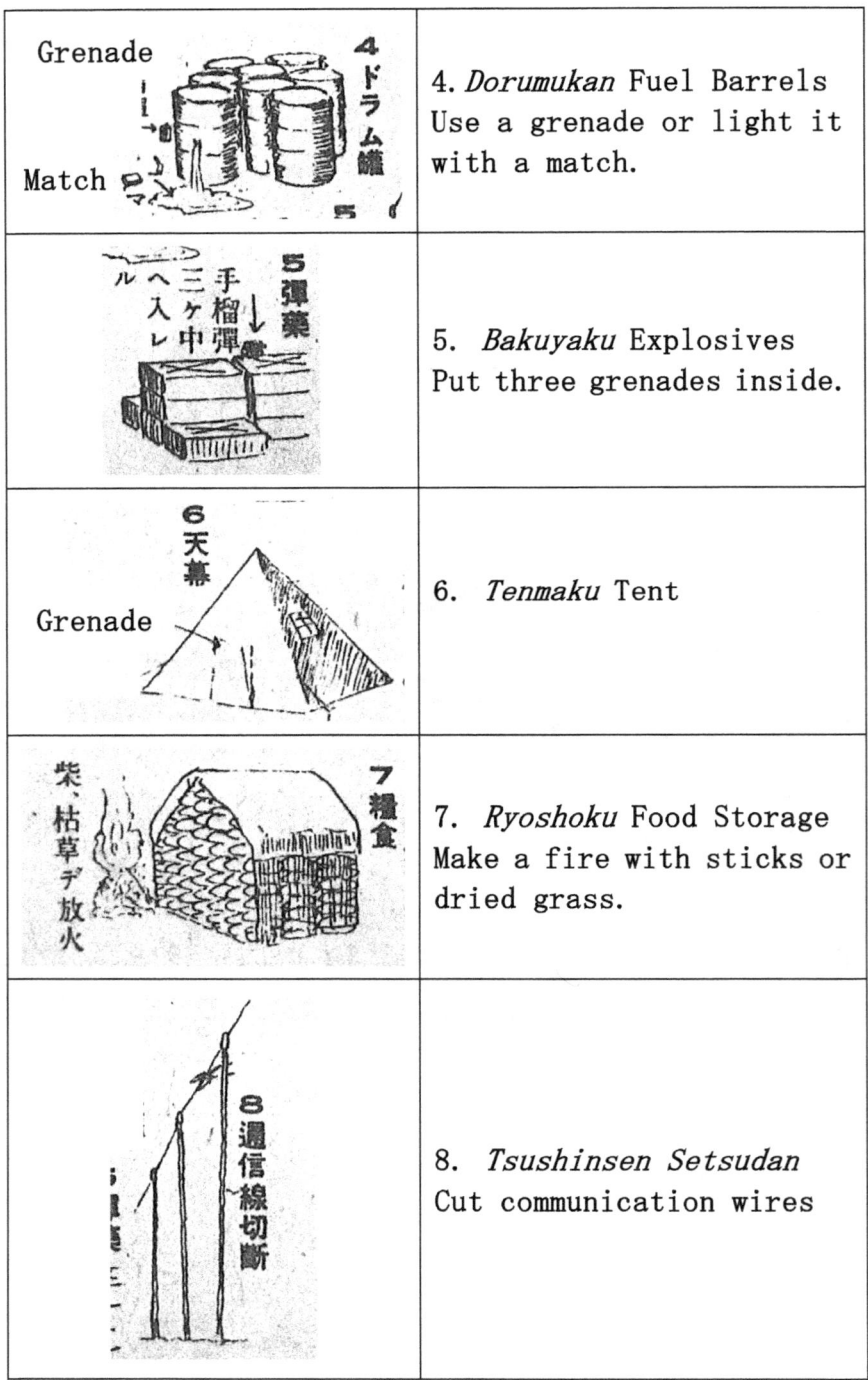

4. *Dorumukan* Fuel Barrels
Use a grenade or light it with a match.

5. *Bakuyaku* Explosives
Put three grenades inside.

6. *Tenmaku* Tent

7. *Ryoshoku* Food Storage
Make a fire with sticks or dried grass.

8. *Tsushinsen Setsudan*
Cut communication wires

Newspaper Article 5
Seizing the Chance:
Adapting to the Requirements of the Moment

4. *Machibuse Yugeki* Ambushes and Raids

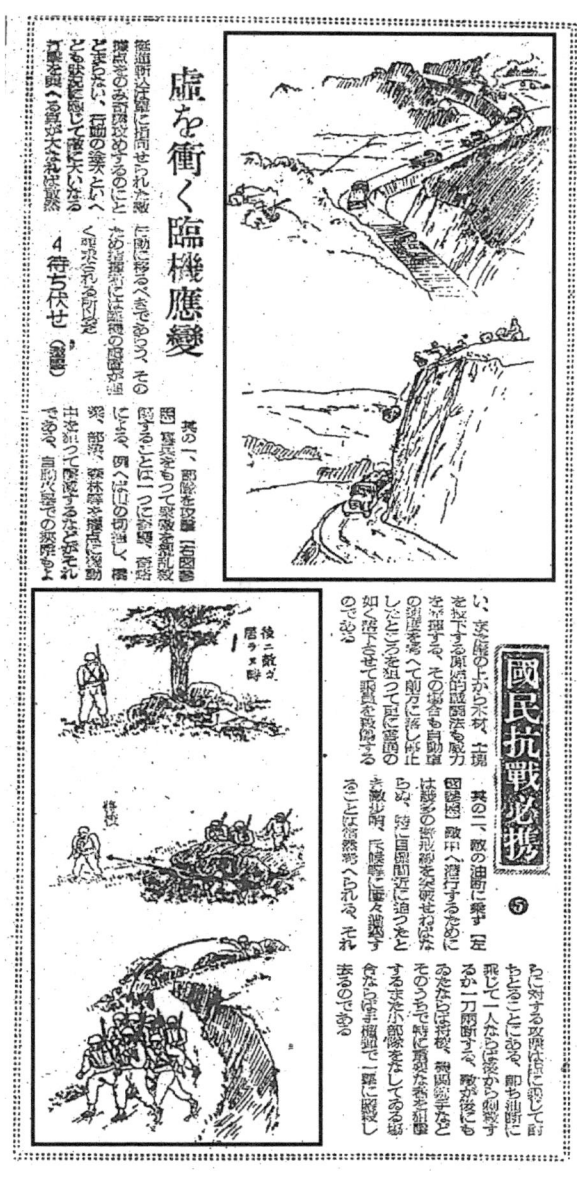

4. *Machibuse Yugeki*
Ambushes and Raids

Overview

Members of Volunteer Attack Units should not solely follow their directive to launch surprise attacks on enemy positions. During the course of your mission, if you see a chance to strike the enemy that will result in great damage, you should take decisive action. Thus commanders are very much in favor of units acting on targets of opportunity that may present themselves.

4. *Machibuse Yugeki*
Ambushes and Raids

1. Attacking a Unit

A small force attacking a group of enemy soldiers, throwing them into confusion as you kill them can only be achieved by a surprise attack using an unconventional plan.

For example, setting up a base of operations near a road cut through a mountain, a bridge near a village or in the woods and keeping watch will allow you to decimate the enemy. Using automatic weapons to fire on the enemy in a pincer's movement is best.

Further, if you are on top of a cliff you can drop lumber or chunks of earth down on the enemy. This shows that primitive fighting methods can be effective.

When doing this, consider the convoy's speed and drop material in front of them to stop the column. Then dump more material on them like an avalanche. This will kill or wound all those riding in the convoy.

2. Make Use of the Enemy's Inattention

In order to sneak into the midst of the enemy, it is first necessary to overcome several security nets.
In particular, as you approach your objective, no doubt you will soon encounter scouts on patrol as well as enemy guards. Attack when you find an opportune moment, and strike them down.
In other words, if you find a solitary enemy who is inattentive, stab him to death from behind, or cut him down with one sword cut, splitting him cleanly into two parts. If the enemy is unaware anyone is behind him, particularly if it is an officer or man armed with a machine gun, then such an important individual should be killed with sniper fire.
Further, if the enemy is formed into a small unit, then the explosion of a hand grenade will kill them all.

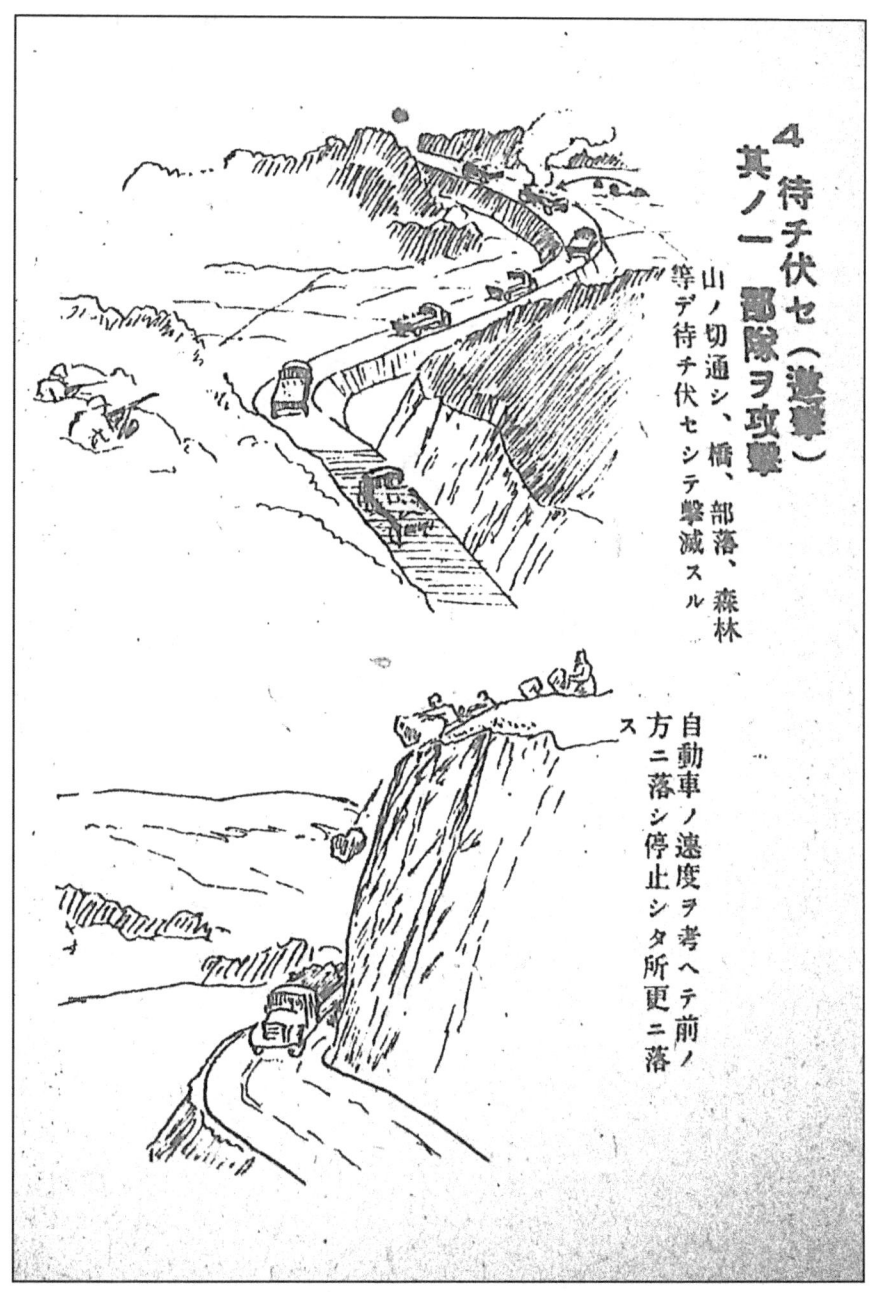

Wait where the road cuts through the mountains, near a bridge, a small village, forest or other such place and cut them down.

Consider the speed a vehicle is moving and drop objects in front. When the vehicles stop, drop more.

If the enemy is alone then kill him by stabbing (cutting) him from behind.

When the enemy does not think anyone is behind him.

If you can see the backs of the enemy and there is an important person there (an officer, a machine gun operator and so on) then try to snipe him.

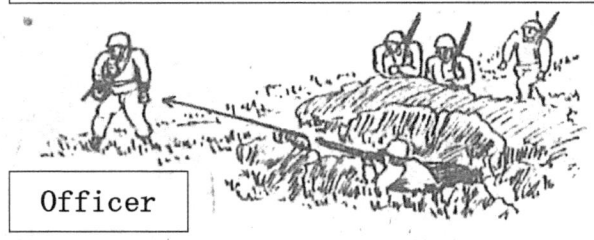

Officer

If there is a large group in close formation then throw a grenade. No matter what you do, ensure that you are not discovered before you attack.

Newspaper Article 6
Obliterate Enemy Camps in One Stroke
5. Volunteer Attack Units
Part One : General Outline

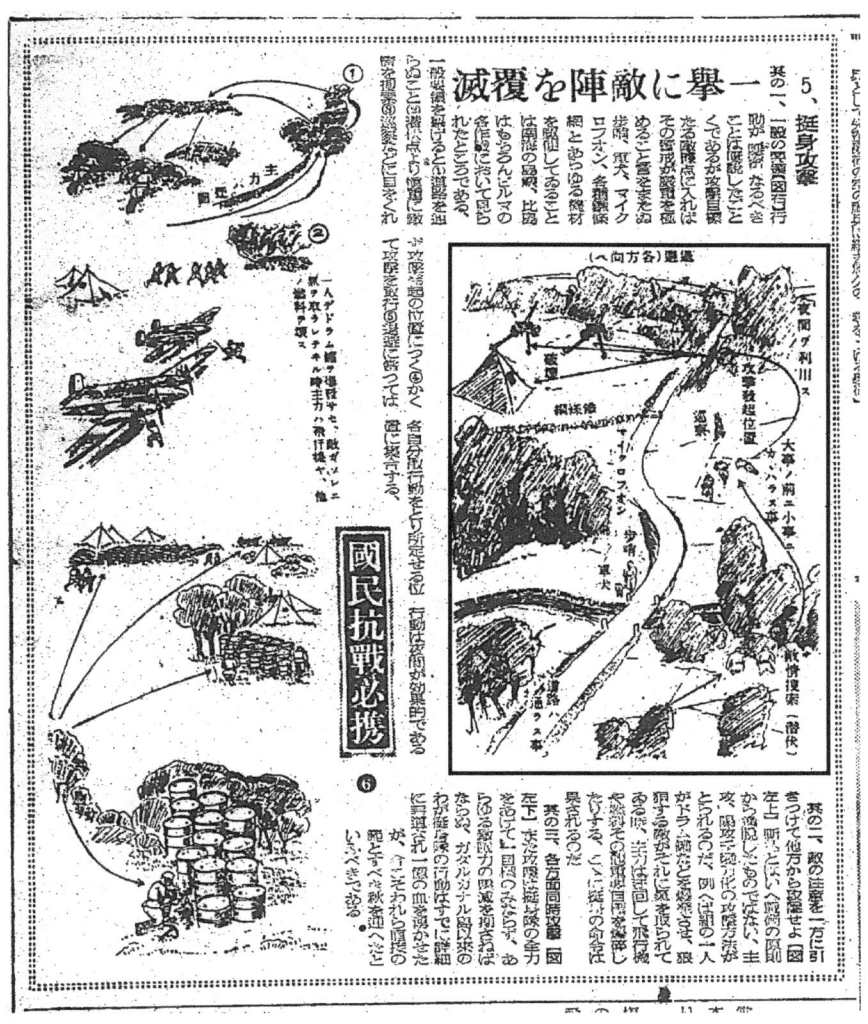

5. Volunteer Attack Units
Part One : General Outline

As was previously mentioned your activities and movements should be completely covert, however as you enter the area of your target, the enemy stronghold, it goes without saying that you need to absolutely be on your highest possible guard.
The fact that the enemy uses foot patrols, military guard dogs, loudspeakers, along with all manner of barbed wire and other equipment, was all seen on the islands in the south seas. This was not just in the Philippines but also seen in all operations in Burma and other places.

To give a general outline:
1. Don't use roads
2. Once you have infiltrated behind enemy lines, carefully observe the enemy.
3. Keeping an eye out for roving patrols, decide on the place you will launch your attack.
4. Commit to your method of attack
5. Withdraw and split up, with each member moving on their own. Meet back at a pre-arranged spot.

It is more effective to implement your plan at night.

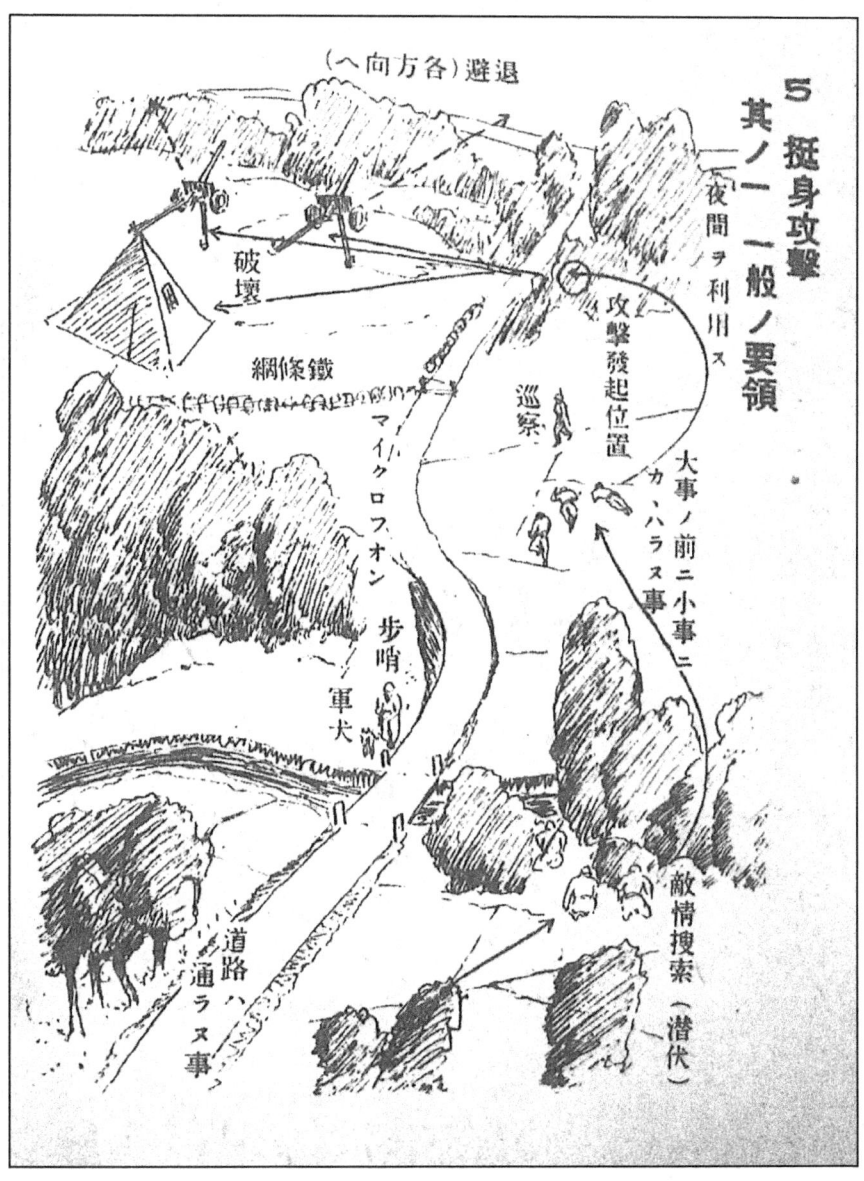

Part One: General Outline

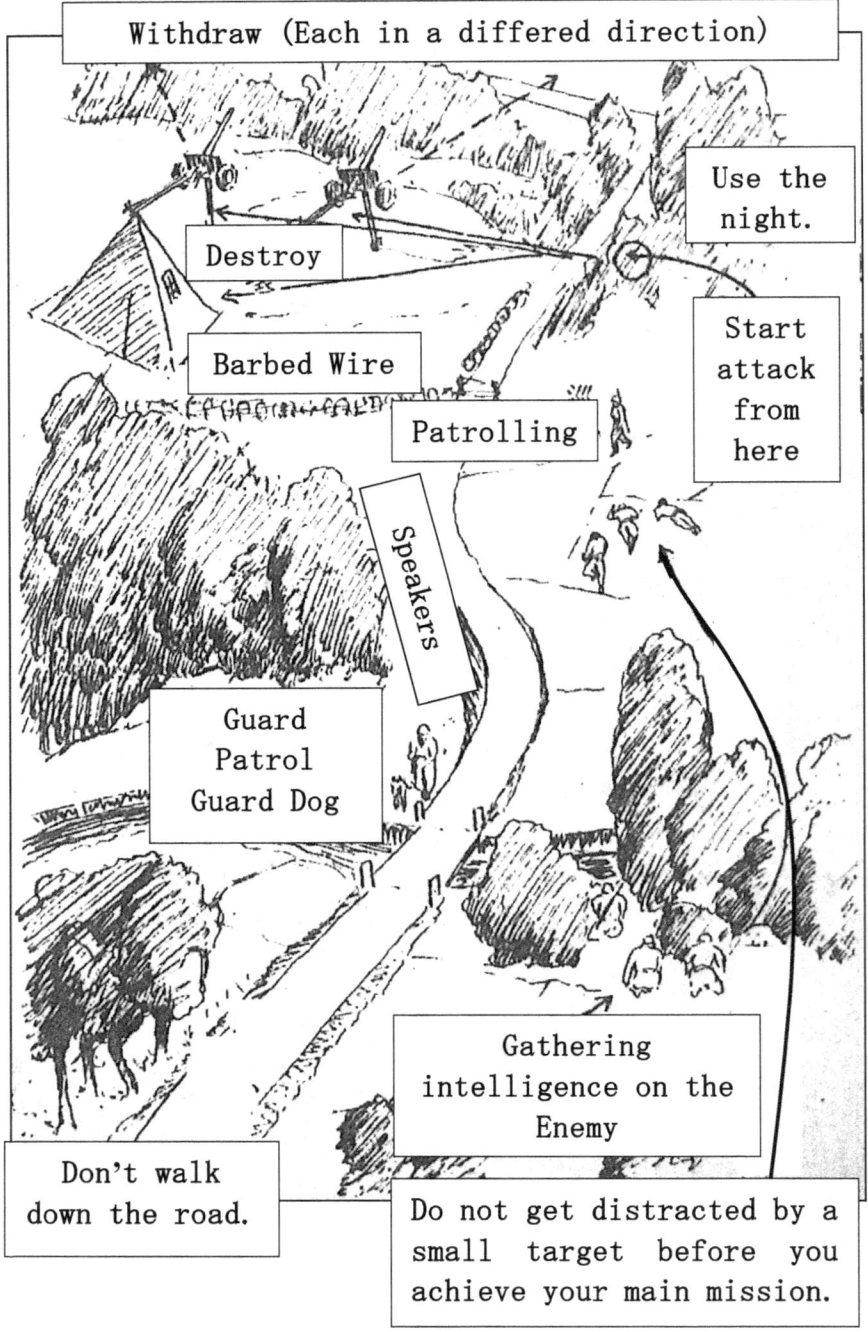

DEFENSE OF THE JAPANESE HOMELAND

Newspaper Article 6
Obliterate Enemy Camps in One Stroke

Part Two
Draw the enemy's attention in one direction before attacking from another.

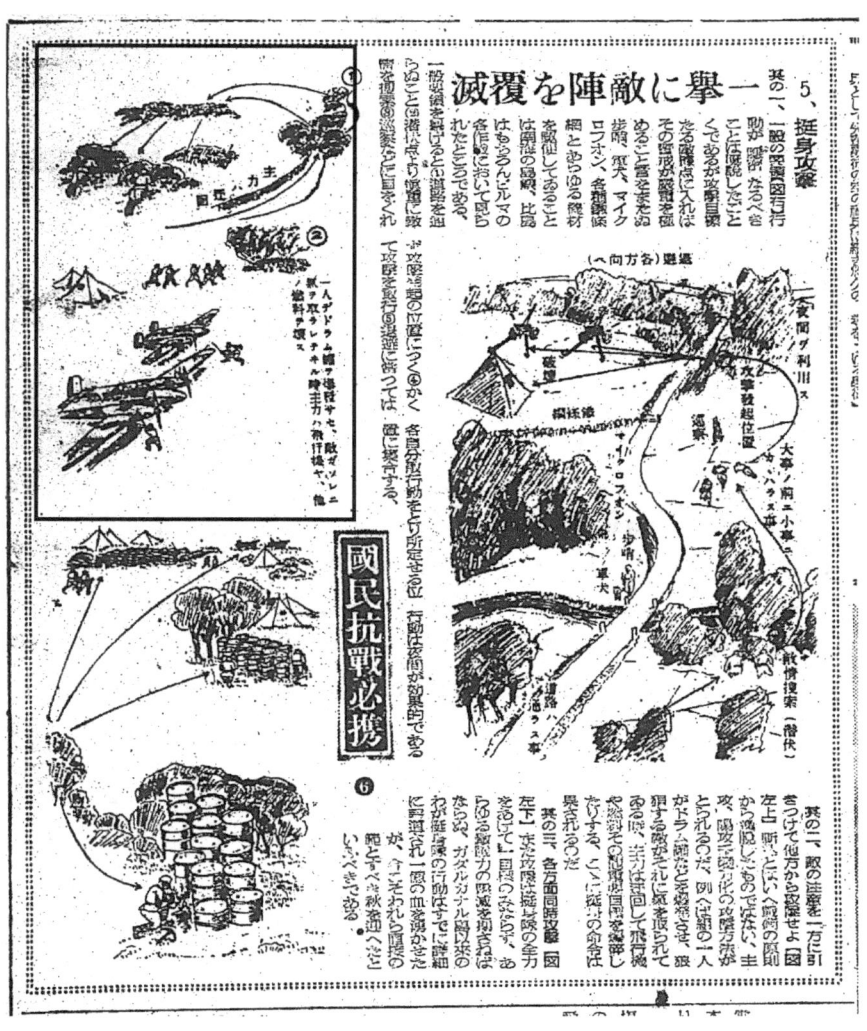

Part Two
Draw the enemy's attention in one direction before attacking from another.

Even though this is a "cutting in" attack it does not deviate from the fundamentals of battle. There is the true focus of your attack and the false attack which you use to distract. As history teaches us, when crafting this strategy there are a thousand variations of 10,000 possible approaches.
For example, one member of a group can blow up some fuel barrels sewing confusion in the enemy. While they are concentrating on that disturbance the main force takes a different route and blows up airplanes or another important objective.
This is how Volunteer Attack Units complete their mission as ordered.

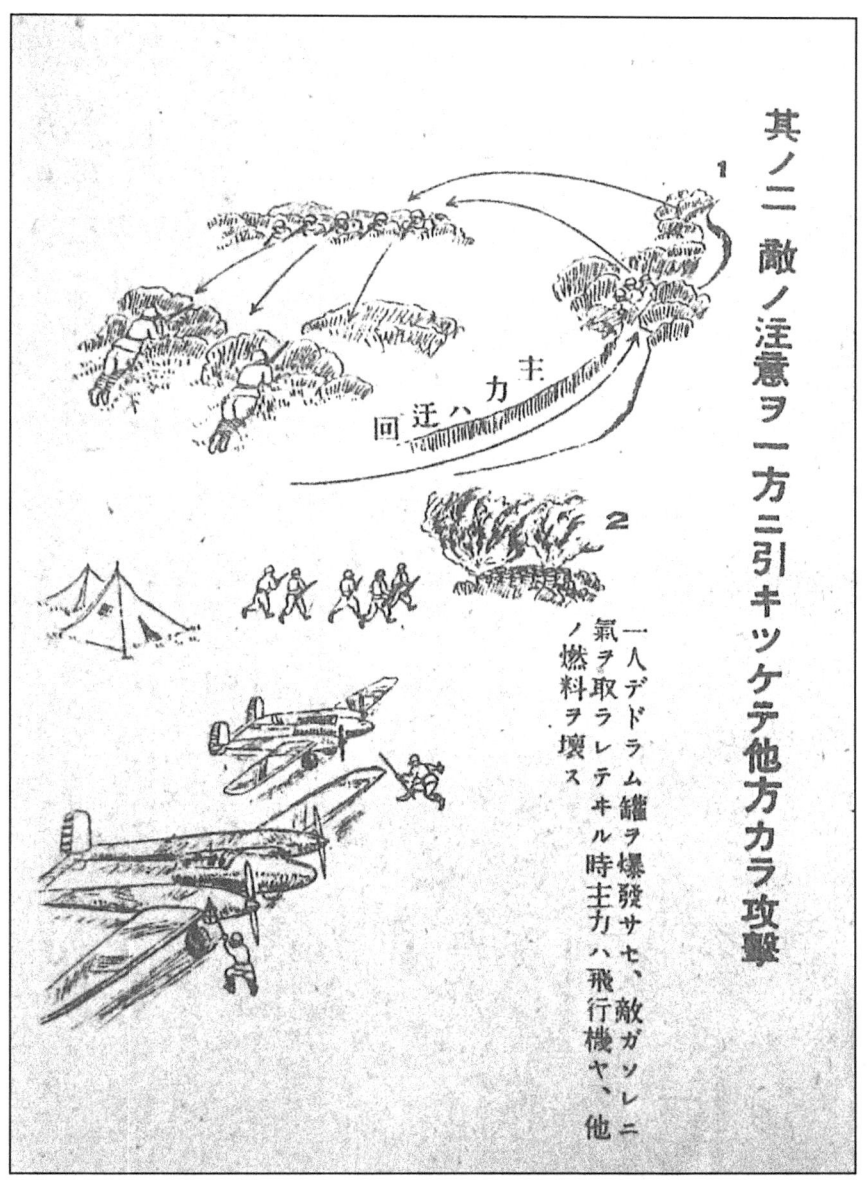

Part Two : Draw the enemy's attention in one direction while you launch your assault in another.
1. The main force should take an alternate route.

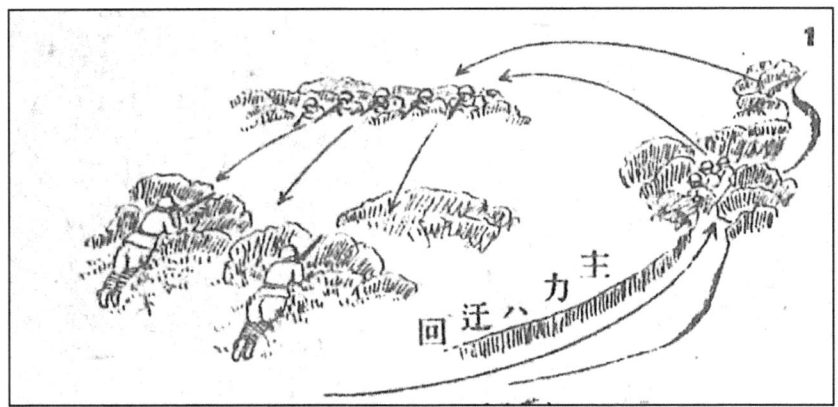

2. Have one person blow up some barrels of fuel. While the enemy is busy dealing with that, your main force attacks airplanes or other fuel storage tanks.

Newspaper Article 6
Obliterate Enemy Camps in One Stroke

Part Three
Attacking from multiple directions at the same time.

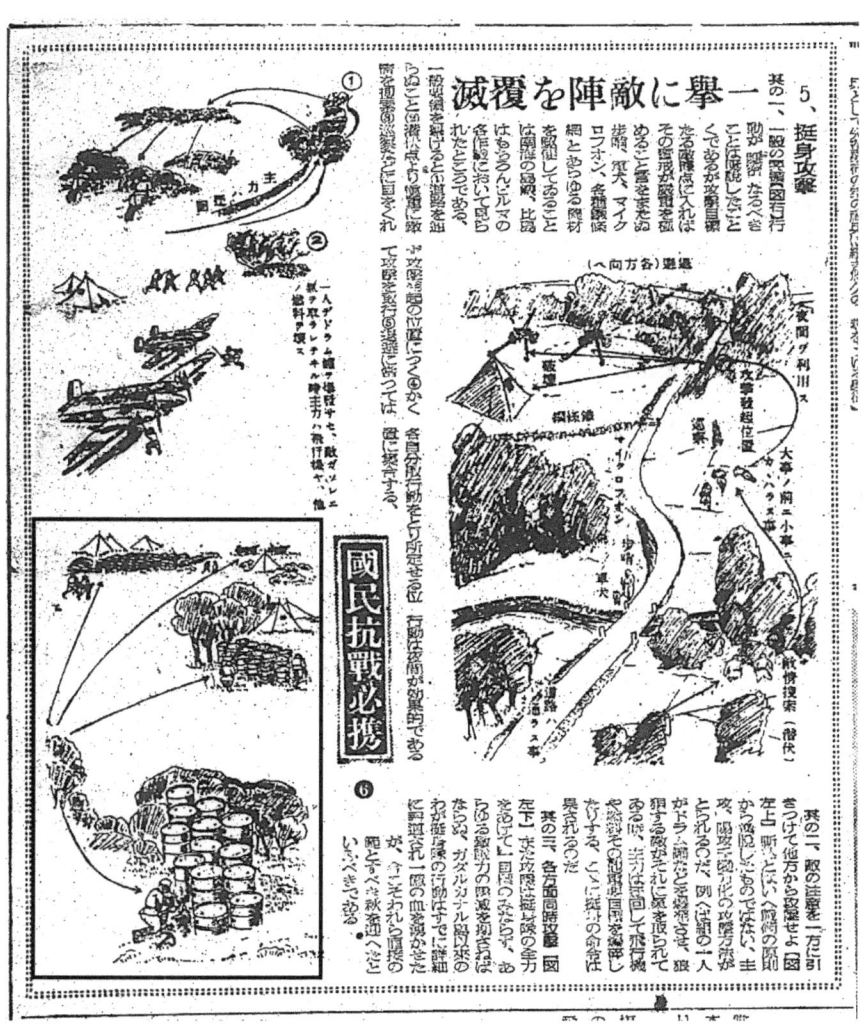

Part Three
Attacking from multiple directions at the same time.

Volunteer Attack Units do not devote all their energy solely to assaulting their main objective, rather they decimate the enemy's fighting strength at every turn. Stories of the Volunteer Attack Units in Guadalcanal have already been widely reported which caused the blood of a hundred-million citizens to go wild. Thus we should emulate that model as we face the coming autumn.

DEFENSE OF THE JAPANESE HOMELAND

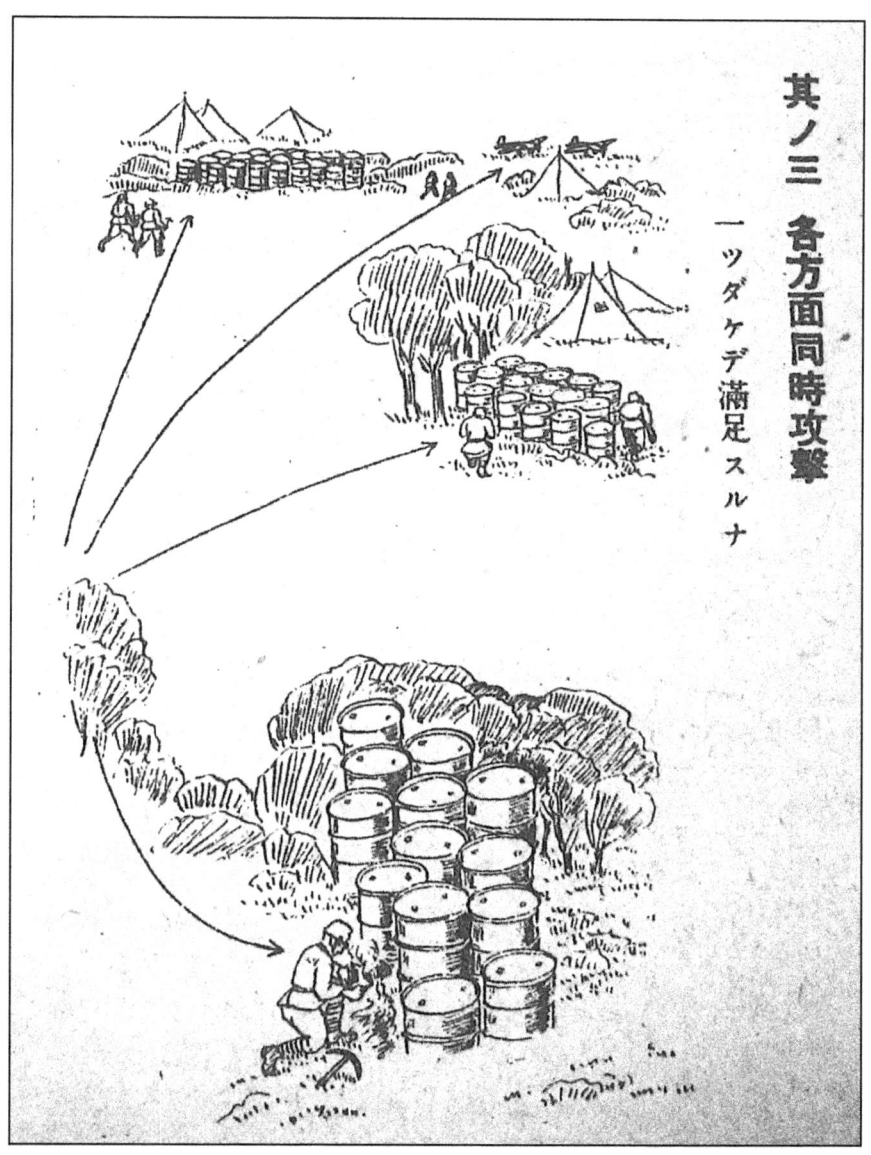

Part Three: Attacking from multiple directions at the same time.

Don't be satisfied with just one!

Newspaper Article 7
Obliterating Airborne Units Requires Fast and Decisive Action

1. *Shogaibutsu*: Obstacles

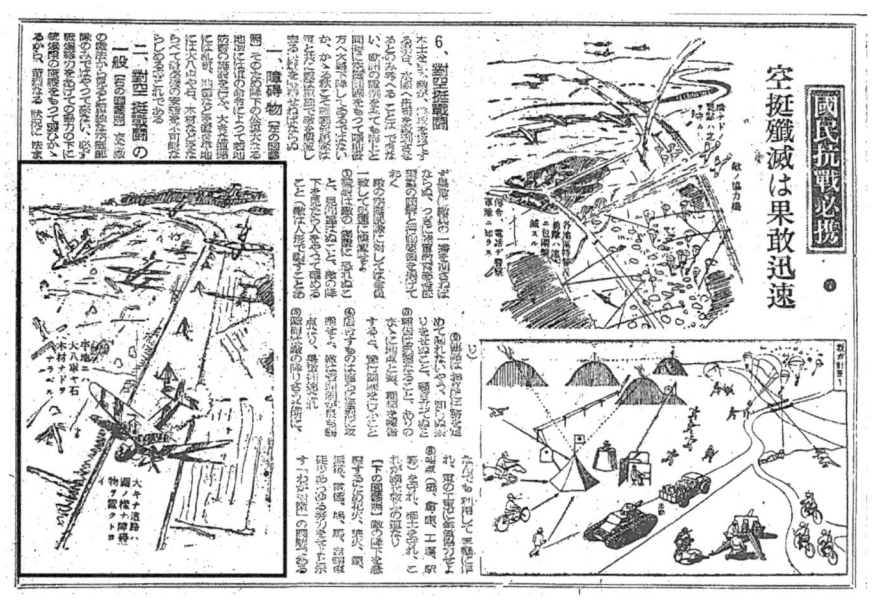

1. *Shogaibutsu*: Obstacles

Areas that are considered to have a high likelihood of being the target of airborne assault should, if ordered to by the military, take measures to obstruct their landing.
On large roads, construct a series of irregularly placed and angled wooden stakes in combination with mines. On flat areas place wooden cards, rocks and lumber to prevent gliders from being able to land successfully.

DEFENSE OF THE JAPANESE HOMELAND

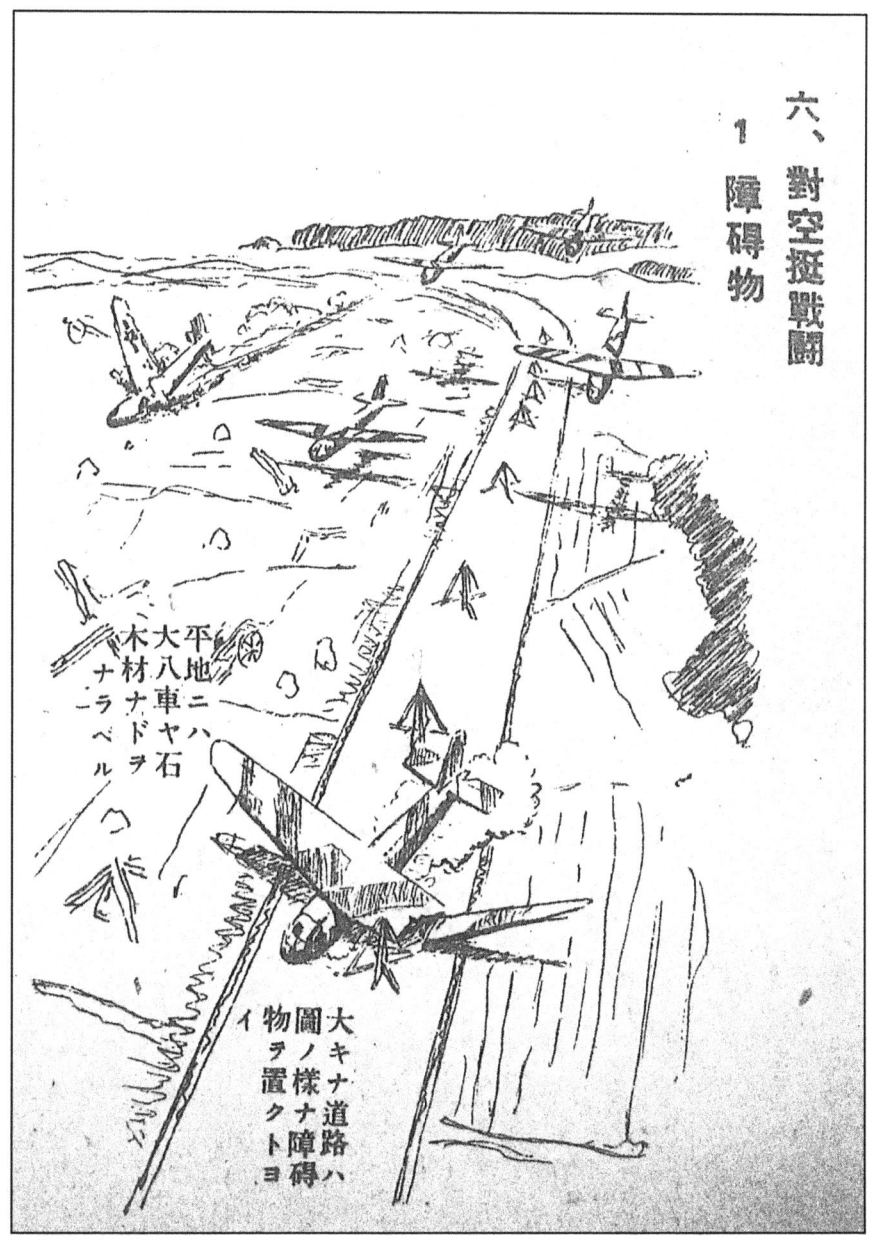

Six, Fighting Against Military Aircraft
1. *Shogaibutsu*
Obstacles

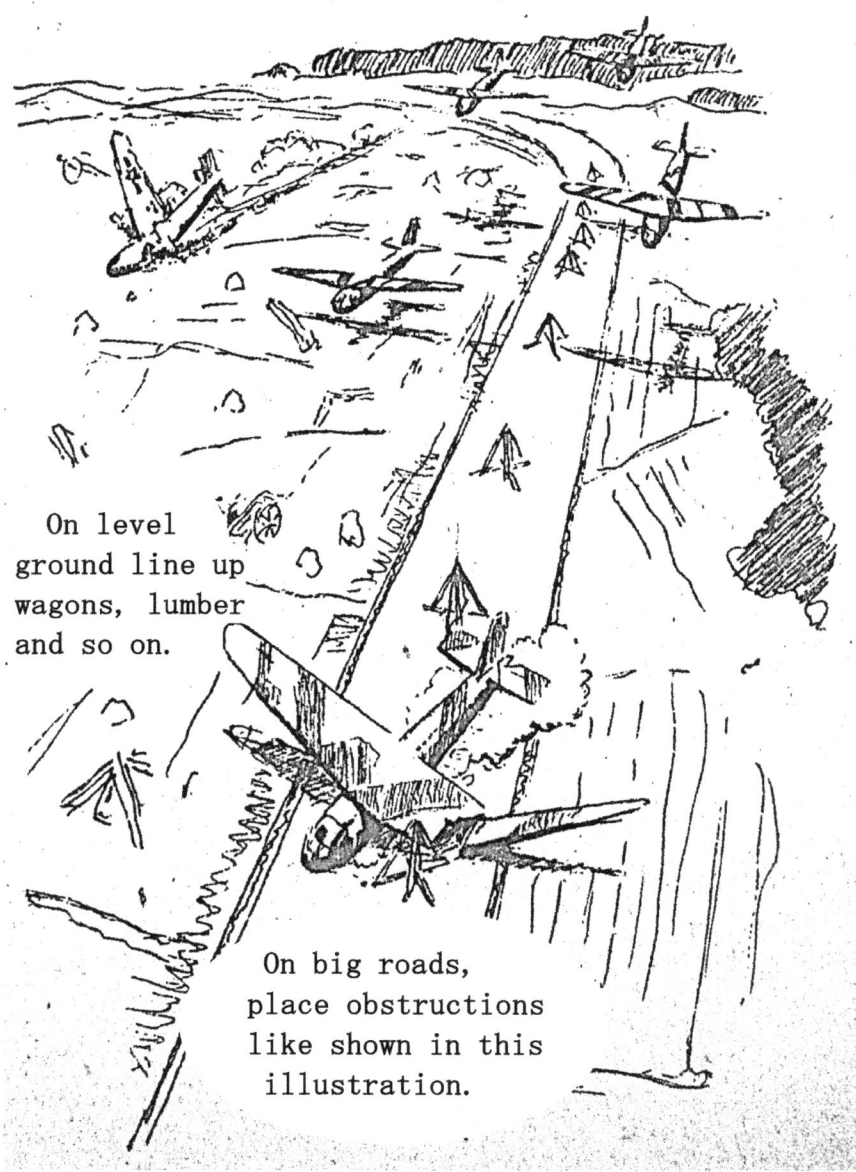

On level ground line up wagons, lumber and so on.

On big roads, place obstructions like shown in this illustration.

DEFENSE OF THE JAPANESE HOMELAND

Newspaper Article 7
Obliterating Airborne Units Requires Fast and Decisive Action

2. General knowledge regarding fighting against airborne units

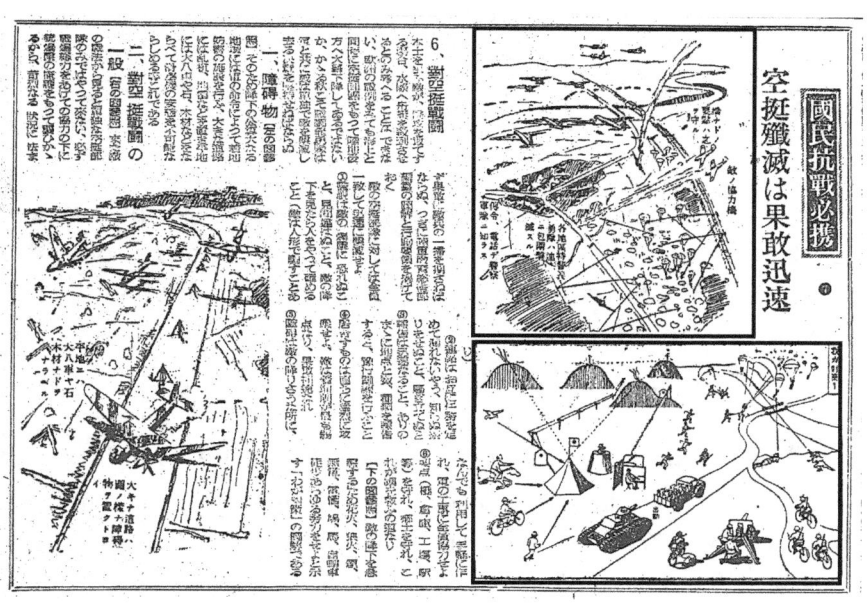

2. General knowledge regarding fighting against airborne units

Looking at the enemy's military strategy it is clear that they will not rely solely on sending individual airborne units. It goes without saying the enemy will attack with its full explosive power using gun and bomb attacks to support their assault. We cannot hesitate in the face of this intense assault, but must remain firm and sweep the enemy soldiers away.
Next, the Inspectorate General of Military Training has prepared an illustrated guide outlining what actions need to be taken.

In order for us to obliterate the enemy's airborne infantry units we must all move quickly and in unison.

1. If tasked with observing you should not be afraid of the enemy's bombing attacks. You should observe accurately. If you see figures being dropped from aircraft, confirm that they are human. (The enemy may try to fool you with mannequins.)

2. When passing information, both the sender and receiver should do their duty and not allow any communications to be missed. Do not ignore any communications and do not panic.

3. Make your reports quickly and be sure to describe the scene and report the number and type of what you see. This type of reporting should be practiced beforehand.

4. If what you see matches an enemy target, then immediately attack it with ferocious intensity. Airborne troops are most vulnerable in the time before they touch the ground. Be daring and quick, even if you don't hit every target.

5. When building obstructions in an area the enemy is likely to land, make use of anything that may be at and don't concern yourself with a specific method of construction. Everyone should cooperate with military construction efforts.

6. Protect important places (bridges, storehouses, factories, train stations etc…) Defend your hometown, this is the way to save the nation.

In order to make emergency reports of enemy paratroopers, use fireworks, signal fires, smoke, radios, phones, pigeons, horses, bicycles or make your way on foot. The efforts you make, as shown in the illustrations, are our countermeasures.

Our Strategy 1

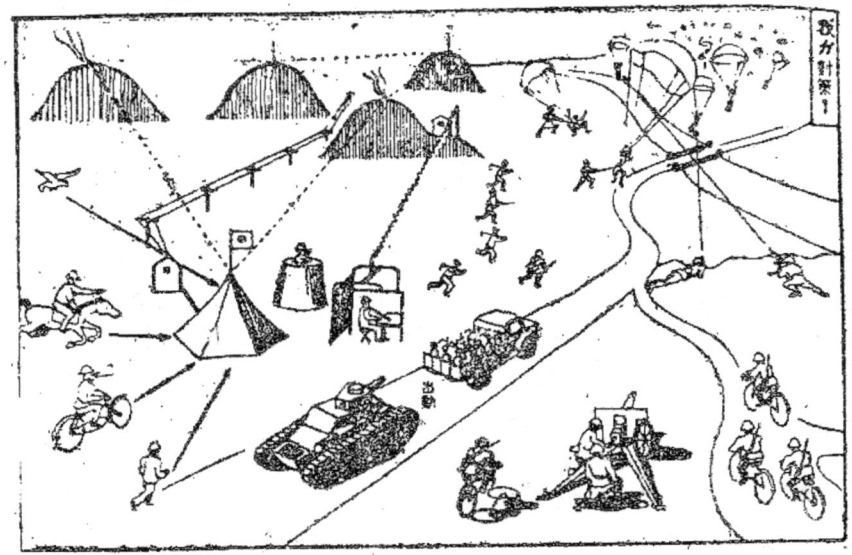

![bird]	Messenger Pigeon	![snipers]	Snipers
![horse]	Messenger on Horseback		
![bicycle]	Making announcements by bicycle.		
![bicycles]	Soldiers advancing by bicycle.		
![advancing]	出勤 *Shukkin* Advancing		

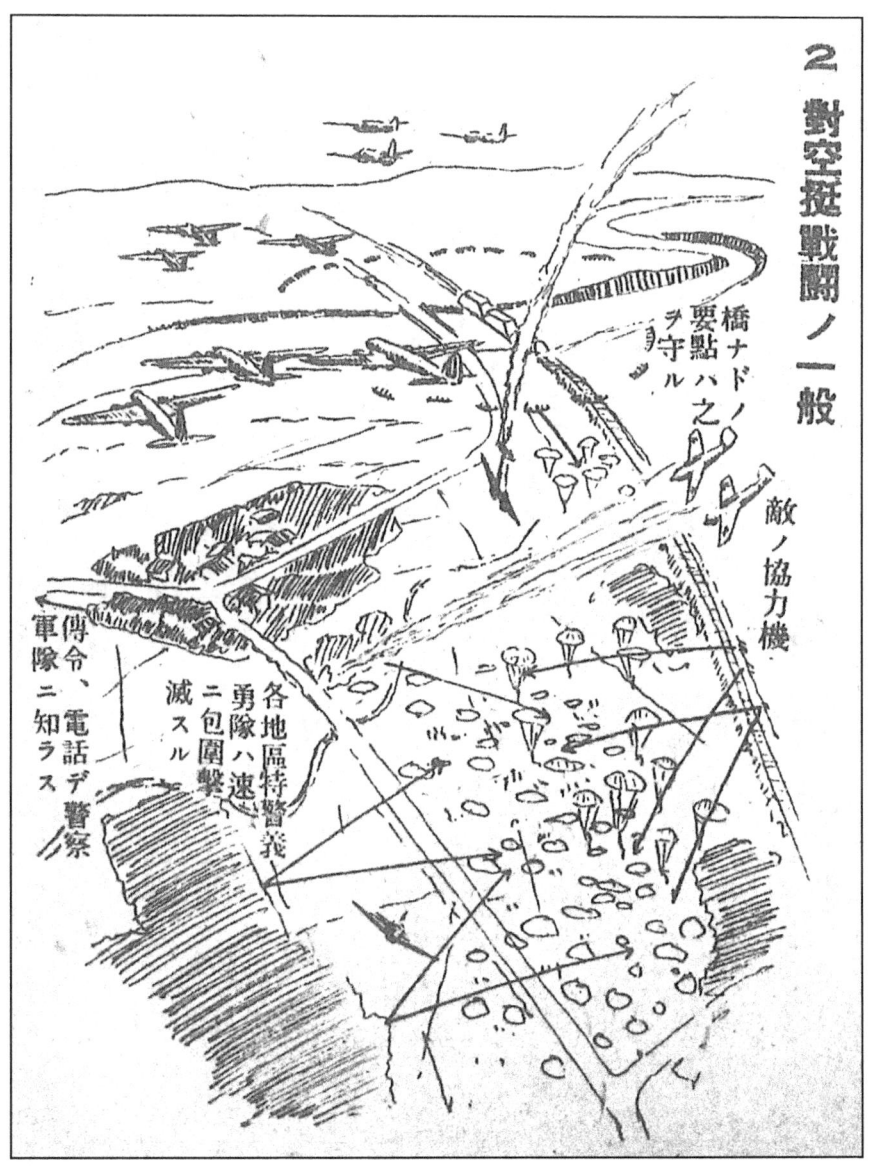

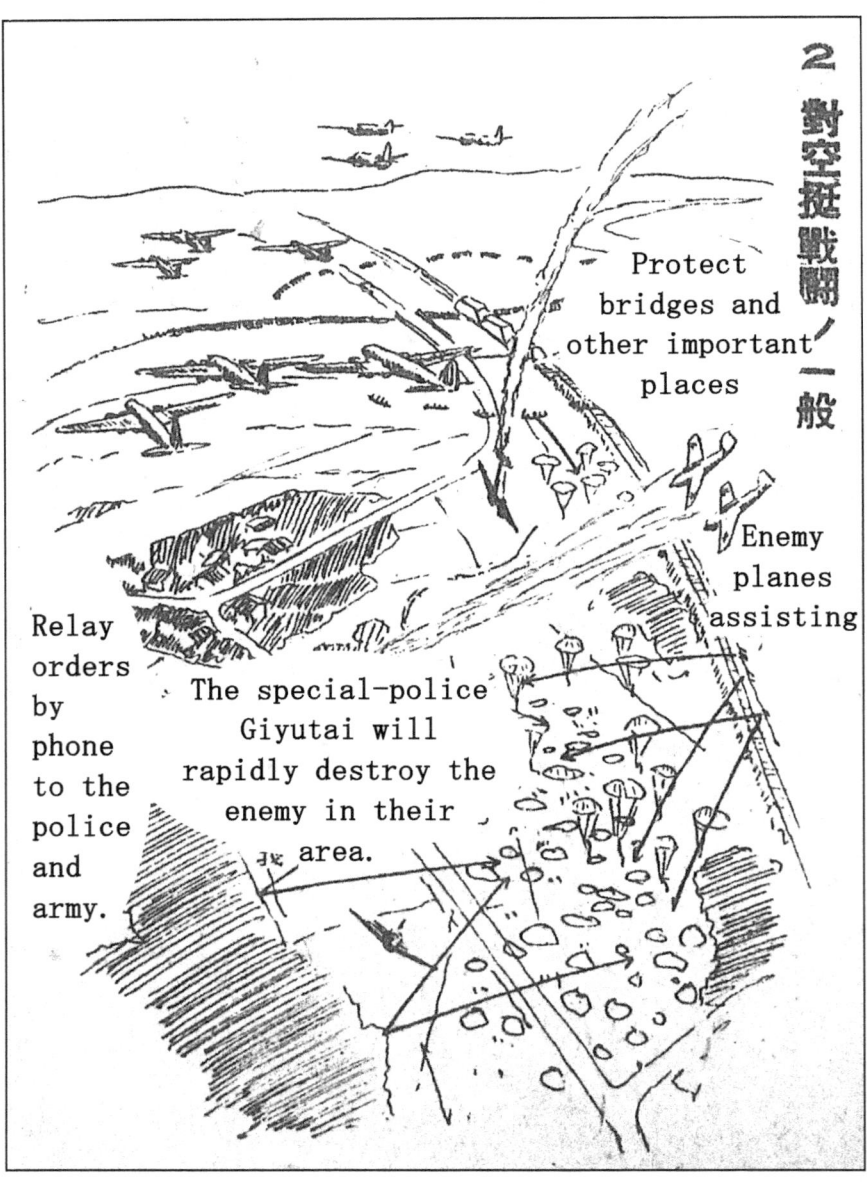

Newspaper Article 8
We Are Not Afraid of Anything
7. Gas・Defending Against Flamethrowers

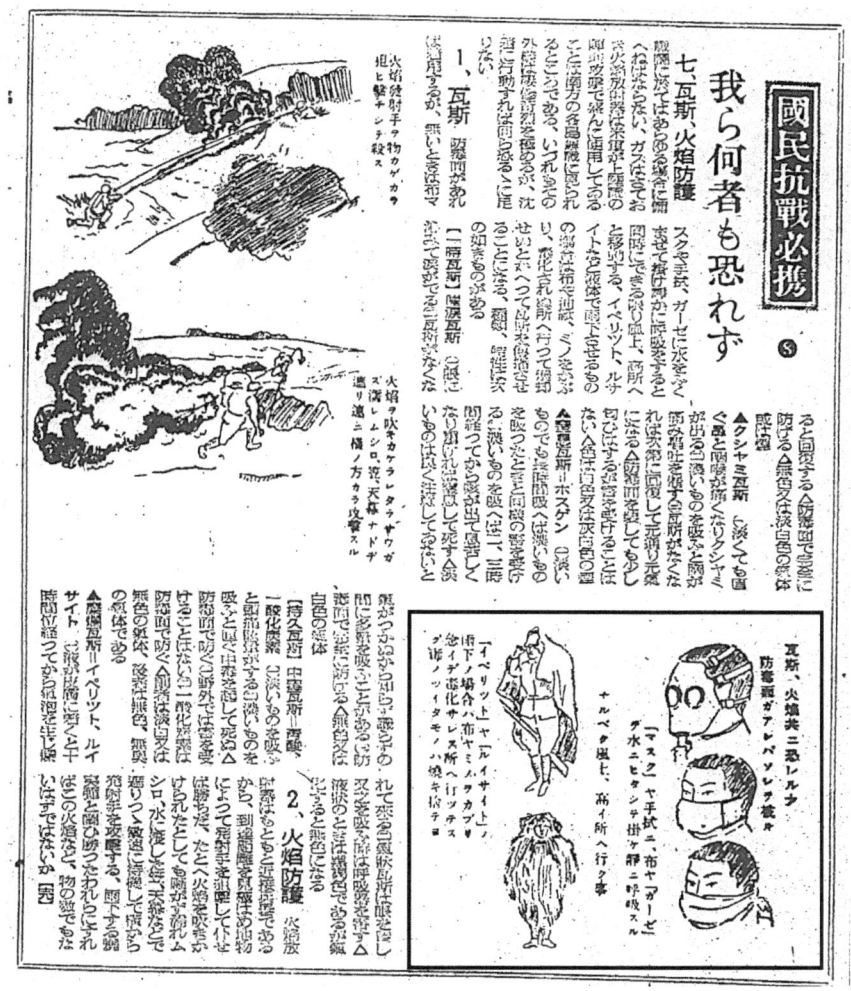

In war, you need to be prepared for any situation. Setting aside the gas attacks for now, it is important to note that the American military makes extensive use of flamethrowers in land battles. This is particularly true when they attack encampments, as was seen in the battles on each of the southern islands.

No matter where you encounter it, the flamethrower will at first appear to be a weapon of astounding intensity, however if you remain calm and act properly there is nothing to fear.

1. Gas

If you have a mask that prevents poison gas then wear that. If not, then you can use a Tenugui, general purpose cloth, or a piece of gauze. Soak it in water and tie it around your mouth and nose, breathing slowly. At the same time try to move upwind and to a spot with higher elevation.

If liquid forms of mustard gas or Lewisite gas are being dropped like rain from above, then cover your body with cloth, oiled paper or straw. Move to a place that has not been exposed to the liquid and allow the gas to dissipate rather than trying to incinerate it. The characteristics of each are as follows.

Gas Weapons that Quickly Dissipate

Tear gas
1. If it coats your eyes, it will cause tears to flow
2. When the gas disperses, you will recover
You can completely protect yourself with a gas mask. It is colorless or appears as a thin white colored vapor or smoke.

Sneezing Gas
1. Even if the gas is diffuse your nose and throat will begin to hurt and you will sneeze.
2. If the gas is thick and you breath it in, your chest will hurt and you will start to throw up.
3. Once the gas clears you will recover and return to your usual level of energy.
With a gas mask on you may still be able to smell the gas but you will not be adversely affected.
It is a colorless gas for the most part but may appear like greyish white smoke.

Suffocating Gas: Carbonyl Chloride

1. Breathing in the diffuse gas for a long period of time results in the same amount of damage as breathing in a dense gas for a short period of time.
2. If you breath in when the gas is thick around you, after two or three hours you will develop a cough. Breathing will become difficult and in severe cases can cause you to suffocate to death.
3. Be aware if you are in an area with diffuse gas. If you do not pay attention, or take preventive measures, you will end up breathing in a large dose.

A gasmask will completely protect you. The gas is usually colorless but can appear as a white vapor.

Gas Weapons That Linger

Poison Gas: Hydrogen Cyanide • Carbon Monoxide

1. If the gas is diffuse and you breath it in, your head will hurt and you will become dizzy.
2. If the gas is dense and you breath it in, you will be poisoned and die.

You can protect yourself with a gasmask.
1. You will not be injured if you are outside.
2. You can protect against carbon monoxide with a gasmask.

The former appears as a pale white or colorless vapor. The latter is a colorless and odorless vapor.

Blister Gas : Mustard Gas • Lewisite Gas

1. If the liquid gets on your skin, in 10 hours it will begin to become inflamed and blister.
2. If any of the above are in gas form they will damage the eyes. If inhaled, they can all damage the lungs.

When these are in liquid form they appear dark brown, however in gas form they are colorless.

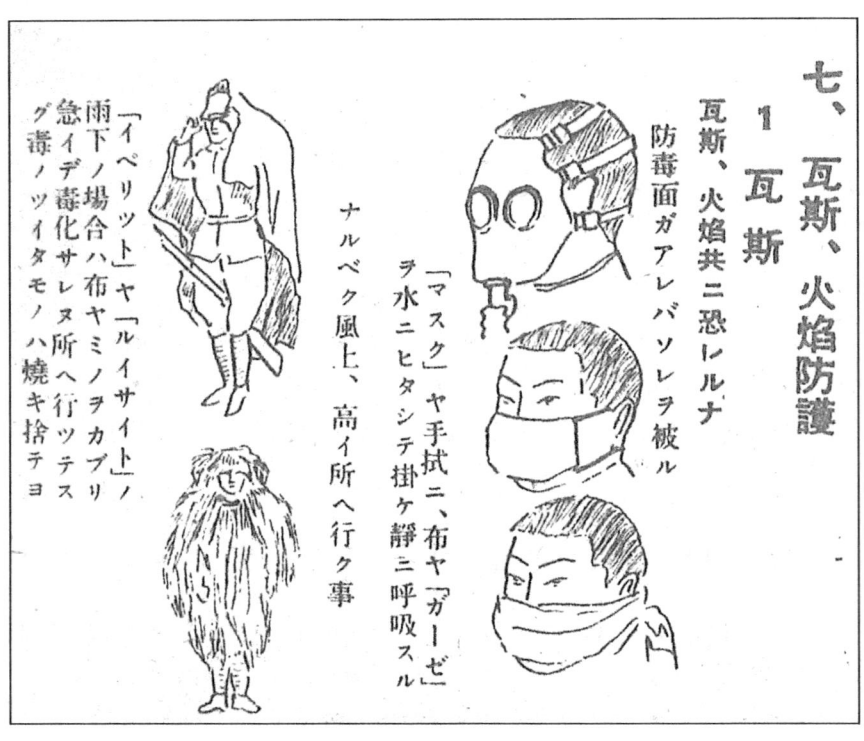

七、瓦斯、火焰防護

1 瓦斯

瓦斯、火焰共ニ恐ルルナ
防毒面ガアレバソレヲ被ル

「マスク」ヤ手拭ニ、布ヤ「ガーゼ」
ヲ水ニヒタシテ掛ケ靜ニ呼吸スル

ナルベク風上、高イ所ヘ行ク事

「イペリット」ヤ「ルイサイト」ノ
雨下ノ場合ハ布ヤミノヲカブリ
急イデ毒化サレヌ所ヘ行ッテス
グ毒ノツイタモノハ燒キ捨テヨ

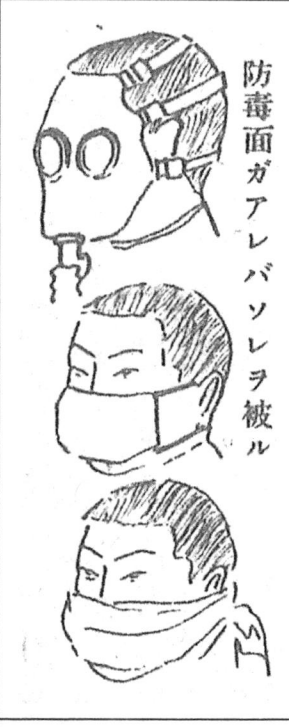

1. Do not be afraid of gas or flamethrowers.

If you have a gas-mask, wear that. You can make a mask out of a Tenugui, multipurpose towel, a piece of cloth or gauze. Soak it in water and tie it around your face. Breathe calmly and try to move upwind and to a higher elevation.

If mustard gas or lewisite is raining down, cover yourself with a piece of cloth or a straw raincoat. Move quickly to an area that has not been exposed to the poison and burn everything that the poison touched.

Newspaper Article 8
We Are Not Afraid of Anything
2. Defending Against Flamethrowers

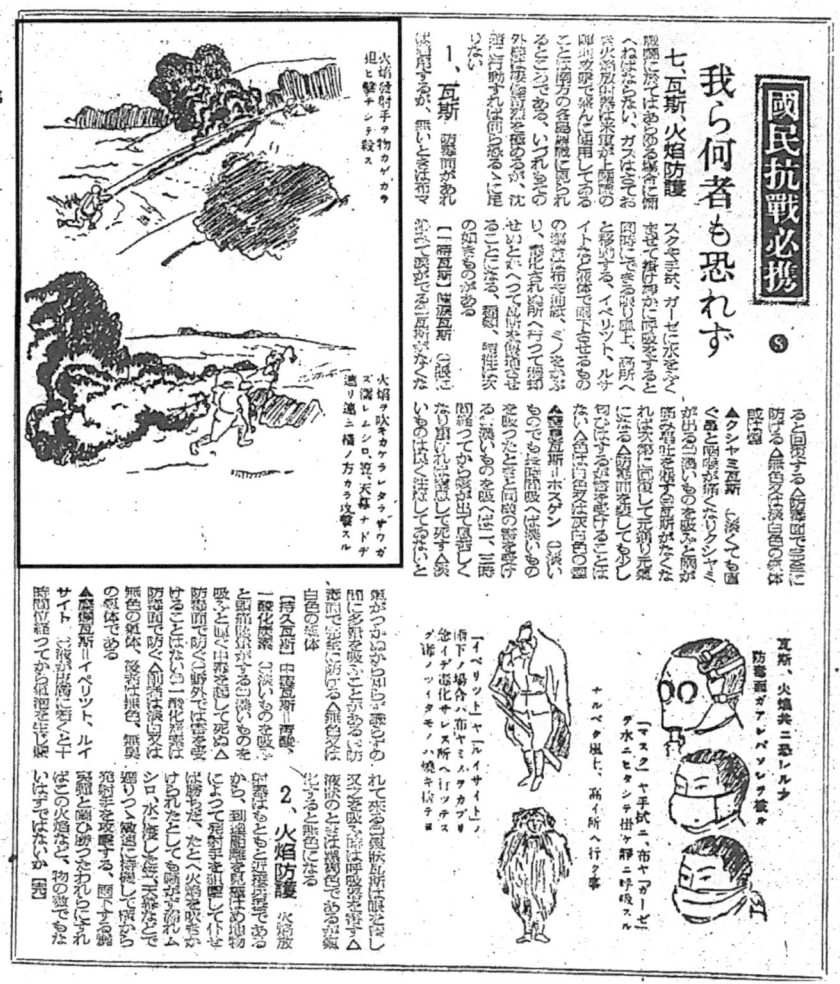

2. Defending Against Flamethrowers

Fundamentally the flamethrower is a close-range weapon. If you understand the range the weapon can reach and use objects and land features to hide behind, you can take the user out with sniper fire. For example, even if flames from the weapon reach you, do not panic. Instead, pour water on a woven grass mat, or even pour water on a straw hat or a tent. Use that as a shield. Waiting for an opportunity, attack the flamethrower user from the side.

The fact that despite incendiary bombs being dropped on us, we emerged victorious, so a flamethrower is nothing in comparison.

2. Defending against a flame thrower

Shoot and kill the flamethrower operator from behind an obstruction.

When the flamethrower operator shoots fire, do not panic. Use a wet hat, tent and so on as a shield. Move quickly to the side and attack from there.

ERIC SHAHAN

DEFENSE OF THE JAPANESE HOMELAND

ERIC SHAHAN

Weekly Photo Report Magazine (excerpt)

July 1945
Weekly Photo Report Magazine
Number 374/375
July 11th Showa 20 (1945)

Weekly Photo Report Magazine
Number 374/375
July 11th Showa 20 (1945) (excerpt)[6]

With the situation similar to Rabaul, officers are gathered in an underground encampment.[7] The phrase *Danjite Yare*, Absolutely determined to go through with it can be seen hanging above. Overflowing with intense concentration and determination the commissioned officers refine their strategy

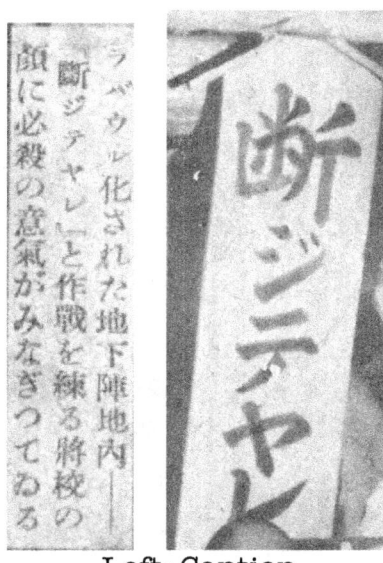

Left: Caption
Right: *Danjite Yare* Absolutely determined to go through with it

---

[6] Other articles in this issue were titled, "Soldiers and Citizens Continue (the fight) in Okinawa!" and "Wild Vegetables You Can Consume in Summer." This was the final issue of this magazine as the printing facility was destroyed in a bombing raid.

[7] This refers to how the Japanese air on Rabaul, in Papua New Guinea, were cut off after being surrounded by allied forces but continued to resist.

をドらつないやりにすする

朝顔に對し注意すべき點

武器としては、長さ約九〇センチ乃第ーメートル、太さ直徑三センチ位の丸太、木刀、竹刀がよい斬撃の際には剛手首の内側胞をもって、棒の上方より下方に變化するやう に力をいれ、斬堅した振に兩膝の輕くのびるやうに斬撃する

二、體當（前方突と前踢をいふ、前方突は

體當は、朝力の强さる張い體力と不撓の闘魂で培ひ、徒手搏闘に必要な技術を鍛成するがが目的であるから、先に足をあげて同じ動作を繰返して行ふ（第六圖）

一、突、蹴

右足を前にして傍へ、右足先端をもって對手の投閣に蹴上げ、次に足を換へて同じ動作を数回繰返す（第七圖）これは柔技として最もすぐれた技術であるが、何れも身心の總力を一時に集結して行ふものであるから、一般必殺の威力を發揮させることが出來る

二、押倒

敵に投し體當をためて、彈丸のやらりに突進して行くも敵の受入れと、一氣に押切らうといふのが目的である。始めに相對立させ、敵入が對手に向つて突進して來たならが敵入の兩脇胞を雙手で押さゆへ、又は兩手で敵の兩肩胞上部をしつかり掘へ、左右に開いて踏みこみ、胯を落し、爪先、足先に力を入れて、浮き足しないやうにし、敵人の運動を殺ぐやうにして、對手の股を目掛けて、對手を押えつける、引込みつつ對手の腰を浮かせるやうにし、一氣に押し下ろせば、前踢熊を蹴らうと飛び上って來るから、一氣に足をかゆ入れて擦り倒す...

三、投倒、對手の體力が劣つてゐるか、體勢が...

實豫上の注意

投擲力を練り高度の揮射力を修得せしめるのか目的である。始めに練りびの距離約二十メートルの距離よりを行ふ。試合場の時は地面に描いた距離約四メートル乃至十メートルの間隔で實施する投擲は出來るだけ軽裝にし、少くとも上半身捕接である。何手にも多少の練習を要するが最も瞬時で實用のある物々如き投擲物の得物となっては大切である。投擲物の如き得物になつては狭い場所でも手軽の得ものとなった掩作にかなふことが有利である、二人で一側の球を用ゐて適度の間合から投

四、擲

五、護身

實豫上の注意

大事に直面して冷靜沈着に行動し、身を護り得る能力を養ふのが目的である。大きさには古布で作った懷に、松脂、松殻、古酒などを球は古布で直徑六センチ方乃至八センチにし、眞綿を容物にするため、着衣のかくしに何時も一個入れて置き練習する

方法は(イ) 突、片足を少し側に開いて立ち、左右両方及び前方を突く（第十一圖

(ロ) 蹴、片足を少し側に開いて立ち、左右の膝關をもって、なるだけ高く蹴上げる

DEFENSE OF THE JAPANESE HOMELAND

醜敵を叩き砕かん

一億國民總蹶起し國土防衛に生産に
各自が強い戰意と不屈の闘志力をもって
死力を盡くすべき秋は來た

闘力の秋を迎する烈々の闘魂は、日々の鍛錬を通して達成される

闘技の強力

闘技には、體力が必要である。それは體力の増進に役立つとともに、格闘力の増大を目的とするもので「闘技」と呼ぶ。後者は徒手で行うものと、武器を使用するものと区別し、武器としては丸太（刀、竹槍、銃劍、丸石、手榴彈）等が使はれる。これらは何れも格闘に必要な基本技術であるから、これらを十分に鍛ふれば、實地の格闘に必要な基本技術を極めて容易に修得することができる。鍛成の容易なるもののみであるから、男子は勿論、女性に於いても十分鍛成し得る氣慨のものである。中には男子とともに職場に於ける問・製造される場合に、女性の補助とするのみでなく、我國古來の女性、その手中にいささかの刃物もて弱し強し敵の一人二人を倒すことを得ば、その樂しさ、愉快なることを想ひみる時、婦人の心得と鍛練に意を盡くさなければならぬ。

一、歩走

步走の鍛錬は、行軍力を練り、高度の機動性を確保させるのが目的である。特に交通機關の利用不能となった場合、國民の機動性は歩行軍力に因るから、日常に於て十分心掛けて行ふことが肝要で、この鍛錬は極めて必要である。それには二つの方法がある。出來るだけ長距離を掛ける方法と、一定距離內に於ける時間を短縮する方法である。練成の方法として、キロ距離に二キロの疲労に堪へる體力を獲得し、その練步以上、一本の疲勞困憊の上にて、この長距離練歩の場合、その長距離に影響すやうな仰がみと働くやうな休みをとってはならない、むしろこれを禁とし、短時間の休憩は必要であるが、出來る限り氣樂に歩行をなすやうに心掛けて行ふ。（第一圖）

二、斬突

斬突の鍛錬は、旺盛なる武魂を養ひ、一撃必殺の術を體得せしめるのが目的である。從來劍技は刀を用ひて實施するが、今回は、簡易な設備と用具で實施する格闘の必須の鍛練として、これを劍道に代替するもので、その他の武器に關連する諸々の斬突に應用し得るものである。

斬突の修練は、從來主として劍道を通して會得されるが、今回は、簡單な設備と用具で實行し得る上に、短期の修練で十分に役立つものを探して行ふ。

一、據誰斬擊

それには二つの方法がある。即ち（地上約九〇センチ）に結束した枝丸（輪束家）に對し丸太が斬れる刀を持ち、足を前後に開いた姿勢（第二圖）正面斬

二、

擊を行ふのと、約一・五メートルの高さの橫梗（斬擊家）に對し、丸太を兩手に持ち、足を前後に開いた姿（第三圖）に出し、橫梗に對して十分な氣慨をもって斬擊を行ふとする（第三圖）

三、殺橫斬突

四方八方に敵を假想し、これを抹殺する修練した丸太（刀）の操法、體の開きなどを應用し、氣に乗じて斬撃を横縱に斬りまくる（第五圖）。直正斬擊敵は、每回少くとも貳本

一、基本斬突

斬突の基本である正面斬撃、斜斬撃及び正面刺突のみについて、丸太をもって斬撃刺突する。正面刺突の場合には刺擊刺突を加

Knocking the Grotesque Enemy to Pieces

With the coming of fall, a hundred million citizens have leaped to action, mobilizing in an all-out effort to produce what is necessary to defend the homeland. Every one of us possesses a powerful fighting spirit and an unsurpassed capacity for battle which will enable us to fight with vigor.

The root of combat power is having a burning fighting spirt. Developing this spirit into a powerful technique requires intensive training.

There are two components necessary for fighting techniques. The first is increasing mobility through *Hoso Undo*, Marching and Running Exercises and the second is strengthening the body and improving combat ability through learning *Tohgi*, Fighting Techniques.

Further, the latter is divided into both unarmed and armed combat. The weapons that have been selected are wooden poles which serve as Katana, bamboo spears which serve as bayonets, pieces of roof tile and rocks which serve as hand grenades. These are all fundamental skills required for fighting. Since the training method is extremely simple, this system is easy to follow.

As for girls, when one looks at their nature, clearly the way their training is conducted is quite different, however from ancient times in our country, women possessed an awe-inspiring fighting spirt, meaning not only are they are undaunted going head to head against men, but there are more than a few that charged onto the battlefield alongside men.

Thus, since there is no shortage of tales regarding the martial bravery of women, it is time to discard the old way thinking that women are weak. In preparation for the final battle, we should endeavor to ensure women are trained properly to craft them into strong and resolute female representatives of imperial Japan.

Picture One

I. *Hoso* : Marching and Running

The purpose of training both marching and running is to develop your ability to travel long distances on foot, thereby achieving a high level of reliable mobility. In particular, if the situation arises where using public transportation becomes difficult, you will only be able to move about by relying your feet, thus this type of training is extremely necessary.

There are many ways to train marching and running, however it is essential that you utilize the simplest method possible to successfully develop this ability. For example, decide on a training program consisting of a one to two kilometer/ 0.0~1.2 mile, fast run followed by a two kilometer-long walk.[8] Depending on how the people you are training with react, you may adjust the distance of either the run, the walk or both. By doing this you can reduce the amount of time required to train while also reducing fatigue while simultaneously not having to worry about it affecting workers' production.

Generally speaking, when training running and walking, you should select a spot where the participants can run out and back enabling them to exercise while also becoming more familiar with their surroundings. This is shown in Picture One.

---

[8] The article uses the metric system. The imperial system measurements are for reference.

Picture Two

II. *Zantotsu* : Cutting and Stabbing

The purpose of *Zantotsu*, cutting and stabbing training, is to develop a vigorous martial spirit while ensuring your learners are ingrained in *Ichi Geki Hissatsu*, attacking with one violent blow that is invariably fatal. In order to succeed at close quarters fighting, you will need not only strength but also to be able to fight with various weapons.

Typically, Kendo training would serve as the base for *Zantotsu* training, however in place of that we have found a way to use a simple set up and equipment to allow anyone to training anywhere. Further, this method was chosen as anyone can become effective in battle after a short amount of training.

1. *Tanren Zangeki*: Training For Attacking With Cuts

There are two ways to train this. The first is setting up a target about waist height (this should be about 90 centimeters/ 3 feet) off the ground.) Position a bundle of branches at that height (this is known as a *Zangeki Dai*, target for cutting attacks.) Hold a *Maruta*, wooden pole, in both hands and stand with one leg forward and the other back. Then strike powerfully down onto the cutting attack target as shown in Picture Two.

Picture Three

For attacks to *Men*, the face or head, set up a wooden pole 1.5 meters/ 5 feet high (this is known as a *Zangeki Bo*, cutting attack pole.) Hold your wooden pole with both hands and face the pole. Stand with one leg forward and the other back. While facing the pole ensure you have generated sufficient fighting spirit before cutting down diagonally. This is shown in Picture Three.

Picture Four

2. *Kihon Zantotsu* : Basic Cutting and Stabbing

The Basic Cutting and Stabbing Attacks, which consist of cutting straight down, cutting at an angle along with a straight thrust should each be trained individually with a wooden pole. When training *Shomen Sattotsu*, Straight Stabbing Thrust, stabbing with the bayonet should be done at the same time. This is shown in Picture Four.

Picture Five

3. *Juo Zantotsu* : Cutting and Stabbing in Every Direction

Imagine that you are surrounded by opponents on all sides. Use the wooden pole (which represents a Katana) and cut using the previously introduced basic stabbing and cutting methods. Be sure to use your body effectively as you cut down all the opponents surrounding you. This is shown in Picture Five. Note that when training, you should not do less than a hundred repetitions.

Things you should be careful of when cutting:

Whether you are making a Maruta, wooden pole, a Bokuto, wooden sword, or Shinai, bamboo sword, it is best to craft one that is between 90 centimeters to 1 meter in length/2.9~3.2 feet and about 3 centimeters/ 1.1 inches in diameter.

When cutting hold your weapon with the base of your palms and as you swing down from above, grip it tightly with both hands. At the end of your cut extend both elbows slightly.

Picture Six

Picture Seven

III. *Tai Atari* : Striking

Striking is the foundation of making a strong body and an indomitable fighting spirt. The goal of this training is to develop the necessary skills to fight barehanded.

1. Tsuki·Keri : Punching and Kicking

How to train Train Zenpo Tsuki, front punch, and Maegeri, front kick.

To do a front punch stand with your left leg in front and your body facing to the right. Use your right fist to strike sharply forward towards your opponent's abdomen. After several repetitions switch your feet around and practice with your left fist in the same manner. Practice these types of attacks repeatedly.
This is shown in Picture Six.

To train a front kick, stand with your left foot in front and use your right foot to kick up into your opponent's groin. Next, switch your feet around and kick with your right foot in the same way. Repeat this several times. This is shown in Picture Seven.

In Judo these techniques are called *Atemi Waza*, striking techniques, and are highly prized. Whenever you train them, in order to be most effective you should focus your mind and all your power on one point. Thus you will be striking with enough power so that one attack will invariably be a killing blow.

Picture Eight

2. *Oshi Taoshi*: Shoving Down

The objective of this training is to learn how to compress your body into a ball and then blast forward like a bullet, striking your opponent with a sharp blow using all your body weight. This will enable you to topple your opponent in one blow.

First of all, each pair should be divided into two roles, *Kojin*, the attacker, and *Ukenin*, the defender. Both combatants should stand several spaces apart and face each other in *Nakagoshi*, mid-hips, or squatting with the knees and hips off the ground before standing. If you are in the role of the attacker you charge straight at your opponent with your hands open and slam your forehead into his right collarbone while shoving both hands under his armpits or against his forearms and forcing him up off the ground. However, be sure not to allow your own feet to come off the ground. Be sure to keep the balls of your feet on the ground and your power focused in your hips as you shove your opponent up off the ground and slam him down.

When you in the role of the defender, shift your left foot back slightly as the attacker charges and use both hands to lightly hold the attacker's forearm and pull him towards you until his forehead contacts your right collarbone. Ensure that you are focusing your power in the balls of your feet and that your right kneecap is facing your opponent's kneecap. Resist to a degree, however allow yourself to be pushed back. This is shown in Picture Eight.

Picture Nine

3. *Hineri Daoshi* : Twisting and Toppling

If your opponent is weaker than you or is positioned poorly, you have a good chance of knocking him down with the previous Shoving Down technique. However, if your opponent is of vastly greater strength or has positioned himself well, you are likely to be pushed back. In this situation you should use *Hineri Daoshi*, Twisting and Toppling. By rapidly twisting your body to the side, you can secure victory.

This is done in a way similar to how Shoving Down is done. If you are the attacker, you charge at the defender, full speed and shove him. The defender judges his timing and shoves you back. The moment he does this rapidly rotate your upper body to the side, twisting and toppling your opponent.

Practice this technique up to the point where you have taken your opponent's balance and then stop. So, in the end you are supporting your opponent at the moment you are about to throw. This is shown in Picture Nine.

Cautions When Training

a. When practicing throwing techniques, start about one meter apart. When doing regular training or bouts, draw a circle on the earth from 4 to 10 meters/ 13~32 feet in diameter and conduct the training or competition within the circle.

b. Competitors should wear minimal clothing and, at the very least, the upper body should be bare.

Picture Ten

VI. *Tohteki* : Throwing Projectiles

The purpose of this training is to improve throwing power and to develop accurate grenade throwing ability. When involved in close quarters battle it is absolutely essential to know how to throw hand grenades and other explosives.

The simplest way to develop throwing power is to play catch ball. It is important to practice this skill anytime and anyplace. This is helped by the fact that finding something to throw is easy and simple to carry around. It is important to remember that you should also practice in narrow spaces.

The way you do this is to pair off with a partner and stand an appropriate distance apart before throwing the ball back and forth. You can make the ball from a piece of old cloth stuffed with paper. In addition to throwing the ball back and forth with a partner you should also practice throwing it at a wall or pole. This will enable you to increase your throwing accuracy. This is shown in Picture Ten.

Cautions regarding throwing practice

The ball is basically a sack made from a piece of old cloth stuffed with scraps of paper, rice husks, old cloth or other such material. it should be between 6 and 8 centimeters in diameter so it is easy to use and one of these can be kept inside the clothing so that you can take it out and practice anytime.

Picture Eleven

V. *Goshin* : Self-defense

The purpose of this training is to learn how to face a dangerous situation calmly and coolly while developing the ability to defend yourself.

The way to do this is as follows:

a. Tsuki – Striking

Step slightly to the side with one foot. Strike forward while alternating between left and right fists. Also practice striking to the sides. This is shown in Picture Eleven.

b. Keri – Kicking

Step slightly out to the side with one foot. Kick upward by raising your kneecap. Alternate kicking with your left and right while trying to lift your knees as high as possible.

www.ingramcontent.com/pod-product-compliance
Lightning Source LLC
Chambersburg PA
CBHW070336240426